*Understanding and Teaching
the Civil Rights Movement*

The Harvey Goldberg Series
for Understanding and Teaching History

The Harvey Goldberg Series for Understanding and Teaching History gives college and secondary history instructors a deeper understanding of the past as well as the tools to help them teach it creatively and effectively. Named for Harvey Goldberg, a professor renowned for his history teaching at Oberlin College, Ohio State University, and the University of Wisconsin from the 1960s to the 1980s, the series reflects Goldberg's commitment to helping students think critically about the past with the goal of creating a better future. For more information, please visit www.GoldbergSeries.org.

Understanding and Teaching the Civil Rights Movement

Edited by

HASAN KWAME JEFFRIES

The University of Wisconsin Press

The University of Wisconsin Press
728 State Street, Suite 443
Madison, Wisconsin 53706
uwpress.wisc.edu

Gray's Inn House, 127 Clerkenwell Road
London EC1R 5DB, United Kingdom
eurospanbookstore.com

Printed in the United States of America

This book may be available in a digital edition.

Library of Congress Cataloging-in-Publication Data
Names: Jeffries, Hasan Kwame, 1973– editor.
Title: Understanding and teaching the civil rights movement / edited
    by Hasan Kwame Jeffries.
Other titles: Harvey Goldberg series for understanding and teaching
    history.
Description: Madison, Wisconsin: The University of Wisconsin Press,
    [2019] | Series: The Harvey Goldberg series for understanding and
    teaching history | Includes bibliographical references and index.
Identifiers: LCCN 2019009206 | ISBN 9780299321901 (cloth: alk. paper)
Subjects: LCSH: African Americans—Civil rights—History—Study and
    teaching. | Civil rights movements—History—20th century—Study
    and teaching—United States. | United States—Race relations—
    Study and teaching.
Classification: LCC E185.61 .U54 2019 | DDC 323.1196/073—dc23
LC record available at https://lccn.loc.gov/2019009206

ISBN 978-0-299-32194-9 (pbk.: alk. paper)

On the cover: Fannie Lou Hamer, center, sings at a Mississippi Freedom
Democratic Party rally on the Atlantic City boardwalk during the
1964 Democratic National Convention with Emory Harris, Stokely
Carmichael, Roland Sherrod, Eleanor Holmes Norton, and Ella Baker.

*For Marland and Laneda Jeffries,
my first teachers.*

To accept one's past—one's history—is not the same thing as drowning in it; it is learning how to use it. An invented past can never be used; it cracks and crumbles under the pressures of life like clay in a season of drought.

JAMES BALDWIN

Contents

Contents

Contents

**Part Four. "The essence of scholarship is
truth": Sources for Teaching
the Civil Rights Movement**

Contents

Part Five. "Strong people don't need strong leaders": Methods for Teaching the Civil Rights Movement

Preface

The students who enrolled in my civil rights class at The Ohio State University in autumn 2016 fell into one of three categories. There were those who took the class to acquire new knowledge about grassroots organizing. These young social justice advocates were students driven by a sincere desire to apply the lessons of the past to the problems of the present. As it tended to be, this group was small, fewer than a half-dozen students. Then there were those who signed up for the class to fulfill a graduation requirement. Most had a genuine interest in the subject, but progress toward degree was as much on their minds as anything else. As usual, the majority of the students in the class, around twenty out of thirty-five, belonged to this group. And finally, there were those who took the class simply because it fit their schedule. For the dozen or so in this category, it did not really matter what I was teaching. They worked forty-plus hours a week and the midday class made it possible for them to get to their jobs on time.

Only a handful of the enrollees in this class were African American, which is not surprising given the marked decline in the admission rate of black students at Ohio State over the last decade. As a consequence, the vast majority in the class were white. And unlike the black students who came from Ohio's major urban centers, the white students hailed from Ohio's wealthy white suburbs and much poorer rural white communities. But regardless of their race or hometown, foremost on the minds of all the students was the 2016 presidential election, which pitted upstart Republican Party nominee Donald J. Trump against former U.S. Secretary of State and Democratic Party nominee Hillary Rodham Clinton.

On the first day of class, the students wanted to know who I thought would win the White House. Like everyone else, I had been following the election closely, watching the debates, reviewing polling data, and tuning in to *Saturday Night Live*, so I predicted that not only would Secretary Clinton win but she would win big. It was basic math, I explained. Trump simply did not have the votes. His racism had turned off black voters and people of color. And if his appeals to white supremacy failed to sufficiently alienate white voters, then surely his sexism, xenophobia, Islamophobia, and dictatorial foreign policy pronouncements would disqualify him in their eyes.

But my white students had their doubts. Trump fever, they reported, was running high among their friends and family back home. And their skepticism about a Clinton victory only grew stronger as Election Day neared. I listened to what they had to say but I did not put much stock into it. "Trump's not going to win," I continued to insist. But of course, he did.

I was just as shocked by Trump's victory as everyone else. But as a historian of the civil rights movement, I really should not have been. The black past teaches us that periods of racial progress, whether real or perceived, are followed by periods of racial retrenchment. Soon after the expansion of government protections for African American voting rights during the civil rights era, political conservatives attempted to roll back that which had helped African Americans triumph over Jim Crow. And so it was that after the two-term presidency of Barack Obama, the nation's first black head of state, white Americans voted a white supremacist into the highest office in the land.

I quickly realized why I had not foreseen what history had foretold. To begin, I had grossly underestimated how many white voters would be energized by Trump's appeal to white supremacy. I should have seen this coming, though, because white supremacy is the most effective political organizing tool in American history. It has advanced political careers and reshaped political parties from the nation's founding through the present. Although new to politics, Trump was no novice to deploying white supremacy to raise his public profile. "Maybe hate is what we need if we're gonna get something done," he told CNN's Larry King in a 1989 interview about the Central Park Five, the group of African American and Latino boys wrongfully accused and convicted of raping a white woman in New York City's Central Park.

At the same time, I significantly overestimated the number of white voters willing to set aside their own professed moral standards to send a Republican to the White House. Some of them dismissed Trump's litany of "isms" as irrelevant, while others spun them as a function of the times. And still others rationalized Trump's racial demagoguery and immoral behavior by insisting that once in office he would become "presidential."

A great number of people shared my miscalculation, but a great many more were blinded by one of the most powerful myths in the American imagination, the myth of perpetual racial progress. In the minds of most Americans, racial progress has proceeded uninterrupted since the founding of the country. If plotted on a graph, it would look like a straight line in a steep, unbroken, upward climb from slavery, to emancipation, to the civil rights movement, to the election of Obama.

But the notion of perpetual racial progress is a false one. A graph of actual racial progress would have short inclines, long declines, and extended flat lines. What's more, the lack of racial progress was a direct result of efforts by those who wanted to preserve the racial status quo, people who sought to maintain social systems and economic structures that reinforced and perpetuated inequality.

The widespread belief in the myth of perpetual racial progress helps explain why the outcome of the 2016 presidential election shook so many people to the core, leaving quite a few grief stricken. "How could this happen?" asked my students, even the ones who saw it coming. And they were not alone. People struggled to make sense of the nation's turn from hope to hate. And they feared what was to come.

One year later, in the fall of 2017, I taught my civil rights class again. The students who enrolled in it this time did so with Trump as president. And although he had not been in office very long, he had already tried to enact the Muslim ban, repeal the Affordable Care Act, and build a wall along the border with Mexico. He had also withdrawn the United States from the Paris Climate Agreement, fired FBI director James Comey under dubious circumstances, pardoned the contemptible Arizona sheriff Joe Arpaio, and ended Deferred Action for Childhood Arrivals (DACA).

Once again, the students who took the class fell into one of three categories. They were either trying to figure out how to change the world, fulfilling a college requirement, or scheduling around a job. But the distribution within these categories was markedly different. The overwhelming majority in this class, easily thirty out of forty-three students, fit squarely within the social justice advocates category. To be sure, most were not frontline activists, nor would they ever be. But they all wanted to figure out why the nation was moving backward instead of forward, and they were determined to do something about it.

The racial demographics of the class had changed as well. More than a quarter of the class was African American, easily the most I had ever had in a class that size at Ohio State. But the powerful new sense of purpose that animated the students was not confined solely to the black students; it crossed racial lines. The white students, Asian students, continental African students, and Latinx students, in addition to the African American students, were all thinking about society in profoundly new ways. Indeed, the level of social awareness in the class greatly exceeded that of my previous classes. At first I did not realize that a fundamental shift had occurred in the way these students viewed the world, but it did not take me long to figure out a significant change had occurred. Channeling my inner Mahatma Gandhi, I thought: "There go my students, I must hurry to catch up with them for I am their teacher."

The Age of Trump has created a great many challenges for all sorts of people, not the least of whom are teachers, who have had to explain to their students the resurgence of hate speech in the public square and the murder of innocents at the hands of white nationalists in places like Charlottesville, Virginia, and Pittsburgh, Pennsylvania.

But for those who have the privilege of teaching civil rights history, the Age of Trump has also created a unique opportunity, a true teachable moment. Students are energized, more eager than ever to learn all there is to know about America's past, in order to understand the complexities of America's present, so they can adequately address the challenges to come in America's future. And they are looking to the civil rights movement as they search for a blueprint for how to end racial prejudice and stamp out racial inequality.

As teachers, we are dutybound to provide students the unvarnished truth. And the times in which we live demand that we do so. To do anything less is to commit educational malpractice. Fortunately, the tools and techniques needed to teach the civil rights movement accurately and effectively are at our disposal. We just have to have the courage to use them.

Acknowledgments

This project was not my idea. It was the brainchild of John Day Tully, Brad Austin, and Matthew Masur, the visionary editors of the award-winning Harvey Goldberg Series for Understanding and Teaching History. But as soon as they invited me to serve as the editor of this volume, I leapt at the opportunity. Like them, I recognized the need for a book on how to teach civil rights history accurately and effectively. Indeed, I wish someone would have handed me a book just like this when I first began teaching.

For their vision and enthusiasm for this project, as well as for the invitation to help lead it, I am forever grateful to John, Brad and Matt. I am also deeply appreciative of Gwen Walker, Adam Mehring, and the staff and faculty board at the University of Wisconsin Press for all they have done to turn this idea into the book that you are now reading.

All the contributors to this volume eagerly joined this project. They too saw the importance of creating this resource to help others teach civil rights history properly. For their time, effort, scholarship, pedagogical insights, and friendship, I thank: Shawn Leigh Alexander, Julie Buckner Armstrong, Steve Bandura, Stephen Berry, Nicole Burrowes, Charlie Cobb, Emilye Crosby, Karlyn Forner, John Gartrell, Michelle Herczog, Wesley Hogan, Charles Hughes, Patrick Jones, Shannon King, Clarence Lang, La TaSha Levy, Charles "Brother Doctor" McKinney, Leonard Moore, Todd "Let's get ready to rumble!" Moye, John Rury, Adam Sanchez, Chris Strain, and Jakobi Williams.

In the summer of 2018, nearly all the contributors to this volume gathered at The Ohio State University for "We who believe in freedom cannot rest": A Symposium on Teaching the Civil Rights Movement. It was an inspiring and energizing gathering. For providing the initial funding for the symposium and for her wise counsel throughout the convening, I thank Simone Drake, my friend and colleague in Ohio State's Department of African American and African Studies. I offer special thanks as well to Ohio State's College of Arts and Sciences for the Large Grant Award for Arts and Humanities, which provided the remaining funding for the symposium. For their able assistance behind the scenes, I thank students Sheneese Thompson, Meghan DeVol, Kyle Huffman, and Karla Haddad, as well as Ohio State history department faculty and staff Scott Levi, Chris Adams, Rhonda Maynard, Laura Seeger, and Steven McCann. Thanks too to Kate Shuster and Maureen Costello of the Southern Poverty Law Center's Teaching Tolerance project for helping us draw connections to K-12 curricula.

Finally, on behalf of everyone who had a hand in creating this book, I humbly thank the many generations of activists and ordinary people who sacrificed so much to make America live up to its professed ideals. I extend sincere gratitude to all of the teachers who taught us, and to all of the teachers who are in the classroom today, keeping the light of freedom burning brightly. And I thank all of our students, to whom the future belongs, for inspiring us to teach civil rights history the best way we know how.

*Understanding and Teaching
the Civil Rights Movement*

Introduction

HASAN KWAME JEFFRIES

The civil rights movement transformed America. It remade public schools by ending de jure segregation in education. It reconfigured the nation's political landscape by enfranchising black southerners. It reshaped public spaces by banning racial discrimination in public accommodations. It reformed the criminal justice system by eliminating all-white juries. It redefined public safety by neutralizing racial terror groups. It reimagined the social safety net by spurring new government-sponsored social services. And it refashioned neighborhoods by opening up housing on a nondiscriminatory basis.

These advances materialized quickly in the 1950s and 1960s, but the struggle to obtain them was many generations old, reaching as far back as the end of slavery. The battle to secure these rights involved a wide range of strategies and tactics, from nonviolent direct action to armed self-defense. And the effort to gain them was hard fought. African Americans were unyielding in their determination to upend the racist status quo, while whites were equally relentless in their defense of it. From Brooklyn to Los Angeles and from Selma to Detroit, African Americans contested labor systems that exploited black workers, challenged political structures that excluded black voters, and confronted social systems that perpetuated white supremacy. Their opponents, meanwhile, did everything in their power, including resorting to mob violence, to maintain and strengthen racially discriminatory systems and structures. But the opposition's efforts were not enough. In the end, those who believed in freedom prevailed, eliminating the most egregious forms of racial discrimination. From the vantage point of the twenty-first century, this outcome seems inevitable, but it was far from a sure thing.

3

Those who led the charge for change were almost always everyday people. They were sharecroppers on white-owned land in Mississippi and factory workers on assembly lines in Ohio. They were domestics in white folks' homes in Louisiana and stevedores in shipyards in Oakland. Still, quite a few extraordinary people emerged from among them. Out of the Virginia Tidewater came Ella Baker. From the Mississippi Delta emerged Fannie Lou Hamer. And Sweet Auburn produced Martin Luther King Jr. Together they organized family, friends, neighbors, and strangers in sustained challenges to the racial order, and they mobilized the masses for dramatic protest marches and demonstrations. But no matter who they were or where they were from, each possessed a vision of a more just society that they articulated through word and deed.

This account of the civil rights movement, which places ordinary black folk at the center of the struggle, reflects consensus thinking among leading civil rights scholars, who over the last twenty-five years have reimagined the movement by looking at it from the bottom up and the inside out. Chief among these scholars are the contributors to this book, who through their research, writing, and teaching have demonstrated the importance of expanding the circle of civil rights leaders beyond Dr. King. They have made clear the significance of emphasizing both mobilizing events and organizing efforts. They have highlighted the necessity of recognizing the full range of movement goals. They have pointed out the need to acknowledge the depth and breadth of white supremacy. And they have revealed that the movement was much more than a nonviolent crusade.

Framing the movement as principally a grassroots struggle, one in which everyday people were the primary catalysts, is the conceptual thread that binds together the twenty-three chapters of *Understanding and Teaching the Civil Rights Movement*. But this account of the movement is not what most students know. They are much more familiar with the deeply flawed version of the movement that veteran activist Julian Bond dubbed the Master Narrative. In this fiction, the movement begins in 1954 when the U.S. Supreme Court concedes that segregation is wrong. It gains momentum when an interracial coalition, inspired by the court's bold action, engages in noble acts of nonviolent protest, ranging from bus boycotts to sit-ins. Dr. King leads this moral crusade and receives the unwavering support of Presidents John F. Kennedy and Lyndon B. Johnson, who put the full weight of the federal government, including

4

the vast resources of the FBI, behind it. It reaches its peak when northern whites learn the disgraceful extent of racial discrimination in the South and southern whites realize that racial prejudice is morally wrong. Then Congress passes landmark legislation designed to end racial discrimination. Unfortunately, African Americans are dissatisfied with the remarkable progress and undermine the movement by rejecting nonviolence, shunning well-meaning whites, and embracing Black Power. Finally, in 1968, Dr. King is killed, effectively ending the movement. But thankfully, by that time, America had essentially righted its racial wrongs, thereby leveling the playing field for future generations and paving the way for Barack Obama.[1]

Students learn about the Master Narrative in the classroom. When the Southern Poverty Law Center (SPLC) reviewed public school curricula for every state in the Union, it found coverage of the civil rights movement to be "woefully inadequate." The problem was that state standards mirrored the Master Narrative. According to the SPLC, many states failed to recognize "the profound national significance of the civil rights movement," choosing instead to see it as "a regional matter." Others saw it as a "topic of interest mainly for black students." The SPLC also reported that there was a tendency to reduce the movement to "lessons about a handful of heroic figures and the four words, 'I have a dream.'" What's more, many states simply promoted a false historical narrative, one that "ignores the nation's blemishes and misrepresents struggles for social justice," which allowed for denials of "the nation's legacy of institutionalized oppression."[2]

Colleges tend to reinforce the Master Narrative. It is not uncommon, especially in American history textbooks, for course content to focus mainly on Dr. King; to overemphasize marches and mass demonstrations; to inflate the support of the federal government; to limit the movement's goals to the pursuit of federal legislation; to reduce the movement's opposition to the Ku Klux Klan and a handful of racist sheriffs; and to overstate African Americans' adherence to nonviolence.

But the Master Narrative is not confined solely to the classroom. It holds a prominent place in popular culture. In fact, popular culture reinforces the fictional version of the movement that the Master Narrative embodies. Every January, when the nation pauses to celebrate the life and legacy of Dr. King, the Master Narrative gets retold. On these occasions, politicians, preachers, teachers, and parents offer King-centric versions of the movement, ones that marginalize, or totally ignore, people, places, programs, and protests not directly connected to the preacher from Georgia. And between King holidays, the media perpetuates the Master Narrative through films that claim to tell the history of the movement, such as Lee Daniels's *The Butler*, and those that only touch on it tangentially but distort it completely, such as *The Help*.

The Master Narrative is stubbornly persistent. It endures in part because it was the first popular version of movement history. When white journalists covered civil rights protests, they explained what they witnessed in terms of the Master Narrative: King spoke; black people followed. The Master Narrative also reinforces the myth of perpetual racial progress. Yes, racial discrimination existed, but Americans, as is their custom, rallied to defeat it. It is "feel good" history, or at the very least, "don't feel so bad" history.

The popularity of the Master Narrative creates real pedagogical challenges for those teaching civil rights history. Not surprisingly, students accept what they have been taught about the essential leadership of preachers and presidents. They embrace what they have been told about the ubiquity of nonviolence and northern colorblindness. And they reiterate what they have learned about the primacy of integration and federal legislation. Having never been presented with a counternarrative, they have no reason to question received wisdom.

Understanding and Teaching the Civil Rights Movement challenges the Master Narrative directly by drawing on the very best civil rights scholarship and pedagogy to provide teachers with what they need to teach civil rights history accurately and effectively. Paying close attention to the particular needs of college-level, American history instructors, as well as to their students' most common knowledge gaps, this book offers detailed overviews of essential civil rights content, suggests practical strategies for teaching civil rights icons, identifies and explains the best ways to use key source material, and presents proven tools for engaging and exciting students.

Understanding and Teaching the Civil Rights Movement is divided into five sections. Each section is organized around a central unifying theme. The themes are teaching experiences, historical context, movement iconography, essential sources, and pedagogical techniques. The first section, "Dispatches from the Frontline," contains four reflections on experiences with teaching civil rights history in traditional and nontraditional settings. In the opening essay, SNCC veteran Charles E.

Cobb Jr., a journalist by profession, offers insightful observations and lessons learned from teaching civil rights in formal and informal settings ever since organizing freedom schools in Mississippi in 1964. In a past life, Steve Bandura taught middle school. Now he coaches little league baseball. Trading in his attendance book for a scorecard has not kept him from teaching. Here he shares a travelogue of the whirlwind civil rights barnstorming tour on which he took his South Philadelphia base-ball team a few summers back, an inspiring twenty-three-day, twenty-one-city journey through the Deep South, Midwest, and Northeast, during which his thirteen-year-olds visited civil rights museums and memorials, met civil rights heroes and heroines, and played exhibition games against local ball clubs. Adam Sanchez, who teaches U.S. history at Harvest Collegiate High School in New York City, discusses the challenges he has faced teaching students more than the Master Narrative and shares some of the imaginative and innovative ways he has been able to push beyond the "Rosa sat, Martin dreamed" framework. In many ways, Sanchez's classroom in Greenwich Village is a world away from history professor Leonard N. Moore's large lecture hall at the University of Texas at Austin, but their curricular aims are remarkably similar—teach a version of civil rights history that reveals rather than obscures, that empowers instead of marginalizes. Moore, who regularly teaches a course on civil rights and Black Power, lets us peer over his shoulder as he teaches nearly two hundred mostly white students shortly after the Ferguson, Missouri, uprising. In each of these essays, teachers will hear echoes of their own interactions with students, as well as glimpse refreshing and exciting possibilities for civil rights instruction.

The second section, "Bigger than a hamburger," offers essential new ways of thinking about the movement. These informational chapters draw inspiration from veteran civil rights activist Ella Baker's 1960 article of the same name in which she chides those who thought the student sit-ins were merely about being able to purchase "a giant sized coke." She points instead to more nuanced economic and political objectives. Stephen A. Berrey opens this section with a close analysis of Jim Crow practices and culture, including the pervasive use of violence to maintain the status quo, making clear the obstacles to civil rights. Students cannot possibly understand what African Americans were fighting for unless they understand what they were fighting against. My chapter on reframing the movement's goals and objectives follows. In it I suggest thinking about the movement as a struggle for freedom

7

rights, the combination of civil and human rights rooted in black protest dating back to slavery, as a way to push beyond the simplistic notion that federal legislation and colorblindness were the movement's
driving objectives. Meanwhile, Christopher B. Strain considers civil
rights strategies and tactics, breaking from the narrow, false dichotomy
of nonviolence versus violence and looking instead at the range of approaches to change embraced by freedom fighters, as well as the ways
these strategies and tactics reinforced one another. Lastly, Patrick D.
Jones directs our attention to the importance of place in civil rights history, emphasizing the absolute need to examine civil rights activism
that occurred beyond Dixie's borders.

When Malcolm X was murdered, Carl Wendell Hines penned "Now
that he is safely dead, let us praise him," a cautionary poem about the
dangers of depoliticizing civil rights martyrs, a fate that has befallen
many movement stalwarts. The chapters in the third section draw on
Hines's keen insight to offer new ways of teaching iconic movement
people, events, and organizations. Charles McKinney and Emilye
Crosby tackle Martin Luther King Jr. and Rosa Parks, the most widely
known and wildly misunderstood movement icons. McKinney revisits
and revises the life and legacy of Dr. King, giving guidance on how to
push beyond the saintly, sanitized version of the man that is typically
taught in classrooms. Crosby, meanwhile, looks anew at Rosa Parks,
suggesting ways to upend the mistaken but long lingering notion that
she was simply a tired seamstress who got swept up in the fast flowing
currents of history. Nicole A. Burrowes and La TaSha B. Levy take on
the 1964 Mississippi Summer Project, the most-written-about event in
civil rights history. Their essay provides a blueprint for how to teach
Freedom Summer in a way that centers local people (rather than white
student volunteers or the federal government), an approach that fundamentally changes how that summer is understood. Clarence Lang
follows with a chapter on Malcolm X and another on the urban uprisings
of the 1960s written with Shawn Leigh Alexander and John Rury. These
two chapters map out how to teach Malcolm as more than Dr. King's
foil, and how to teach the uprisings as more than violence for the sake
of violence. This section ends with Jakobi Williams's curriculum guide
for teaching the Black Panther Party for Self-Defense, the most iconic
movement organization of the 1960s and 1970s. Williams shows how to
use the history of the Panthers to teach the transition from civil rights to
Black Power.

The four chapters in the fourth section build on historian John Hope Franklin's observation that "the essence of scholarship is truth" to examine essential sources for teaching the civil rights movement accurately. J. Todd Moye's opening chapter not only identifies key oral history repositories and explains how to use interviews with movement participants to teach civil rights history, but it also outlines how to construct oral history projects for students of all ages. Among other things, oral histories reveal the singular importance of music to the movement. But the prospect of teaching music in the classroom can be intimidating. Charles L. Hughes provides solutions. He compiles an impressive catalog of freedom songs and popular hits in a "civil rights playlist" and offers easy-to-follow instructions for using these songs to teach civil rights history. Similarly, in "Two Thumbs Up," I identify civil rights movies and documentaries that could and should be used in the classroom, as well as ones to avoid. I also explain how to pair, order, and discuss these films for maximum effectiveness. Movies and music reveal a special kind of truth about the civil rights movement, and like oral history, they complement the usual kinds of primary sources found in archives. Historical collections can play an important role in effective civil rights instruction, but the massive volume of material contained therein can be intimidating. John B. Gartrell demystifies traditional archives, spelling out what goes into them and explaining what kinds of material is best suited for classroom exploration and student assignments. Karlyn Forner concludes this section with a look at civil rights websites, exploring the strengths and weaknesses of high-volume ones such as crmvet.org, a site organized by movement veterans, and taking a deeper dive into the SNCC Digital Gateway, an innovative, online, civil rights archive and portal centered on the organizing experiences of SNCC activists.

Ella Baker's mantra—"strong people don't need strong leaders"—ties together the chapters in the fifth and final section, which considers student-centered and student-led approaches to teaching and learning civil rights history. In "Stay Woke," Julie Buckner Armstrong offers insights into how to use the rich body of civil rights autobiographies, memoirs, novels, short stories, and essays to teach movement history. Literature is just one way to make the movement come alive. Creating an immersive classroom experience is another important way. Wesley Hogan details how to use role-playing to create the kinds of in-class experiences that students can draw upon to better understand the decisions people made during the civil rights era, choices that fundamentally shaped the evolution and trajectory of the movement. The last two chapters in this section use examples of student-centered democratic initiatives to teach civil rights history. Michelle M. Herczog offers the California Democracy School Civic Learning Initiative as a model for teaching civil rights to elementary and high school students, while Shannon King provides insightful instruction on how to use the contemporary #BlackLivesMatter movement to make sense of 1960s era activism.

Civil rights history can teach us about the practice and potential of democracy in the United States. But deciphering its insights requires teaching it accurately and effectively. *Understanding and Teaching the Civil Rights Movement* provides teachers with the necessary analytical framework and proper pedagogical tools and techniques to give full meaning to the African American struggle for freedom and to unlock the unfulfilled promise of democracy in America.

Notes

1. Steven F. Lawson and Charles Payne, *Debating the Civil Rights Movement, 1945–1968* (Lanham, MD: Rowman and Littlefield, 2006), 124–25.

2. *Teaching the Movement: The State of Civil Rights Education 2014* (Montgomery, AL: Southern Poverty Law Center, 2014).

PART ONE

Dispatches from the Frontline

Reflections on Teaching the Civil Rights Movement

Who Is Fannie Lou Hamer?

A Movement Veteran Reflects on Teaching Civil Rights History

CHARLES E. COBB JR.

In order for us as poor and oppressed people to become a part of a society that is meaningful, the system under which we now exist has to be radically changed. That means we are going to have to learn to think in radical terms. I use the term radical in its original meaning—getting down to and understanding the root cause. It means facing a system that does not lend itself to your needs and devising means by which you change that system. That is easier said than done. But one of the things that has to be faced is, in the process of wanting to change that system, how much have we got to do to find out who we are, where we have come from and where we are going. . . . I am saying as you must say too, that in order to see where we are going, we not only must remember where we have been, but we must understand where we have been.

ELLA BAKER, 1969

Nearly two decades ago, I returned to Mississippi, where I had been an organizer for the Student

Nonviolent Coordinating Committee (SNCC). I traveled back to the Magnolia State to hand-deliver copies of *Radical Equations*, a book I had just written with legendary SNCC activist Bob Moses, to friends from my movement days. One of the first people I visited was Shae Goodman Robinson, the principal of Brinkley Middle School. Her school is located in the heart of the capital city of Jackson. My visit was delightful, and afterward, as I sat on the front steps of the school building waiting for my ride, I could not help but think about the many movement people who had sacrificed so much in the fight for freedom. National Association for the Advancement of Colored People (NAACP) activist Medgar Evers, who was shot dead in the driveway of his home very near where I was sitting, came immediately to mind.

As I reflected on Evers, I wondered what the half dozen or so middle school students who were sitting with me knew about him. So I decided to engage them in what I only half-jokingly call "old guy" talk. After I told them that Medgar Evers's home was not far away, I asked, "Can anyone tell me something about him?" I waited eagerly for an answer, but my question was met with stony silence. "You mean none of you can tell me anything about Medgar Evers?" I asked incredulously. Again, nothing. Then one kid finally said, "Didn't he get killed?"

Directly across the street from the school is the Fannie Lou Hamer Public Library. In every way, Mrs. Hamer represented the heart and soul of the Mississippi movement. She was an ordinary person who faced extraordinary circumstances yet never yielded to fear or failure. The youngest of twenty children, she dropped out of school after the sixth grade to work on the cotton plantations of Sunflower County. She was evicted from her home after attempting to register to vote, but that didn't keep her from getting involved in the movement. In fact, it deepened her commitment to fighting for freedom. With a powerful singing voice and keen organizing skills, Mrs. Hamer partnered with young SNCC organizers to help transform Mississippi by challenging the power of southern segregationists and northern liberals. Without Mrs. Hamer, the movement in Mississippi would not have been nearly as effective as it was.

So, having gotten nowhere with Medgar Evers, I decided to shift gears. Nodding toward the library, I asked, "How about Fannie Lou Hamer? Who can say something about her?" But once again, no one said a word.

Civil rights activist and Mississippi Freedom Democratic Party delegate Fannie Lou Hamer speaking at the Democratic National Convention in Atlantic City, New Jersey, on August 22, 1964. (Library of Congress, Prints & Photographs Division, LC-DIG-ppmsc-01267 [digital file from original negative] LC-U9-12470B-17)

By then, my ride had arrived, and as I got up I pointed at the library and told the kids that black Mississippians made a big difference in the civil rights struggle and that Mrs. Hamer was one of the people they needed to learn about if they wanted to understand how those African Americans did it. She was a native Mississippian, I added for emphasis. I also told them that I would be happy to share my remembrances of Mrs. Hamer since I knew her personally.

Just then, as I was about to tell a story that I thought might bring them back to the school's steps when I returned in few days, one of the kids leapt to his feet and in sheer amazement exclaimed, "Mr. Cobb! You was *alive* back then!"

The student's surprise at discovering that I knew Mrs. Hamer personally is easy to understand. After all, her name was chiseled into the facade of a public building, albeit a modest one. For a middle school student at the beginning of the twenty-first century, the 1960s were ancient times. Anybody who knew someone whose name was on a library was most likely dead or tottering on the brink of death, and certainly not likely to be sitting on the steps of their school talking to them.

At the same time, the student's reaction, and the entire conversation for that matter, disturbed me greatly. I had increasingly become distressed over how very little civil rights history the generation to whom the twenty-first century would belong actually knew, and this conversation only intensified my anxiety. But it also changed me forever.

Up to that point, my career as a journalist and writer had revolved around foreign affairs. I had bounced all over the world as a writer for *National Geographic* and as diplomatic correspondent for AllAfrica.com. Yet, with the exception of my book with Bob Moses, I had written almost nothing about the southern freedom movement. The kids on the steps of Brinkley Middle School forced me to face up to the fact that I had an obligation as a writer with a movement background to figure out how best to convey movement history and culture as I understood it. But this charge presented serious challenges, something I learned as a writer and as an occasional college professor.

As a former SNCC organizer, I was inclined to approach telling movement history the way I had organized, from the bottom up and inside out. But despite an expanding body of scholarship stressing the importance of an approach centering on the tradition of grassroots community organizing, elementary and secondary schools across the country continue to stress a top-down and outside-in approach. As a result, a handful of charismatic leaders receive all of the attention to the exclusion of nearly everyone else.

At the same time, the movement is often taught in such a way as to separate and isolate it from the broader American story. Indeed, black protest is usually confined to the South and separated from the much longer history of black protest. The truth is that civil rights era protest was national and a part of an organizing tradition—largely at the grassroots—that includes enslaved revolts, the Underground Railroad, and continuous efforts to challenge the double standards of law and custom under which African Americans have been expected to live since the colonial era. In other words, insisting that "Black Lives Matter" is not new to the struggle.

Similarly, white opposition is frequently reduced to a handful of mad dog sheriffs. Generally speaking, the idea that the movement was a popular challenge to core American values, systems, and institutions that were firmly rooted in the soil of white supremacy is ignored. So too is the fact that America was founded on a great contradiction, immortalized in the words and actions of Thomas Jefferson, who famously declared "that all men are created equal" and infamously held black men, women, and children in bondage. Rather than ignoring these connections, they should be explored, since reconciling this fundamental contradiction has been a motivating factor in the black freedom struggle since the colonial era.

Civil rights history needs to be conveyed in a connected way. Although today it is taught much better in colleges and universities, it is still not taught the way it should be, especially at the elementary and middle school levels. Indeed, having students memorize Martin Luther King Jr.'s "I Have a Dream" speech or sing "Lift Every Voice" during Black History Month is no substitute for learning the intricacies of civil rights history. And using textbooks that barely mention the black experience during the rest of the year does not help either.

There are other challenges aside from these. For several years, I conducted a seminar at Brown University that I titled "The Organizing Tradition of the Southern Civil Rights Movement." The purpose of the seminar was to look beyond protest and carefully examine the tradition of grassroots organizing. Generating interest was not a problem. I was stunned, however, with how wide the knowledge gap was even among the most interested students, a fact that became abundantly clear at the beginning of each semester.

During the very first class session, I would put a dozen or so names on the board and ask students to share, for the class's benefit, what they knew about these people. The technique was not too dissimilar from what I had done on the steps of Brinkley Middle School. I always included a couple of names I was sure would be familiar. Rosa Parks, for example, made the list every time, and Stokely Carmichael joined her often. Most of the names, however, were drawn from the deep currents of community organizing: Amzie Moore, John Hulett, Jo Ann Robinson, or Annie "Mama Dollie" Raines. These were the names of people I was certain would be unfamiliar to the students. When the class completed its "I don't knows," I would explain who these people were. I would also inform them that through our readings and class discussions we would not only learn more about them but also learn about many others just like them. After the roll call of movement notables, I immediately posed two questions. I asked why aren't these names more familiar, and why are these people important? We would return to these questions throughout the semester.

Two things are important to understand with regard to how I conducted this seminar. First, although the class met only once a week, it lasted for two and a half hours, allowing time for thorough discussion. Second, the semester was thirteen weeks long, and I required the students to read a book a week. I was a bit ambivalent about requiring this reading load because, realistically, absorbing an entire book in a week well enough to discuss it analytically is in some regards an unfair ask, especially lengthy books like Stokely Carmichael's autobiography *Ready for Revolution* or James Forman's *The Making of Black Revolutionaries*.[1] I rationalized this requirement by saying to myself that it was important to substantially introduce the students to these books. Generally, in class, I focused discussion on sections of the book that I considered the most important, sometimes directing them in advance to those sections.

I chose not to use audiovisual material, which may have been a modern subconscious rendering of Socrates's aversion to using books. The ancient Athenian philosopher's feeling was that they got in the way of thinking. I have no special pedagogical reason, certainly not in that manner, for avoiding audiovisual material except that the writer in me wanted discussion and conversation, and, perhaps, I am just a little old-fashioned. Notably, the students did not seem to miss the absence of audiovisual material.

I was, however, able to make movement history come alive by bringing civil rights veterans to class. And when they came, I simply introduced them and handed them the reins. Their guest lectures and facilitated discussions thrilled the students by making civil rights history, which the students had been studying, real in a very personal way.

The Africana Studies Department at Brown also allowed me to organize symposia through which I brought many other movement veterans to campus for public forums and classroom interaction. One especially popular symposium was *My Sixties Were Not Your Sixties*. Another symposium took place on the fiftieth anniversary of the founding of SNCC. The presentations at the symposia, unlike the guest lectures, were recorded. The opportunity to hear directly from movement veterans is fading fast as they age, but in the recordings of their interactions and presentations, their thoughts, ideas and remembrances are preserved for future classroom use.

A lot of civil rights scholarship uses movement veterans to track or confirm events, which is valuable. The greatest need, as well as the greatest shortcoming, however, revolves around digging into the thinking and culture of the movement. It is, in the final analysis, the only way that the movement can be meaningfully understood or taught. It is what I found that students know the least about and what they want to know the most about. Sometimes their questions came from a straightforward desire to understand something that does not make sense based on their lived experiences, although they had a kind of intellectual grasp of it. The clearest example of this is nonviolence. Students often asked: "What made you decide to practice nonviolence?"

This same question has come up repeatedly over the years, including once when I was talking to a group of Mississippi high school students about my experiences in the state. I told them that when I decided to stay in Mississippi and work with the movement, I tried to get a Mississippi driver's license. In those days—it was 1962—one had to go to a state Highway Patrol office to get a license. A friend took me to one in Jackson, and I walked inside much like I would have done in my hometown of Washington, DC. "Is this where you get a driving license?" I called out to no one in particular. The next thing I knew a highway patrolman had snatched me up by my shirt, threw me against the wall, slapped me, and then tossed me out the door. As I lay sprawled out on the ground, he leaned over me and snarled: "Nigger, don't ever come in here without saying sir!"

Hearing this story, one of the students asked: "Then what did you do?"

"The only thing I could do," I replied. "I got up, dusted myself off, got back in the car, and left."

"You let him disrespect you like that?" the student asked.

"Well," I chuckled, "I wanted to be around to tell you this story."

The ensuing conversation led to a discussion about young black people and the police. It was not a big leap for them to understand my situation at the highway patrol headquarters and their own sometimes dangerous interactions with police. And that discussion led to another about the practicalities of survival in fraught movement situations.

In Mississippi, we not only had to constantly think about our situation, but also about the situation of the people we were asking to work with us, who often had more at risk than we did. *Thinking* is the key word. I write this some fifty years after Stokely Carmichael's call for Black Power, arguably one of the most misunderstood manifestations of the modern black freedom movement. Much of the negative reaction to Stokely's call grew from people's inability to recognize how and why movement thinking had evolved. It also stemmed from people's failure to appreciate that something much more than anger formed the basis for his call.

The irrational response to Stokely's call was not a historical anomaly. It was a part of a consistent response pattern to radical black critiques of white supremacy. We see much the same thing today in some people's reaction to the Black Lives Matter (BLM) movement. A kind of howl has been emerging in reaction to BLM protests against police violence. "Don't all lives matter?" and "Your slogan is racist!" critics say. It is as if there is no rational reason for these protests. American history confirms that black lives have never mattered much. In a generous mood I will attribute these negative reactions to ignorance rather than hypocrisy, but this ignorance reinforces the case for the need for better education about the freedom movement so that students learn far more than the Master Narrative.

Among the most important things that I have learned through the years is that the struggle continues. It did not end with the passage of new federal civil rights laws in the 1960s or the formation of the Congressional Black Caucus (CBC) in the 1970s. We cannot teach civil rights history if we allow ourselves to become trapped in a narrow timeframe. Furthermore, we would do well to place the "Freedom Rights" postulation of historian Hasan Kwame Jeffries high in our thinking of how to teach the movement. He explains:

> Framing the civil rights movement as a fight for freedom rights acknowledges the centrality of slavery and emancipation to conceptualizations of freedom; incorporates the long history of black protest dating back to the daybreak of freedom and extending beyond the Black Power era; recognizes African Americans' civil and human rights objectives; and captures the universality of these goals. Moreover, it allows for regional and temporal differentiation, moments of ideological radicalization, and periods of social movement formation.[2]

20

My experiences in the movement and in the classroom have convinced me that if we want civil rights history to be useful to young people, then what we teach has to portray black people in meaningful ways. This can and should be done at every educational level, for it is the usefulness of history—what history teaches us to understand about ourselves—more than classroom exercises or syllabi that determines a history lesson's ultimate value. I speak here not as an academic, because I am not one. Instead, I speak as a veteran of the southern freedom movement and as someone still committed to fighting for freedom. What's more, it is clear to me that in the very near future, if not already, we will need to incorporate the current wave of activism and organization by young people into our discussions of the movement. After all, #BlackLivesMatter, Dream Defenders, Moral Mondays, and the many other newly formed organizations of the twenty-first century that have taken up the struggle for change are history in the making.

NOTES

1. Stokely Carmichael, with Ekwueme Michael Thelwell, *Ready for Revolution: The Life and Struggles of Stokely Carmichael (Kwame Ture)* (New York: Scribner, 2005); James Forman, *The Making of Black Revolutionaries* (Seattle: University of Washington Press, 1997).

2. Hasan Kwame Jeffries, *Bloody Lowndes: Civil Rights and Black Power in Alabama's Black Belt* (New York: New York University Press, 2009), 4.

"They won't just be reading about history— they'll be living it"

The Anderson Monarchs Civil Rights Barnstorming Tour

STEVE BANDURA

During the summer of 2015, I took the Anderson Monarchs, a predominantly African American little league baseball team from South Philadelphia, on the journey of a lifetime. For twenty-three days, we rode together in an antique 1947 Flexible Clipper touring bus, the same type of bus that Negro League baseball clubs barnstormed in during the Jim Crow era. The sixty-eight-year-old time capsule, which had no air conditioning, took us to twenty-one cities in the Deep South, Midwest, and Northeast to visit historic civil rights sites, memorials, and museums, to meet veteran civil rights activists, and to play the game we loved.

We traveled 4,500 miles that summer, but what was more impressive than the distance we traversed was the history we covered. The trip was a journey into the past. We set out to discover for ourselves the people, places, and events that defined the civil rights movement, one of the most significant eras in our nation's history. For one month, we made civil rights sites our classroom in order to better understand the movement. Although civil rights struggles cropped up all over the country, the South is where the movement is memorialized most, so that is where we spent the most time exploring historic movement sites. And we came away from the experience with a profoundly richer and deeper knowledge of civil rights history.

Most Americans know very little about this period, and what they do know tends to be grossly oversimplified or just plain wrong. For those who appreciate civil rights history, it is hard to imagine how so many people can know so little about such an important chapter in our nation's past. But I get it. It was not that long ago that I was among that number. Looking back at my own personal history and examining what it took to finally open my eyes to the diversity and complexity of the American experience helps make clear why this period is so often misunderstood and ignored. It also reveals why taking fifteen little leaguers on a civil rights barnstorming tour was so important and impactful.

I was born in 1961, which means that I was alive for a good portion of the modern civil rights movement. But for the life of me I cannot recall civil rights ever being mentioned in my home or anyplace else in my Irish Catholic neighborhood. The nuns in the Catholic school I attended certainly never discussed it publicly; I guess they thought it did not concern us since we were white and lived in one of northeast Philadelphia's all-white, working-class neighborhoods. Life was good, and we did our part. We put money in the collection basket every Sunday to help the poor in countries around the world, but we never took up a collection for people trapped in similarly desperate circumstances here at home. We ignored what was going on in our own country as if no problems existed. And we did not consider whatever problems we thought might have existed to be ours. Later in life I learned that they most certainly were ours.

Growing up, everything I knew, or thought I knew, about race and religion was taught to me by the older kids in my neighborhood, who got their information from eavesdropping on adult conversations and picking up fragments of information from the news. I never questioned what they said. I assumed they just knew about those things because they were older. But they really did not know much. And many of them still do not know much. We lived in a little bubble, rarely, if ever, interacting with people who looked or thought differently than us. Sadly, this was the case for the majority of white Americans. We did not know, and we did not want to know, which is why we find ourselves in the

23

place we are now—in a country deeply divided along racial lines and blinded by hate, with little to no capacity for understanding what has fueled the fires that have burned in places like Ferguson, Missouri, and Baltimore, Maryland.

In 1989 I headed to South Philly to start a boxing program for the Philadelphia Youth Organization. I had so many preconceived notions about the neighborhood as a result of the segregated world in which I lived that it was as if I had traveled to another country. I did not know it at the time, but my true education was about to begin.

Sport, particularly baseball, was an important part of my childhood. It provided me with so many life lessons that I am not sure what my life would have been like without it. I had always assumed that every neighborhood had sports programs for kids, much like the ones I had participated in while growing up. I soon found out that I was terribly mistaken. There were no baseball programs in South Philly, at least none in the African American parts of town. As a result, the kids did not know the game.

This had not always been the case. I learned from some of the older residents in the community that baseball had been a huge part of the community during the 1950s and 1960s. In fact, the Marian Anderson Recreation Center, which had been called McCoach Playground until 1953, had been a hotbed for black baseball during the first half of the twentieth century. But over the years, baseball had faded from everyday life in South Philly. Knowing the positive impact that the sport could have on young people's lives, I was determined to bring it back. I knew that it would not be easy, but I also knew exactly how to begin. The first step was helping the community reconnect with its own rich baseball history.

In 1993, I started the Jackie Robinson Baseball League with a dozen teams composed of five-to-eight-year-olds I had recruited from neighborhood schools. Many of the kids, especially the youngest ones, had never heard of Jackie Robinson or the Negro Leagues. Since they knew almost nothing about this chapter in African American history, I named each of the twelve teams in the league after Negro League ball clubs. I also gave every player a copy of *Jackie Robinson and the Story of All-Black Baseball*, which they had to read and then write a report on before they could play ball. The kids instantly fell in love with the game, as I knew they would, and their parents embraced the program, as I hoped they would.

Two years later, I formed a travel team from the league's all-stars. I named the team the Anderson Monarchs after the Kansas City Monarchs, the Negro League's most famous team, and the ball club that Robinson had played on before joining Major League Baseball's Brooklyn Dodgers. I registered the team to compete in the city's best league—the Devlin League. I had grown up playing Devlin League baseball and knew that we would be the first and only African American team to play in that league. I also knew the kinds of racist attitudes we would encounter when playing the other teams, so I again turned to history to motivate, encourage, and prepare our players for what was to come. I talked to them about the injustices that Negro Leaguers faced in order to pave the way for Robinson, and about what Robinson had to endure to open doors for us. We discussed how he had to struggle on his own, but how we had each other to lean on as we made our own history and paved the way for other African American little league ball clubs. History prepared our kids for their barrier-breaking mission, filling them with immense pride as they carried on Robinson's legacy. They too were baseball pioneers.

Two years after the Monarchs desegregated the Devlin League, the baseball world paused to celebrate the fiftieth anniversary of Robinson breaking Major League Baseball's color barrier. To pay tribute to Robinson and the Negro Leaguers, the eleven-year-old Monarchs boarded a vintage 1947 bus and set out on a barnstorming adventure, just like the Negro League teams had done, playing games, visiting historic sites, and talking to former Negro League players about their experiences. They visited Robinson's gravesite in Brooklyn, stopped at the Negro League Baseball Museum in Kansas City, and finished the tour in Cooperstown, New York, at the National Baseball Hall of Fame. They did not just read about history—they experienced it.

During the summer of 2014, I began thinking about that barnstorming tour. With the protests and unrest in Ferguson and elsewhere around the country, I felt that the current players needed a better understanding of what was going on. So I began planning another trip.

It was of the utmost importance that the kids learned as much as possible about the key events, places, and people of the movement *before* we set out on our journey. This way, their experiences on the tour would enhance and deepen what they already knew. So beginning in December 2014, we gathered every Friday evening in an old locker room in the recreation center and studied African American history. Since young people today are such visual learners, and because textbook accounts of the movement tend to be severely flawed, we examined the black past primarily through documentary films and movies and then discussed what we had watched afterward.

We began our crash course in African American history with the epic television mini-series *Roots* because without understanding slavery and its long-term effects on people and place one can not fully appreciate the need for, and purpose of, the civil rights movement. I also knew that I could not begin teaching the movement by starting with Dr. King, as nearly all textbooks do. There is no way kids can put the movement into proper perspective when it is divorced from its historical context.

After *Roots*, we watched the documentary *Slavery by Another Name*, which explores convict leasing. This film allowed us to discuss the lost opportunities of Reconstruction and the tragic beginning of Jim Crow. Next I showed *Eyes on the Prize: America's Civil Rights Years 1954–1965*, pausing midway through the six-part series on the history of the movement to watch *Freedom Riders*, which examines the effort to desegregate interstate transportation, and Spike Lee's *4 Little Girls*, which tells the heartrending story of the young victims of the 16th Street Baptist Church bombing in Birmingham in 1963. We finished with *Malcolm X: Make It Plain*, a documentary about the life and death of the outspoken Black Nationalist Malcolm X.

Between these films, we had special "movie nights" where we watched historical dramatizations of the black experience. We screened *Glory*, *The Tuskegee Airmen*, *The Court Martial of Jackie Robinson*, *42*, and *Selma*. The kids also read *Claudette Colvin: Twice toward Justice*, the story of the life of a fifteen-year-old resident of Montgomery, Alabama, who in 1955 refused to give up her seat to a white woman, an act of resistance that both preceded and inspired Rosa Parks. This was an especially important book for the kids to read because the number one lesson that I wanted them to take away from our sessions was that young people can create change. We always hear about the contributions of adults and veteran activists, most commonly Martin Luther King Jr. and Rosa Parks, but the movement was fueled by young people—college, high school, and even middle school students—who were willing to sacrifice everything, including their lives, in the fight for freedom and justice.

We spent six months preparing for the trip, studying African American history almost as much as we practiced baseball. When summer rolled around, we were ready to hit the road.

June 17, 2015, Philadelphia, Pennsylvania

I am sitting in the back of an antique 1947 Flexible Clipper touring bus outside of the Marian Anderson Recreation Center in South Philly. With me are the Anderson Monarchs—fourteen boys and one reluctantly famous girl, Mo'ne Davis, the pitching phenom. With tremendous anticipation, and more than a little bit of trepidation, we all handed over our cellphones, waved goodbye to our loved ones, and set out toward Washington, DC, the first stop on our tour.

June 18 and 19, Washington, DC

We were eating breakfast in the hotel lobby when we first heard the horrific news that a white supremacist had shot and killed nine African Americans at Emanuel African Methodist Episcopal Church in Charleston, South Carolina. We sat there as a group, in stunned silence, as the television news anchor described the deadly events of the previous night. "It's like Birmingham all over again," I heard one of the kids say. We all agreed.

A goal of the trip was to get the kids to understand that the movement was not ancient history. Most of the events that they had been studying had taken place in *my* lifetime. In fact, the first Freedom Rides took place during the very week I was born. I also wanted the kids to realize that when laws change, people's attitudes do not necessarily change with them. The Charleston killings made that point all too clear.

We were hoping to start our day by touring 1600 Pennsylvania Avenue and meeting the First Family, the Obamas. I had received a phone call from the White House the week before, confirming the day and time of our tour, which led me to believe that we might be meeting President Barack Obama. Unfortunately, the events in Charleston the night before put an end to that hope.

As great as it would have been to meet the president, it could not have possibly topped the meeting we had later that morning with Congressman John Lewis. Meeting him was, hands down, one of the highlights of the tour. Lewis was already a legend in the kids' minds, a kind of rock star, in fact, because of the films we had watched and the books we had read. They knew that he had been a Freedom Rider, had spoken at the March on Washington, and had attempted to march across Selma's Edmund Pettus Bridge on Bloody Sunday. So when the

Congressman John Lewis discusses his involvement in the civil rights movement with the team. (photo by Al Tielemans)

kids finally met him, they were awestruck. And when he talked about his experiences in the movement, they were mesmerized.

One story in particular had the kids on the verge of tears. Lewis told them about the time an older white man and his son visited his office. The older man confessed that he had been one of the people who had attacked Lewis during one of the many civil rights demonstrations in which Lewis had participated. He came to apologize and ask for forgiveness. When Lewis forgave him, the man started crying and hugged him, prompting the son to start crying and Lewis to do the same. By the end of the story, we were all holding back tears.

During the short question and answer period that followed, the kids did not disappoint. We never discussed possible questions with them, but they were genuinely curious, which came across in their thoughtful queries. "What was your first reaction to the shooting in Charleston last night?" "How did you feel when you decided to continue the Freedom Rides against the wishes of Dr. King? Was it a hard decision?" There were several more questions that I could tell impressed the congressman and his staff because they showed that the kids had been studying the movement. Before we departed, the kids presented Lewis with an official Anderson Monarchs tie. He told them to keep an eye out because he would wear it proudly on the floor of the House of Representatives.

June 23, Atlanta, Georgia

In Atlanta, we visited Dr. King's birthplace, his church, Ebenezer Baptist Church, and his final resting place at the Martin Luther King, Jr. Center for Nonviolent Social Change. The reflecting pond at the King Center, which contains the crypt of Dr. King and his wife, Coretta Scott King, gave the kids a chance to ponder the life, accomplishments, and mortality of Dr. King. It was a much more powerful moment than I had expected.

From there we went to the new National Center for Civil and Human Rights, which turned out to be another highlight. The lunch counter interactive exhibit was haunting. It is one thing to read about the sit-ins and to look at pictures of the protests, but another thing entirely to sit at a replica lunch counter and get a genuine sense of the fear and humiliation that those brave young people endured. The experience made nonviolent direct action come alive. It was scary and upsetting, but a history lesson they will not soon forget.

We also had the honor of meeting Major League Baseball Hall of Famer Hank Aaron. The Atlanta Braves were out of town, but Aaron met us at Turner Field, where the team played their home games. We had studied the history of baseball and the Negro Leagues in great detail, so the kids knew all about Hammerin' Hank's accomplishments on the diamond. Yet, when they talked to Aaron, they were just as interested, perhaps even more so, with his life off the field. They especially wanted to know what it was like growing up in segregated Alabama, and what it was like playing baseball during the Jim Crow era. They asked him about his time playing for the Indianapolis Clowns of the Negro Leagues, and about the death threats he received when he was on the cusp of breaking Babe Ruth's career home run record. Like Representative Lewis, Aaron was deeply impressed with the kids' questions and general knowledge, and he was just as impressed with our ace pitcher, Mo'ne, whom he asked for an autograph.

Our next stop was along Highway 202 in Anniston, Alabama, to see a historical marker commemorating the Freedom Rides, which had begun in May 1961. The marker is located on the exact spot where the

29

Freedom Riders' first bus was ambushed and burned. The Freedom Rides held special meaning for the kids because our bus was following the route that the Freedom Riders had taken. When we stepped off the bus to read the marker and snap a few photos, the kids noticed that the house next door had a large Confederate flag hanging prominently in the front picture window. This was one day after activist Bree Newsome had climbed the flagpole outside of the South Carolina State Capitol and removed the Confederate flag flying there. A CNN reporter who was traveling with us knocked on the door to interview the resident about the flag, but he refused to comment. For the kids, seeing that flag drove home the point that attitudes are harder to change than laws.

June 24, Birmingham, Alabama

Birmingham was the epicenter of the southern movement, so it had a lot of history for the kids to absorb. Our first stop was the 16th Street Baptist Church where the four young girls were murdered by Ku Klux Klansmen in 1963 when a bomb planted at the church exploded shortly after Sunday School had ended. We had been introduced to the bombing in *Eyes on the Prize* and learned more about it in *4 Little Girls*. Three of the girls who died were fourteen years old, and that day Mo'ne turned fourteen, an ironic twist of fate that made the visit especially sobering.

Imagining someone like Mo'ne, a sweet kid with her entire life ahead of her, being taken from us for no reason other than racial hatred, is unfathomable. When a reporter interviewed Mo'ne, she explained that the bombing made her "so sad because we'll never know what those girls could've accomplished."[1] We also got to visit with Denise McNair, one of the victims' sisters. She told us about the void that her sister's death had left in her family and the effect that it had on her and her parents. It was a very emotional moment.

Next we visited Kelly Ingram Park, which is located across the street from the 16th Street Baptist Church. The park served as a central staging ground for mass demonstrations in the city. It was here, during the first week of May 1963, that Birmingham police and firefighters, under orders from Commissioner of Public Safety Eugene "Bull" Connor, confronted the student demonstrators, turning water cannons on them, letting loose police dogs, and arresting thousands. Images of those confrontations were broadcast around the world, garnering the kind of attention

Anderson Monarchs exploring the civil rights sculptures in Kelly Ingrahm Park in Birmingham, Alabama. (photo by Al Tielemans)

that sparked a public outcry and generated sympathy and support for the freedom struggle. The demonstrations in Birmingham brought city leaders to the negotiating table, leading to an agreement to end public segregation locally and increasing momentum for a federal civil rights law to ban segregation. For our kids, the Birmingham crusade underscored the fact that young people helped propel the movement and reinforced the notion that they too could be agents of change.

In the park, there are several sculptures flanking a circular "Freedom Walk." They capture the drama of the 1963 protests. The sculpture titled *I Ain't Afraid of Your Jail*, which depicts a young boy and girl standing behind the bars of a jail cell, was both moving and inspiring.

My favorite photo from the tour is the one of our kids standing behind those bars, staring defiantly out into the world. Looking at their faces, they really "felt" the gravity of this history and the weight of the moment.

There are also sculptures depicting the water cannons and police dogs that had been used on the children, and an emotionally stirring sculpture called *The Four Spirits*, which serves as a memorial to the four girls killed in the church bombing. Walking through the park and standing on the same ground where the student protests had taken place fifty years earlier made the movement come alive.

That night, we paid tribute to the Negro Leagues by playing a game at historic Rickwood Field. The ballpark had been the home of the Birmingham Black Barons of the Negro Leagues and had recently been restored to look as it did during its heyday, when the team featured a young centerfielder and future Hall of Famer named Willie Mays. To make the experience even more realistic, our kids wore throwback uniforms bearing the name of the Negro Leagues' Philadelphia Stars, while the Birmingham team wore Black Barons uniforms. Peering out from the dugout during the game, it was as if, for an hour or two, we had actually traveled back to 1945.

June 25, Montgomery, Alabama

From Birmingham, we drove south to Montgomery, where we visited the Rosa Parks Museum and delved deeper into the people and events surrounding the Montgomery Bus Boycott. The kids found the exhibits in the children's wing especially interesting. I am willing to bet too that we are still the only group to visit the museum in a bus older than the one on which Parks was riding when she was arrested. Many of our kids also brought up Claudette Colvin's protest while we were there.

We did not go very far after we left the Parks museum. We rode only a few blocks away to the Southern Poverty Law Center's (SPLC) Civil Rights Memorial, where its founders, Joe Levin and Morris Dees, welcomed us. The kids were visibly moved by the memorial, which features a circular black granite table bearing the names of the forty-one people, black and white, women and men, known to have died during the civil rights movement. The table also chronicles the history of the movement in lines that radiate outward like the hands of a clock. Water springs from the table's center and flows evenly across its top. Etched into the curved black granite wall behind the table is one of Dr. King's most famous quotes. Drawing on Amos 5:24, Dr. King said, "We will not be satisfied until justice rolls down like waters and righteousness like a mighty stream." Like the Vietnam Veterans Memorial in Washington, DC, which was designed by the same artist, Maya Lin, the Civil Rights Memorial invites visitors to touch the engraved names. Lin envisioned the memorial's plaza as "a contemplative area—a place to remember the Civil Rights Movement, to honor those killed during the struggle, to appreciate how far the country has come in its quest for equality, and to consider how far it has to go." The kids moved slowly around the table, reading the names and running their fingers across each one.

Inside the SPLC museum, the kids eagerly added their names and those of their family members to the "Wall of Tolerance," which displays, in digital form, the names of more than half a million people who have pledged to take a stand against hate and to work for justice and tolerance in their daily lives. Their names flow continuously down the twenty-by-forty-foot wall.

June 26, Selma, Alabama

The next day we drove to Selma, where we were greeted by Mayor George Evans, who escorted us across the Edmund Pettus Bridge. Having seen *Selma*, watched the episode from *Eyes on the Prize* about the Selma voting rights campaign, and listened to John Lewis describe his experiences on Bloody Sunday, all we could think about as we crested the steeply arched span was what it must have been like for the marchers on that terrible day in 1965 as they approached the line of state troopers. It was chilling and powerful. Before leaving, we stopped at the National Voting Rights Museum and Institute, where we talked to others who had been on the bridge that terrible day. This was living history, and the kids were enthralled.

June 27, Jackson, Mississippi

As we crossed the Alabama state line into Mississippi, we discussed Emmett Till, the fourteen-year-old Chicago boy who had been kidnapped and brutally murdered in Money, Mississippi, in 1955. His only offense was being accused of flirting with a white woman.

Anderson Monarchs crossing the Edmund Pettus Bridge in Selma, Alabama. (photo by Al Tielemans)

Till's badly disfigured body had been dumped in the Tallahatchie River. I can still remember the kids' gasps of horror when we were watching *Eyes on the Prize*, and the photo of Till's open casket flashed on the screen. All of the boys on the trip were Till's age when he was lynched.

When we arrived in Jackson, we visited the home of NAACP activist Medgar Evers, who was slain in his driveway in 1963. This stop had a profound impact on the group. During our study sessions, we talked about what it must have been like for the Evers children to see their father gunned down in front of their home. But standing there, in the driveway, on the exact spot where Evers fell, and imagining his wife, Myrlie, running out of the house and seeing her husband lying in a pool of his own blood, was chilling. As we walked through the house and saw where a bullet had torn through the wall in the kitchen, the kids were noticeably upset, imagining what his children must have gone through that night.

Anderson Monarchs learning about the life and death of Mississippi NAACP leader Medgar Evers. (photo by Al Tielemans)

June 28, Little Rock, Arkansas

Our next stop was Little Rock's Central High School, the site of the 1957 school desegregation crisis. As soon as we got there, we watched a short introductory video on the history of the conflict. The video introduced the Little Rock Nine, the intrepid African American students who attempted to desegregate the school. Amazingly, they were only slightly older than our kids. Then a National Park Service ranger led us along the same path to the school's main entrance that the Little Rock Nine had taken when they tried to enter the school. As we approached, we were struck by its size—it was enormous; pictures do not do it justice. The ranger explained that the nine students faced an angry mob of whites on their first day, and for many days after that, and needed a military escort just to enter the building safely.

After we left the school, we met with another unsung hero of the movement, Sybil Jordan Hampton, who attended Little Rock Central soon after the Little Rock Nine. She described how not a single white student spoke to her in the three years she was at the school, and how the white teachers and administrators refused to protect her from physical and verbal abuse. She explained that long after the national press had left Little Rock, the struggle for equal education remained a difficult, uphill climb. Although the story she shared was dispiriting, her message was hopeful. She spoke of forgiveness and understanding. She encouraged our kids to be agents of change, to be leaders in a society desperate for leadership, and to look for ways to promote peace. Her words were moving and inspiring. I could tell that the kids were really "getting it" and I was very proud of them. When Hampton finished speaking, all of the kids stood and hugged her.

June 29, Memphis, Tennessee

We had been on the road for almost two weeks by the time we reached Memphis, and we still had another two weeks to go. But Memphis was our last stop in the Deep South, which was fitting, because we spent our time there touring the National Civil Rights Museum at the Lorraine Motel. This is where Dr. King spent his final night and drew his last breath. In Atlanta, we had reflected on Dr. King's accomplishments. Now, as we peered into Room 306, where Dr. King had stayed, and looked out onto the balcony where he had been gunned down, we thought about everything he had not been able to accomplish because his life had been cut short. Being in that solemn space felt eerie and clearly saddened the kids. Knowing that they were standing where Dr. King's journey had ended cast a pall over the day's activities.

After Memphis, the civil rights side of our trip was mainly over. We made our way north and east, attending professional baseball games, playing little league games of our own, and visiting the Baseball Hall of Fame in Cooperstown, New York. All in all, it was an amazing journey, one in which the kids learned an incredible amount about the past—about the struggles and sacrifices of those who fought for civil and human rights for everyone. They also learned a great deal about the present—about the origins of the problems facing the nation today and about possible solutions. And they learned a lot about themselves—about their own ability to achieve, despite whatever hurdles life put in their way, and about their responsibility to become role models and leaders not only for their community but also for the country.

Anderson Monarchs exploring the March on Washington for Jobs and Freedom Exhibit at the National Civil Rights Museum at the Lorraine Motel in Memphis, Tennessee. (photo by Al Tielemans)

There is a lot of anger in our country today. Indeed, there is a lot of anger around the world. What is lacking, but needed most of all, is empathy. We are quick to judge and quick to blame. We have little tolerance for others who do not look or talk like us. I was one of those people. I lived in the dark, in my comfortable bubble, but now I am determined to do everything in my power to make sure that our kids live in the light. We must make an effort to understand others instead of simply judging them. President Obama once challenged Americans to "cultivate a sense of empathy." He encouraged us to put ourselves "in other people's shoes—to see the world from their eyes." "Empathy," he said, "is a quality of character that can change the world."[2]

As educators, we must strive to meet President Obama's charge, to cultivate a sense of empathy in our students to better prepare them to change the world. Traveling to civil rights sites allowed our kids to see more clearly what it is like to sacrifice and suffer for one's beliefs, strengthening their sense of empathy. Now more than ever they are better prepared to change the world. Indeed, they already have.

NOTES

During our civil rights barnstorming tour, we were extremely fortunate to meet and learn from some of the most highly respected civil rights experts in the country. Their knowledge, insights, and perspectives were invaluable to the success of our trip and our deepening understanding of the movement. The Monarchs would like to thank Bryant Simon from Temple University, Robert Luckett from Jackson State University, Charles McKinney from Rhodes College, and Hasan Kwame Jeffries from The Ohio State University. We would also like to thank the amazingly dedicated men and women of the US National Park Service. We were guided and educated by extremely knowledgeable and enthusiastic park rangers in Washington, DC, Atlanta, Birmingham, and Little Rock. I was amazed at how much pride they took in educating the kids and how much they genuinely enjoyed it. The park rangers were another key to the success of our trip.

1. Frank Bruni, "Baseball and Black History," *New York Times*, June 12, 2015, https://www.nytimes.com/2015/06/14/opinion/sunday/frank-bruni-baseball-and-black-history.html.

2. http://cultureofempathy.com/Obama/SpeechIndex.htm.

Rosa Did More Than Sit and Martin Did More Than Dream

Pushing beyond the Master Narrative with High School Students

ADAM SANCHEZ

"Martin Luther King!" Tyriq shouted. "Rosa Parks!" Kadi chimed in. The names came in rapid succession, and as they did I wrote each one on the white board. "Tell me about Rosa Parks," I asked. "Why was she important?" Margaret answered: "She refused to give up her seat on the bus." Stephon added, "Yeah, she was part of a boycott." "And Martin Luther King?" I queried. "He was about nonviolence," someone said. "He gave speeches," remarked someone else, while yet another student said simply, "He had a dream!"

I start my unit on civil rights by asking my students to name every person and organization involved in the civil rights movement. Without fail, they name the usual suspects. Martin Luther King Jr. leaps from their lips, as does Rosa Parks, Malcolm X, and Emmett Till. Far fewer students are able to name civil rights organizations, but when they do, it is usually the National Association for the Advancement of Colored People (NAACP) or the Black Panther Party for Self-Defense (BPP).

I teach juniors in high school, and for the most part, when they enter my classroom, they have already learned something about the civil rights movement. But what they have been taught is almost always some version of Julian Bond's Master Narrative. As a result, my students tend to see the movement as a nonviolent struggle against racial segregation in the South that somehow morphed into a violent call for Black Power in the North. What's more, they bookend the struggle with the 1954 Supreme Court ruling in *Brown v. Board of Education* and the 1965 Voting Rights Act. They also frame the movement as being wholly dominated by charismatic leaders such as Dr. King and Malcolm X, rather than as having involved thousands of young people like themselves. And even these leaders are often depicted as caricatures of themselves, with simple, static ideas. Besides not being true, this way of seeing the movement reinforces the mistaken belief that America has already overcome its racist past, which leads many to believe that the movement is devoid of lessons for today's struggle for racial justice.

Textbooks tend to reinforce, rather than challenge, the Master Narrative. The Teachers Curriculum Institute's widely used *History Alive! The United States* is fairly typical. Just one page after extolling the virtues of the 1965 Voting Rights Act, the authors write in their "Black Power" section: "By the time King died, many African Americans had lost faith in his vision of a society in which the color of a person's skin didn't matter. Angry young African Americans looked instead to new leaders who talked about black pride and black power."[1]

Missing from this passage is the radical King who in the final years of his life suggested that his dream had "turned into a nightmare," the King who critiqued segregation in the North, opposed the Vietnam War, advocated for a massive redistribution of wealth, called for black pride, and worked closely with proponents of Black Power. What's more, African Americans—before and after King's death—acted on a sober assessment of, and with justified anger at, systemic racism in the United States, rather than by blind faith in a mythic color-blind society.

Also missing are the civil rights roots of Black Power. In 1965, the Student Nonviolent Coordinating Committee (SNCC) began organizing the Lowndes County Freedom Organization (LCFO)—which became known by its ballot symbol, a Black Panther—as an attempt to build an independent political party that could challenge the ruling Democratic Party in Alabama. Out of SNCC's Lowndes County project sprang the "Black Power" slogan and political program.

So instead of looking to textbooks, teachers need to look to each other to truly challenge the Master Narrative. In addition to creating curriculum with colleagues, I have benefited immensely from working with social justice teaching networks such as Rethinking Schools, Teaching for Change, and the Zinn Education Project.

Because most students learn about the civil rights movement long before they enter high school, many come to my class with the idea that they have already learned all there is to know about it. I have found that a good way to get these students to want to learn more, while simultaneously challenging the myths they have been exposed to, is to immediately complicate some of the civil rights icons they have already learned about.

One way I have done this is by simply handing students a list of quotes from Dr. King and Malcolm X. Students think of these two figures as diametrically opposed—nonviolence versus violence, integration versus separation—yet their real ideas were far more complicated. Their ideas were also never static, but rather constantly evolving. As historian Clayborne Carson concludes in his essay "The Unfinished Dialogue of Martin Luther King, Jr. and Malcolm X": "Had they lived, Malcolm and Martin might have advised their followers that the differences between the two were not as significant as was their shared sense of dedication to the struggle for racial advancement. Malcolm came to realize that nonviolent tactics could be used militantly," Carson continues, while Martin "increasingly recognized that mass militancy driven by positive racial consciousness was essential for African American progress."[2]

Yet most grade schools provide students with only a partial snapshot of Martin and Malcolm, usually from 1963, and fail to discuss their political evolution. So when my students try to figure out who called our government "the greatest purveyor of violence in the world" and who hoped we would "get on the right side of the world revolution," they almost never guess correctly that it was Martin. Likewise, they fail to recognize that it was Malcolm who declared repeatedly that he was for "human rights" and grew "convinced that some American whites do want to help cure the rampant racism" in America.

This is an important moment of realization for my students. After examining ten quotes and getting the authorship repeatedly wrong, my student Jeremy declared, "I feel like everything I've been taught about the civil rights movement is a lie." There is, of course, some truth to what Jeremy has already learned, but this is exactly the kind of revelation that encourages students to ask more probing questions and to rethink what they have accepted as gospel truth. Whether it is learning more about Martin or Malcolm, having students revisit the icons they supposedly know so well can be a truly revelatory experience.

As teachers, we also have to move beyond teaching the movement by focusing solely on prominent leaders. If it had not been for ordinary people, we might not even know the names of people like Martin Luther King Jr. or Malcolm X or the organizations that they spearheaded. Furthermore, in confronting racism in today's world, students need to grasp that social change does not simply occur by choosing the right political leader or finding the right tactic to implement, but through slow, patient organizing that empowers oppressed communities. We need a curriculum and pedagogy that allows students to walk in the shoes of yesterday's activists to better understand the struggles of today and tomorrow.

One of the best ways to do this is through role play. On the Zinn Education Project and Rethinking Schools websites, there are several role plays available that I and others have developed for use in the classroom. A mixer role play can be used to introduce students to many unsung heroes of the movement. I cowrote a mixer on the Black Panther Party with Rethinking Schools editor Jesse Hagopian.[3] In this role play, each student assumes the persona of someone who was a member or supporter of the Black Panthers. The roles give students a thumbnail sketch of the person's life history along with details that help illuminate aspects of the BPP. Students are often blown away by the stories they hear. "My character's a badass!" one student exclaimed after reading about Bobby Seale's defiance in a Chicago courtroom following antiwar demonstrations at the Democratic National Convention in 1968.

When students finish reading their roles, I give them eight questions to answer about others, so they have to move about the room and interview the people their classmates are pretending to be. For example, one question on the handout asks students to "Find someone who has an opinion on the role of women in the BPP. Who is this person and what is their opinion?" The point of the mixer is not only to answer the specific questions, but also to learn from the stories being shared in the room to get a more complex picture of the BPP. At the end the exercise, we discuss what the students learned, talking about the stories they found most interesting and surprising, and unpacking the critiques of the Panthers that surfaced. We also try to answer the new questions that the activity generated. Debriefing in this way draws out major movement themes and surfaces the students' specific interests in the BPP, which can be used to shape future study.

One of my favorite activities when I teach the civil rights movement is a role play where students imagine themselves as members of SNCC and debate key issues that the organization faced.[4] Between 1960 and 1968, SNCC evolved from an organization that was heavily influenced by the Southern Christian Leadership Conference (SCLC) to one that allied with the BPP. By scrutinizing the questions SNCC faced during its organizational life, students gain a deeper understanding of how the movement evolved and what difficulties it faced, and, most importantly, they learn that social movements not only involve ordinary people taking action but also discussing and debating a way forward.

When exploring whether SNCC should focus its efforts on voter registration or direct action, my student Dwell suggested, "I think we should focus on voter registration because if we had some sort of political power we could take out the racist politicians." But Jade disagreed. "I think direct action is more useful. We've seen that the *Brown v. Board* decision didn't actually desegregate schools. It took direct action. Action moves things forward faster and we want change now." Giorgio sided with Dwell. "I agree with Dwell," he said. "Focusing on voter registration is going to create a permanent change that will come from the government, not just changes in a few small places." Finally, Shona chimed in with a crucial observation. "I see voter registration *as* direct action. SNCC members get beaten up whether they are doing sit-ins or voter registration. Both are forms of nonviolent disobedience. Why can't we focus on both?"

Debating the answers to these important questions taught the students critical content as well as crucial lessons in civic engagement. Before we debated I described how SNCC ran its meetings, echoing what I was told by SNCC veteran Judy Richardson: "Each one of us is putting our lives on the line, so we want to try and make sure that we come to a decision that we all feel comfortable with," I said. We chose a student facilitator to call on other students before I wrapped things up with another insight gleaned from Richardson: "Now the last thing you need to know about how SNCC ran meetings is that if things got really heated, they would pause and sing a song. So I'm going to teach you a song that they might have sung, and if our discussion at any point gets really contentious, we can pause and sing to remind us that we are all in this together." I sang "Ain't Gonna Let Nobody Turn Me Around" for the students and encouraged them to sing along with me. This was out of my comfort zone as a teacher, just as singing in a social studies class can be out of a student's comfort zone. But it is an essential and beautiful part of the role play. We also sang to refocus our minds following a lockdown drill, and it pleased me to hear some of my students still singing the song as they walked to their next class. In addition to getting a better sense of the debates that shaped the movement, this role play teaches students how to run their own meetings and how to maintain solidarity in the wake of internal tension and external stress.

I have also created role plays that center on a particular organizing campaign. One of the "case studies" that I developed for my students asks them to debate a series of questions that SNCC faced when organizing in Lowndes County, Alabama. One question asks them to respond as SNCC would have responded to increasing racial terrorism. Annika offered: "I think we should stick to the position we had in Mississippi. That we will remain nonviolent, but if people feel the need to carry guns for protection we won't stop them." Aris responded: "Think about this place. It's nicknamed "Bloody" Lowndes County. Nonviolence is going to get you killed. Nonviolence is over. It's been real, but it's over."

Another question asks students to consider whether newly enfranchised African Americans should cast their lot with the Democratic Party or chart a course toward independent, third-party politics, especially given that the slogan of the Alabama Democratic Party was "White Supremacy for the Right." "It's going to be too hard to build our own party. We should just join the Democrats," said Brianna. "What do you mean?" asked Francisco. "It's going to be way harder to take over the Democratic Party when it's run by a bunch of racists who are going to fight us." Jahlila agreed. "Remember the Mississippi Freedom Democratic Party," she said. "The Democratic Party betrayed us." But Brianna remained unconvinced. "Yeah, but aren't the Democratic primaries really important? That's why they organized within the Democratic Party in Mississippi." "But black people are 80 percent of the county here," countered Elian. "If we organize our own party we would win."

Of course, after we role-play these situations, we read about and discuss what actually happened. But these kinds of debates help students see that movement activists had a wide range of choices, meaning that there was nothing inevitable about the movement's evolution. Furthermore, this kind of role play allows students to see themselves as activists. As my student Nakiyah wrote in her final course evaluation, "Learning about SNCC was so interesting because SNCC was so effective." She added: "Knowing that the racism they experienced still exists in a similar but different way today made me want to make a change and gather my generation to fight."

The other aspect of the Master Narrative that has to be challenged in the classroom is its limited time frame and narrow geographic scope. As historian Jeanne Theoharis has noted, before the Watts Rebellion there were more than two decades of nonviolent activism against legalized segregation in Los Angeles. And in 1963, after what is widely taught as a successful nonviolent struggle to desegregate downtown Birmingham, Alabama, two thousand African Americans, angered by ongoing racial terror, took to the streets in the first urban rebellion of the 1960s. Despite the fact that their actions compelled President John F. Kennedy to give a full-throated public endorsement of what would become the 1964 Civil Rights Act, this part of the Birmingham movement's story is often ignored, just as nonviolent direct action is almost always omitted from the story of the 1965 Watts uprising.[5]

These examples reveal that students are often taught a version of the movement that ignores or marginalizes key aspects of civil rights history that are essential to understanding the movement as a whole. By mythologizing the movement, pretending that it was strictly a nonviolent struggle against racial segregation in the South, we ignore grassroots struggles across the country that operated differently.

We have to replace this mistaken narrative with one that locates the struggles of the 1950s and 1960s on a much longer continuum of black protest that stretches back to slavery, that featured self-defense and nonviolent direct action, that dealt with issues of race *and* class, that forged bonds of international solidarity, and that surfaced deep in the heart of the South and far beyond Dixie's borders.

Doing so is profoundly liberating because it compels teachers to develop curricular content for teaching the movement that focuses on those aspects of the struggle that make civil rights history relevant today. Armed with the knowledge about what came before them, our students can help shape today's social justice movements in truly profound ways and continue the struggle for freedom and justice that is many generations old. As my student Morganne stated after learning that the largest civil rights demonstration of the 1960s was not in Selma or Washington, DC, but in the city she grew up in, "Before I knew that people in New York City were a part of the Civil Rights Movement I couldn't see myself in the movement. It felt like everything happened in the South—and people in the West and the North were just sitting back and watching everything. But now that I know that people in New York City—students like me—were a part of the movement, it feels like we can learn from what they did. It helps me make sense of things that happen today."

NOTES

1. Diane Hart et al., *History Alive! The United States* (Palo Alto, CA: Teachers' Curriculum Institute, 2002), 463.

2. Clayborne Carson, "The Unfinished Dialogue of Martin Luther King, Jr. and Malcolm X," *OAH Magazine of History* 19, no. 1 (2005): 22–26.

3. Jesse Hagopian and Adam Sanchez, "What We Don't Learn about the Black Panther Party—but Should," *Rethinking Schools* 32, no. 1 (Fall 2017): 26–33.

4. Adam Sanchez, "Teaching SNCC: The Organization at the Center of the Civil Rights Revolution," *Rethinking Schools* 32, no. 2 (Winter 2017–18).

5. Jeanne Theoharis, "Hidden in Plain Sight: The Civil Rights Movement outside the South," in *The Myth of Southern Exceptionalism*, ed. Matthew D. Lassiter and Joseph Crespino (New York: Oxford University Press, 2010).

"I had this black professor at UT"

Teaching Civil Rights and Black Power to White and Black College Students

LEONARD N. MOORE

One of the most memorable days I've had in my seventeen years as a professor occurred on November 25, 2014. The night before, the St. Louis County district attorney decided not to indict Ferguson, Missouri, police officer Darren Wilson in the shooting death of eighteen-year-old Michael Brown. My family and I had watched CNN's coverage of the Ferguson protest for several hours that evening. While the commentators and many in America focused on the violence, the looting, and the lack of civil order, my wife and I talked about the long pattern of police brutality in America and why the residents of Ferguson reacted so angrily.

When I went to bed that night I knew my Black Power class would be filled to capacity with my students, students not enrolled in the class, alumni, and interested staff. Generally speaking, white students would want to know why black people would burn down their own communities, and black students would want to know how a white police officer could get away with killing an unarmed black man in 2014. I tried to write down some thoughts, but nothing I came up with was satisfying.

When I arrived on campus that morning one of my graduate students said, "Doc, I'm coming to class today. I gotta hear this." As eleven o'clock approached, I put on my suit jacket and headed across Dean Keeton Street to Burdine Hall, still not knowing what I was going to say. When I walked onto the stage I could see that the auditorium was filled beyond capacity. Those who couldn't find a seat sat in the aisles. And those who couldn't get inside stood outside the classroom's double doors. I put on the microphone and pulled a chair to the front of the stage. "I know what all of you want to talk about, and I'm gonna let you talk to each other," I said. "Remember, you can't get mad, and we will be tolerant and respectful of opinions we don't agree with."

For the next seventy-five minutes students of all races stood up and expressed their opinions on Ferguson while the rest of us listened. Although some students came to class expecting me to preach about Ferguson, afterward they expressed their appreciation for the opportunity to talk. As I left class I saw students of all races standing outside Burdine Hall continuing the discussion in productive ways.

Just like that day, at the start of every semester, I walk from my office in the Student Services Building to the large lecture room in Burdine Hall. As I enter the class for the first time the room is always buzzing with excitement, anticipation, and energy. It's electric. When I look out at all 550 students I see how racially diverse the class is. Black students congregate in the middle center. Football players sit in the first few rows. Nigerian Americans occupy the front left. Latinx are in the front center. White liberals have found their way to the middle left. I see the feminists up near the front. And in the back left a large contingent of white Greeks has taken up residence.

The white fraternity boys and sorority girls are noticeable because of their distinct look—they proudly wear their Greek T-shirts as a status symbol. To find so many white Greeks in my History of the Black Power Movement class is still shocking. When I first started teaching this course at the University of Texas at Austin in the fall of 2008, the class was approximately 80 percent African American and enrolled 150 to 200 students. It was so black that we called the experience a miniature Prairie View A&M University, a nod to the historically black college nearby. But over time, as the class became more popular, more and more whites enrolled.

White students who take my course often experience a series of firsts. It's usually the first time many of them have had a black teacher, let alone a black professor. It's the first time many have ever taken a class on African American history. It's the first time many have been in a classroom with so many black and Latinx students. It's the first time many have taken a class that does not meet their parents' approval. It's the first time many have found themselves not a part of the racial majority. And it's the first time many will be in a class that forces them to acknowledge their whiteness and confront their racial privilege.

The white Greek presence in the class is especially interesting because this population is typically the most conservative and the most privileged; they're the ones who usually host racially themed frat parties on West Campus. I'm not suggesting that these students are racist, just that they have been shielded from any discussion about the black experience in America. For a country that has been shaped by race, we do young people a disservice when we allow them to avoid taking a black history course during their K–12 years because we are afraid to confront the brutal realities of racism in America.

"Welcome to History of the Black Power Movement," I say at the beginning of the first class. "This is HIS 317L, so make sure you are in the right place. To be clear, this is a class about black people, approached from a black perspective, and taught by a black professor. White students? Are we clear about that? This is not a black history class taught from your perspective—this is not black history on white people's terms. You are here because you really want to understand the black experience." The reason I am explicit about how the class will be taught is because on a teaching evaluation several years ago one student wrote that she didn't enjoy the class because it was too focused on black people! I continue:

"As you see, I am not politically correct and don't plan to be. We are overly sensitive about race in this country, and this prevents us from having an open, honest dialogue. Please understand we will deal with sensitive issues in this class that most professors avoid. But I have some ground rules."

"Rule 1: You can say whatever you want in this class. Rule 2: You cannot get mad at another student's comment. Rule 3: There are no stupid questions—we are here to learn. Rule 4: I am very opinionated, but you don't have to agree with me to do well in the class. Rule 5: I am not here to change the way you think—I just want you to look at the black experience through a black lens. Rule 6: We will have fun and create a bond over the next fifteen weeks. Rule 7: You will remember this class thirty years from now. And Rule 8: You will always refer to me as 'the black professor I had at UT.'"

The students always laugh at number eight because many of them don't know me as Dr. Moore or Professor Moore; they know me as "the black guy who teaches the black history class."

The end of the first class is always interesting because I typically have a bunch of students who want to speak to me afterward. They say things like: "My friend told me to take this class, and I know that I am going to like it." "I'm a business major, and I've never had a class like this. I grew up in a very conservative environment so a lot of this will be new to me." "I just want you to know that I probably won't agree with everything you say." "I know I look like the typical white guy, but I have a ton of black friends." "This class will be good for me because I don't know much about black history although I dated a black guy in high school." "I've started to read the assigned books, and this is fascinating."

I typically require the students to read five books over the course of the semester, including *Negroes with Guns* by Robert F. Williams and *Die Nigger Die!* by H. Rap Brown. I have been told by my white students that possessing *Negroes with Guns* and *Die Nigger Die!* sparks instant conversation with their friends and roommates. When I inquire about this phenomenon in class, the white students freely share the questions they are asked. "What are you taking that class for? Is it required?" "Why does this class exist?" "Are there any other white students in the class?" "What does it feel like in there?" And my all-time favorite: "Does the professor hate white people?"

Additionally, some white students have mentioned the responses they receive from parents when they tell them about the class. "Now don't get up to Austin and become a liberal!" "Why would UT offer a class like that?" "I hope the class doesn't teach you that we are to blame for all of their problems; slavery ended a long time ago."

There are always several white students who say that they discuss my lectures with their parents over the phone every evening after class. One parent even obtained a copy of the syllabus and read the books along with her daughter who was enrolled in the course. This same parent sent me a thank-you letter at the end of the semester for helping them gain a different perspective on the black experience. The mom admitted that at first she didn't want her child taking the course, but by the end the semester, she realized that it helped both of them grow in amazing ways.

The class is structured as a lecture, but I do my best to make it engaging. I typically start each meeting by posing a provocative question, such as: "Can white teachers effectively teach black children?" And with that, we're off and running.

I also try to make the class as interactive as possible. Indeed, in an era where Google provides instant access to more content than a student can be reasonably expected to digest, the role of the professor is to facilitate, inspire, and prepare. With 550 students, my class often feels more like a town hall meeting than a large lecture.

There are several times during the semester when white students start to get it. The first occurs on the second day, when I show graphic images of African Americans being lynched. In these photographs and picture postcards, there is usually a group of whites surrounding the victim, smiling and posing for the photographer. When I put up the first image the class becomes eerily silent. Some students stare at the image while others put their heads down. Then I ask: "What could this person have done to deserve this? Why are the people standing next to the corpse smiling? Why do the people appear to be well dressed? Why are children present at this event? If you are a white kid and witness this, how would this affect you the rest of your life? If you are a black kid, how would this affect you?"

Another transformative moment in the class comes when we discuss the reparations movement in America. After establishing that Jim Crow was state-sanctioned violence, I then make a relevant application. "Since black people in Texas could not vote until the mid 1960s, that means white voters had a hundred-year head start on black voters. To address this miscarriage of justice, would it be fair to pass a law stating that white voters could not vote again until 2075?" They all say no, even the black students. "What about all of the advantages this gave the white community?" Still the answer is no. Then I provide the following illustration, which they all understand: "Imagine playing Monopoly with five of your friends. At the start of the game, each player gets $1,500, a token to move about the board, and a chance to roll the dice to see who will go first. But right before the game starts you are told that you cannot buy property until everyone else goes around the board twenty times. But you can roll the dice, move around the board, pick cards from Chance and Community Chest, pass GO, pay taxes, and, of course, you can go to jail. But remember, you cannot buy any property.

So when you do finally have the chance to buy property, all of the property has been purchased. If these were the rules of the game, would you ever be able to catch up to other people in the game? No, because at the beginning of the game, the rules were drafted so that you would never be able to compete. This is what happened to African Americans during the period of slavery and Jim Crow—the rules were drafted so that we would always play catch-up."

This is indeed an "aha" moment for many white students in the class, because for the first time in their lives they are able to see the connection between race and public policy. They are able to see how the present is a product of the past.

Our discussion of affirmative action and race in university admissions really touches a nerve with my students. Someone typically tells the class, "My friend, who is white, got a 1530 on his SATs, but because he wasn't in the top 10 percent of his high school graduating class he didn't get into UT. He went to a competitive high school, so why should someone from an inner-city school with lower test scores get in before him?" Good point. "The Top 10 Percent Law rewards those who were the best in their peer group and those from similar backgrounds. So while your friend did get a 1530, he wasn't among the best in his peer group." This typically transitions us into a discussion about standardized testing and whether these exams are measures of intelligence or culturally biased against black people. I help the students process this question by giving them my own five-question IQ test. I ask them to answer the following questions:

- If I told you that I had to go put some money on my uncle's books, what would I be talking about?
- My friend spent his entire paycheck on some 22's. What does this mean?
- If you are up big in a dice game at what point can you leave?
- What does the acronym HBCU mean?
- My grandmother recently told me that my grandfather had the Sugar. What is she talking about?

Then we discuss the answers. Typically, most of the black students get at least four of the answers correct, while the white students get them all wrong. "Now," I ask, "does that make you dumb or unqualified for college because you failed to answer these questions? No, it just means that the questions weren't relevant to your environment."

One particular semester several members of a white fraternity that threw a racially themed party on campus were students in my class. At the party, attendees could swim from one side of the party to another as if they were swimming across the Rio Grande from Mexico into the United States. This, along with other racial stereotyping, upset many students on campus.

When it was brought to my attention that my students were in the fraternity that had held the party, I met one of the Greek alpha males in my office. I asked him if he understood why people were mad. "Dr. Moore, none of us are racist," he pleaded. "We were just trying to have some fun."

I believe him. I truly believe that he had no idea why people responded so angrily. He then suggested I come by the frat house to have dinner with him and his fraternity brothers. When the appointed time came for the dinner, he told me that we needed to postpone it. I'm still waiting. I think that he was ready to have an open discussion about race and racism in America, but his fraternity brothers were not.

Teaching white students about race, racism, and African American history poses a unique set of challenges. But many people are surprised when I tell them that teaching black students their own history has its own unique set of challenges as well. For the most part, African American students enjoy taking my class and other courses on the black experience. For some, it is the only class that they will take at the University of Texas where they will be surrounded by other students of color. "Doc, I look forward to this class because in all of my other classes there are just two or three of us, and we have to speak for the entire race." So out of a class of 550 students, roughly half will be African American, which represents about 15 percent of the university's black population. When I first arrived at Texas in the fall of 1998, I spent several days before the beginning of the semester passing out fliers about my class to black students. For the most part they were excited and receptive. "I will definitely sign up for the class," was how most of them responded. But I did find some resistance. One African American male student told me, "I'm not gonna take the class because I'm not into that black shit." When I asked why he wasn't interested he explained: "Doc, taking black history is a waste of my time. I was born black and I know what it is to be black. How is this gonna help me in life? I don't see why any black student would take a black studies course." After probing a bit further I learned that he was a student in the business school and that he was singularly focused on getting a job in the corporate world. Unfortunately, these conversations are all too often familiar to many of us who teach black history. Some black students simply find my class and other courses on black history devoid of value. However, when these same students see how many white students are in my course, they tend to adjust their outlook and enroll.

If the attitude from the black male student in the business school represents one type of hostility to black history, then another type of hostility is expressed by some African-born students who were raised in the United States. Unfortunately, many African students at universities across the country were taught to look down upon, and not associate with, African American students. "Dr. Moore, I was constantly told by my parents not to become like y'all." When I asked her why, she stated: "Everything we see in Africa about black people in America is bad. Y'all are lazy, y'all complain a lot, and y'all blame white people for everything. There are so many opportunities here in the United States, but y'all don't take advantage of them." The troubling part of her answer lies in the fact that many African students and their parents have no knowledge of the African American experience. Thus, there is no recognition of, or appreciation for, the sacrifices African Americans made to create the opportunities that African-born students and their parents have access to upon arriving in the United States.

At the end of the semester I want skeptical black students to understand that because they now have a firm grounding in their own history, they are better equipped to navigate the turbulent waters of the world beyond UT's gates. Similarly, I want African students to appreciate the African American struggle and to realize that the life experiences of Africans across the globe are interconnected.

The end of every semester brings about mixed feelings. While I am excited about the holiday break, I realize that I will not see this collection of students again. When I finish the last lecture and thank them for taking the class, the students often applaud. As we say our goodbyes and go our separate ways, I can't help but hope that my students' heightened awareness of the black experience and new understanding of American history better prepares them for internships, jobs, and graduate and professional school. What I know for sure, though, is that when they discuss race in America, they will start the conversation with, "I had this black professor at UT."

NOTE

A version of this chapter was originally published as "Seeing Race" in *Alcalde: The Official Publication of the Texas Exes* (September–October 2015).

PART TWO

"Bigger than a hamburger"

Reframing the Civil Rights Movement

Obstacles to Freedom

Life in Jim Crow America

S T E P H E N A . B E R R E Y

The photograph shows two women sitting together, a seat between them. One of the women is white. She is elegantly attired in a black dress and hat with a turquoise necklace draped around her neck. The woman next to her is black. She wears a crisp white maid's uniform and holds a white baby to her chest. Other white people sit or stand behind them, paying no attention to the women or to the camera. On an assignment for *Life* magazine, African American photographer Gordon Parks captured this moment in a waiting area at the Atlanta airport in 1956. His background notes are minimal. Parks tells us that the photograph was taken at approximately 2 a.m. and that the baby's mother is away getting flight information. He adds this observation: "Although the Negro woman serves as nurse-maid for the white woman's baby, the two would not be allowed to sit and eat a meal together in any Atlanta restaurant."

I often show this photograph in class as a prelude to discussing Jim Crow and the barriers to freedom that activists in the civil rights movement fought to dismantle. I ask students to describe what they see. They always express curiosity about the close proximity of the white woman and black woman and the even closer proximity of the white baby and the black woman. Many of them wonder about a possible emotional intimacy among these individuals. I then ask the students to take on the role of historian and hypothesize what this photograph suggests about segregation. Specifically, I ask them to connect this photo to the images that are most often associated with segregation, such

Gordon Parks's photograph of an Atlanta airport waiting area in 1956. The identities of the individuals seen here are unknown. Jim Crow preserved many interracial spaces defined by unequal power relations, such as this one featuring an unseen white employer, an unidentified white woman, and a black nursemaid. Interracial spaces of inequality reinforced ideas of white superiority and privilege alongside black subordination. (courtesy of the Gordon Parks Foundation)

as burning crosses, hooded Ku Klux Klansmen, and separate water fountains. They struggle to reconcile the quietness of the airport scene with the more familiar and more dramatic moments of violence. Parks, though, compels us to make that connection. Through his camera and his brief note, he has us thinking about airports and restaurants, about white families and black maids. He has us wondering about the lives of these women, and in particular the life of the black woman, who is on the job in the middle of the night and in uniform. He has us asking who her family is and where they are at 2 a.m. Parks has us thinking about Jim Crow as more than signs and separate spaces, as more than a series of isolated acts of violence against African Americans. His photograph is a window onto a complex racial system that seeped into every aspect of life, every day.[1]

Jim Crow refers to a national system of race relations that preserved white supremacy in the United States from the late nineteenth century to the mid-twentieth century. The term, which comes from a blackface character of the minstrel stage, denotes a range of practices designed to control black people through the segregation of public and private spaces, the disfranchisement of voters, and the use of lynching and other forms of violence. On a daily basis, Jim Crow practices, laws, and customs shaped expectations for how black people and white people moved, talked, and interacted. Significantly, a national culture that routinely reproduced dehumanizing caricatures of black people and black life reinforced notions of white superiority and encouraged most Americans to understand racial disparities as natural and normal. Jim Crow existed throughout the country, varying only by degree from one region to the next. In each region, this political, economic, social, and cultural system preserved and disguised white privilege in everyday life.[2]

The roots of Jim Crow can be traced to the mid-nineteenth century.[3] In 1860, nearly 95 percent of the 4.4 million African Americans in the United States lived in the South, and more than 93 percent of that population was enslaved, legally owned by other people. Emancipation and the end of the Civil War in 1865 effectively meant that nearly four million African Americans were newly free. However, it was unclear what that freedom would mean in terms of labor, land ownership, voting, and even everyday interracial interactions. Uncertainty and violence, but also hope, marked the postwar period. In an effort to maintain political power, white mobs and vigilante groups, including a new group formed in 1866 and calling themselves the Ku Klux Klan, attacked black people and their Republican allies. In spite of this vigilantism, the Reconstruction years also signaled the beginnings of a significant racial transformation.

The Thirteenth, Fourteenth, and Fifteenth Amendments formally ended slavery, guaranteed all citizens equal protection under the law, and protected African American men's right to vote, respectively. African Americans formed political clubs and voted in large numbers, and many of them won elected office, including a significant number as state legislators in South Carolina and Mississippi. On the economic front, while some African Americans became entrenched in a sharecropping labor system that favored white landowners, others made considerable economic strides. Within a decade of the abolition of slavery, a black middle class was becoming more visible in the South.

By the 1870s and 1880s, many white southerners observed the economic and political gains of African Americans with increasing alarm. These fears often emerged in everyday life when African Americans laid equal claim to public and privileged spaces, such as on sidewalks where they refused to step aside for passing white walkers (a custom from the slavery days). Similarly, when African Americans boarded first-class train cars, they gained access to spaces populated by elite white men and women. As some white travelers in less expensive seats worried about African Americans moving ahead of them on the social ladder, elite white men found their own authority challenged by a black presence. For many white people, the increasing visibility of independent, successful black people in public space symbolized the erosion of white privilege and a society ruled by white people. Many of these interracial spaces became sites of violence, and they attracted the attention of lawmakers.

In 1881, Tennessee lawmakers passed legislation requiring railroad companies to provide "separate cars, or portions of cars cut off by partition wall" for black travelers with first-class tickets. Over the next two decades, state legislatures and local municipalities throughout the South passed laws and ordinances requiring racially separate spaces in seemingly every public and private space, including in restaurants, on streetcars, and in waiting rooms at train stations. In other cases, such as with water fountains, restrooms, hotels, and schools, these measures mandated separate facilities for "white" people and "colored" people. This proliferation of new laws and ordinances—variations of which appeared outside the South, too—garnered the endorsement of the U.S. Supreme Court in the *Plessy v. Ferguson* decision (1896), which based segregation's constitutionality on the doctrine of separate but equal.[4]

The aforementioned legal measures suggest an effort at racial isolation, an attempt to make black people virtually disappear from white sight. But complete separation was often expensive and impractical, and for many it was never the goal. Instead, many white southerners desired a racial system that promoted particular kinds of interracial togetherness akin to the togetherness Parks captured years later in the Atlanta airport. The roots of that scene can be traced back to the *exceptions* that politicians wrote into the earliest segregation measures. The 1881 Tennessee law that called for separate train cars, for example, made this exception: black servants could ride in the same car with their white employers. Other legal measures made related exceptions for black servants to be in white-only spaces when accompanied by white employers. In short, many segregation laws explicitly allowed black people and white people to occupy shared space as long as the black person occupied that space in a subordinate role, serving and in the care of a white person.

While laws stipulated where black people could go and not go, customs guided how black individuals and white individuals were expected to interact in shared spaces. Even in strictly segregated spaces, such as the interior of a bus with two racially separate sections, passengers in either section could see and hear each other. Jim Crow, then, depended on both black people and white people performing—talking, moving, gesturing—in particular, racially distinct ways. For instance, white southerners rigorously enforced the custom from slavery that required black walkers to step off a sidewalk for approaching white walkers. Similarly, black southerners became accustomed to entering through the back doors of white people's homes, going to the take-out windows on the back sides of restaurants, going to the balcony of theaters, moving toward the back of the bus, and moving further back on the bus if white riders spilled out of the "whites only" front section. Generally, white shoppers could—and were expected to—cut in front of black shoppers in lines at stores. Other customs related to verbal expectations. White people, for example, expected African Americans to address them with titles of respect, such as *Mr., Miss, sir,* and *madam.* Conversely, white people did not address black people with those titles—orally or in writing—but instead called black individuals by their first names or by a condescending or dehumanizing nickname such as *auntie, uncle, mammy,* and *boy.* Every interaction became a performance of the racial hierarchy in which the white person talked and moved as the superior and the black person talked and moved as the subordinate. Disregarding Jim Crow laws and customs invited a verbal or violent reprisal.

These various formal and informal measures brought racial order to daily life. These practices also defined what it meant to be white and what it meant to be black in a Jim Crow world. Material benefits came with being white, such as having access to more comfortable and more convenient seating in theaters and restaurants and being able to live in neighborhoods with full municipal services. Being black meant having access to fewer goods and services, to spaces that were often physically inferior to white spaces, such as public schools for black students that

This segregated bus, like many others in the South, featured a movable sign to increase, if necessary, the number of seats available for white passengers. On this bus the African American riders are crowded in the back, with some standing, while white riders spread out comfortably in the front. On a daily basis Jim Crow created opportunities for white comfort and convenience at the expense of black comfort and convenience. (Birmingham, Alabama, Public Library Archives)

received only a small fraction of funding that public schools for white students received. Movement also defined whiteness and blackness. On a daily basis, being black meant being interrupted and disrupted, from stepping aside for white people on a sidewalk to giving up a seat on the bus for a white passenger when the white section filled. In short, Jim Crow laws and customs routinely required African Americans to sacrifice time, space, and comfort so that life could be more convenient for white people. And just as the legal measures made exceptions to allow black servants to be present in white spaces, the customs similarly imposed rules that envisioned black people as servants and white people as masters, everywhere and always.

In the late nineteenth century, white southerners also turned their attention to growing black political influence. Many white political elites worried especially about a potential alliance between black farmers and white farmers within the Populist Party. Across the South, Democrats responded by disfranchising black voters (and some poor white voters) through a range of new measures, including requiring voters to own property, to pay a poll tax, or to pass a literacy test that often included interpreting the Constitution to the satisfaction of the registrar. Democrats also excluded black voters from party primaries, which in the solidly Democratic South nearly always determined who would win the election. When these methods of disfranchisement failed, white southerners turned to terrorism—intimidation and physical violence—to keep black voters from the polls. Their efforts were stunningly effective. In Louisiana in 1896, 130,000 African Americans registered to vote. By 1904 that number had dropped to 1,000. Similar declines occurred across the South. The political realm had effectively become a whites-only space.[5]

The implementation of new segregation laws and practices and the subsequent enforcement of them were possible only through a great deal of violence, ranging from verbal abuse to beatings to sexual assault to lynchings. From the 1880s to 1968, white people lynched more than three thousand African Americans, with the greatest number coming in the first two decades of Jim Crow (averaging more than one hundred per year in the 1890s). Distinguished from other killings, lynchings are conducted by a group of people with the explicit or tacit support of the larger (white) community, and without recourse for the victims within the legal system.[6] In the Jim Crow era, white people carried out lynchings in every region of the country, with more than 80 percent staged in the South.

White people lynched African Americans for a wide range of alleged offenses from homicide to theft to insulting a white person. Stories of black male rapists threatening white women often became a blanket justification for this practice. However, like Jim Crow laws and customs, lynching was not a response to criminal behavior but rather to a growing fear of black independence after emancipation. Lynchings were often community spectacles, with hundreds or even thousands of men, women, and children attending. Torture nearly always preceded death, which most often came from hanging or burning. Afterward spectators frequently took photographs with the victims and sometimes left with charred body parts as souvenirs. Lynchings were becoming less common and more secretive by the 1920s. Throughout the era, though, they delivered a powerful message to the entire black community: white people had authority over black people and could injure and kill black people as they saw fit. The threat of lynching served to reinforce Jim Crow expectations every day.

Whereas most lynching victims were black men, black women had to worry about another form of violence: sexual assault. Compensation for domestic work was low enough that most middle-class families could afford to hire a black domestic worker, and the girls and women who toiled in the homes of white families were particularly susceptible to sexual assault. Compared to the public nature of lynchings, these acts were intentionally quiet and private, hidden from white family members and the community. Available records, however, indicate that these acts occurred frequently. Like lynching, sexual assault served as a reminder of white authority over black people and their bodies.[7]

Much of the discussion thus far has focused on Jim Crow in the South, in large part because prior to the twentieth century, most African Americans lived in the South. Nonetheless, from its beginnings, Jim Crow was a national institution that emerged from mainstream ideas about race and encompassed specific kinds of racial projects in the North and West.[8]

Beginning long before the nineteenth century, European settlers in North America tapped into ideas of white superiority to justify land claims, violence, and the removal of indigenous people. In the late nineteenth century, notions of white supremacy that informed southern laws and customs also underwrote related practices in other regions and for other ethnic groups.[9] In 1882, only a year after Tennessee passed its first segregation measure, a federal law—the Chinese Exclusion Act—banned Chinese immigration, the first such prohibition to target a group from a particular geographic region. In addition, through local practices and ordinances, Chinese Americans already in the country were confined to particular areas in San Francisco, New York, and elsewhere, giving rise to "Chinatowns" and to segregated neighborhoods. Like the stories that positioned black men as a threat to white women, national narratives depicted Chinese Americans as a dangerous menace.

Similar notions of white superiority also informed U.S. imperial projects at the turn of the century with U.S. involvement in Hawaii,

Cuba, Puerto Rico, and the Philippines, and later in Haiti and the Dominican Republic. Federal officials and the media regularly defined U.S. intervention in racial terms, making the case that nonwhite or non-Western natives were not yet ready—not civilized enough—for self-rule. Segregationists in the South had made similar arguments about African Americans after emancipation.

By the early twentieth century, thousands and eventually millions of African Americans migrated out of the South in search of better opportunities and in hopes of escaping the violence and oppression of Jim Crow. They went north and west to Chicago, St. Louis, Detroit, Pittsburgh, Cleveland, New York, Philadelphia, Boston, San Francisco, Los Angeles, and elsewhere. They encountered highly segregated neighborhoods, which were often preserved through restrictive covenants, clauses in housing contracts that prevented sale to particular racial groups understood as not white. Targeted groups varied by locale, but collectively restrictive covenants prevented many people, including African Americans, Mexican Americans, Japanese Americans, Chinese Americans, and Jewish Americans, from moving into "white" neighborhoods.[10] In addition, in the 1930s, federal agencies established policies that came to be known as *redlining*. Federal officials created color-coded maps of cities across the country, identifying some areas as desirable and others as undesirable for investment. Overwhelmingly, they outlined and shaded majority black communities in red (undesirable) and majority white communities in green (desirable). Banks drew on those determinations to make loan decisions. Redlining fostered economic growth in white areas and stunted that growth in areas with larger numbers of people of color.[11] As a result of these policies, segregated neighborhoods defined by dramatic racial disparities became the norm across the United States.[12]

Even without the more formal segregation laws characteristic of the South, across the nation white people maintained segregated public spaces and entertainment venues. Organizers and proprietors of world's fairs, amusement parks, theaters, baseball stadiums, and many businesses either created separate sections for black visitors or excluded them altogether.[13] This system of racial separation included the military, as U.S. armed forces remained segregated until 1948. Segregation also reached into the private sphere as twenty-nine states passed "anti-miscegenation" laws prohibiting marriage across racial lines. As well, even as lynchings were less frequent in the North and West, racial

Sign in a restaurant window in Lancaster, Ohio, in 1938. While segregation is often associated with the South, Jim Crow practices discriminating against African Americans and
other groups identified as nonwhite prevailed in every region of the country. (Library of
Congress, Prints & Photographs Division, FSA/OWI Collection, LC-DIG-fsa-8a17588
[digital file from original neg.] LC-USF3301-006392-M4 [b&w film dup. neg.])

violence—from mob attacks to police brutality—preserved racial lines
and expectations. Forms of discrimination, violence, and separation
extended beyond the black community, including with the forced re-
location and confinement into camps of people of Japanese descent
during World War II.

Nationally, cultural representations of blackness played a critical
role in justifying discrimination and violence and in making Jim Crow
appear normal and necessary. These depictions drew on nineteenth-
century minstrelsy in which white actors donned blackface and mim-
icked black people. Generally characterized as lazy, ignorant, and child-
like, black people were positioned as best suited as slaves on southern
plantations and out of place as free people in the urban North. The popularity of the professional minstrel show peaked by the twentieth century
but churches, schools, and civic groups across the country continued to
stage their own amateur blackface shows into the 1960s and 1970s. Additionally, virtually every emerging popular culture form—vaudeville,

film, radio, animation, and television—extended the demeaning minstrel depictions of blackness. White cultural creators also characterized black people as violent and as dangerous when not controlled. Thus, Hollywood's first blockbuster hit, *The Birth of a Nation* (1915), retold the story of Reconstruction as one where robed and hooded Ku Klux Klan members saved the South from black rule and saved white women from black male rapists (played by white actors in blackface). Even the more comic representations of African Americans, such as in the immensely popular radio and television show *Amos 'n' Andy* (1928–1960), were destructive because they reduced the entire African American population to a few dehumanizing caricatures and perpetuated myths about black inferiority that sustained Jim Crow practices.

Whereas many portrayals of blackness functioned to justify violence and discrimination, others legitimated a harmonious interracial vision of black people happily serving white people. One of the longest enduring of these portrayals is the advertising icon Aunt Jemima. A variation on the "Mammy" figure, Aunt Jemima was heavyset, asexual, and always smiling. She wore a bandana that evoked the slavery era. Like. the mythical Mammy, in advertisements Aunt Jemima faithfully served breakfast to eager white families. Other brands similarly utilized images of black individuals as cheerful servants, such as in the icons for Uncle Ben's rice and Cream of Wheat cereal. Related depictions of black people serving white people, and especially of a nurturing maternal figure, became a mainstay of film, as seen in *Gone with the Wind* in 1939, and in television, as seen in *Beulah* from 1950 to 1952. Similarly, in the 1930s the new industry of animation became a venue for introducing young viewers to stereotypes of black people as lazy, as asexual or hypersexual, as ignorant, and as loyal servants to white families. Through animation, film, radio, television, advertisements, and literature generations of Americans were daily inundated with limited and dehumanizing representations of blackness that suggested that black people preferred segregation and servitude.

By World War II as civil rights mobilizing intensified, Jim Crow's tendrils reached into law, politics, economics, culture, and everyday life. In the South, African Americans lacked the vote, faced a constant threat of physical violence, and navigated a segregated landscape in which they were always expected to play the part of inferiors. If racial expectations in the North and West were relatively less extreme, African Americans nonetheless found themselves confined to segregated and unequal spaces and subject to vigilante and police violence. Challenging white supremacy represented a massive undertaking that entailed changing laws and attitudes, gaining political and economic power, ending racial violence, and transforming a national culture.

As the civil rights movement developed in the 1950s and 1960s, segregationists deployed familiar tactics to save Jim Crow. The newly re-formed Ku Klux Klan and other groups and individuals used threats, beatings, and murder to silence African Americans and their civil rights allies.[14] In 1954, a new white supremacist organization called the Citizens' Council formed to defend segregation, and chapters quickly spread across the South. This organization publicly disavowed Klan violence and instead employed less visible but equally disturbing forms of violence and intimidation to preserve segregation. The police and court officials, meanwhile, turned to arrests and trials to silence activists. Nationally, the federal government was sometimes an ally of civil rights activists and sometimes an impeder—or even foe—of racial change. For instance, the 1954 *Brown v. Board* decision overturned *Plessy* and deemed segregation in schools unconstitutional, but the court initially issued no plan for implementing its ruling, allowing communities to ignore the decision. Meanwhile, the Federal Bureau of Investigation (FBI) spied on and regularly attempted to silence civil rights activists, including Martin Luther King Jr.

As the civil rights movement unfolded, two other obstacles to freedom became more apparent. First, media coverage of the civil rights movement portrayed racism as a uniquely southern problem. Images and descriptions of violence in the South—such as police dogs let loose on activists and angry white people yelling at black people—were important in winning national public support for civil rights. However, when racial uprisings intensified in the urban North and West in the mid 1960s, many white Americans separated these grievances from the Jim Crow practices in the South. More than that, instead of seeing black protestors and activists as having legitimate concerns, many white Americans saw only black criminals and troublemakers. The linkage between racism and the South hindered efforts to address racism nationally in the 1960s and in the following decades.[15]

A second obstacle involved the way racism became narrowly defined in overt and violent terms. Most Americans came to see "whites only" signs, disfranchisement, and Klan rallies as racist. Those understandings were not expansive enough to include restrictive covenants and redlining in cities throughout the United States, the Mammy stereotype, or a black maid holding a white baby in an airport in the middle of the night. For the mainstream, racism became defined as isolated incidents and as overtly violent ones, instead of as the systemic workings of policies and everyday practices.

On this side of the civil rights movement, Gordon Parks's 1956 photograph is a potent reminder of the complexity and the totality of Jim Crow. That racial system sometimes took the form of lynchings and beatings and sometimes of separate water fountains and voter restrictions. But Jim Crow encompassed much more. In the cultural arena, ranging from cartoons to advertising to film to everything in between, it shaped ideas about blackness and whiteness. It defined where white people and nonwhite people could live throughout the country, how they moved and talked in public and private space, and what quality of life they could expect. Laws, policies, customs, beliefs, and practices functioned together ceaselessly to preserve white supremacy and white privilege. Throughout the Jim Crow era, African Americans and their allies worked to dismantle those barriers to freedom.

NOTES

1. Additional Gordon Parks photographs on segregation work well in the classroom and are available online through the Gordon Parks Foundation, http://www.gordonparksfoundation.org/archive/segregation-story-1956.

2. For an overview of Jim Crow, see Jerrold M. Packard, *American Nightmare: The History of Jim Crow* (New York: St. Martin's Press, 2002). For a legal overview, see Michael J. Klarman, *From Jim Crow to Civil Rights: The Supreme Court and the Struggle for Racial Equality* (Oxford: Oxford University Press, 2004).

3. A useful teaching resource that could be used for a debate activity is John David Smith, *When Did Southern Segregation Begin?* (Boston: Bedford/St. Martin's, 2002).

4. The court ruled that segregation was constitutional if the separate spaces were "equal." Such spaces were virtually never equal in a material or aesthetic sense. Furthermore, given that the motivation for segregation was the exclusion of African Americans, from a psychological perspective these spaces symbolized that black people and white people were not equal. Throughout this era African Americans challenged Jim Crow restrictions. For a turn-of-the-century example, see Blair L. M. Kelley, *Right to Ride: Streetcar Boycotts and African American Citizenship in the Era of Plessy v. Ferguson* (Chapel Hill: University of North Carolina Press, 2010). For everyday challenges, see Robin D. G. Kelley, *Race Rebels: Culture, Politics, and the Black Working Class* (New York: Free Press, 1996).

5. *Smith v. Allwright* (1944) deemed the racially discriminatory white primaries unconstitutional.

6. All-white juries meant that courts were rarely a place of justice for African Americans.

7. On sexual assault, see Danielle L. McGuire, *At the Dark End of the Street: Black Women, Rape, and Resistance—A New History of the Civil Rights Movement from Rosa Parks to the Rise of Black Power* (New York: Alfred A. Knopf, 2010).

8. For an overview of responses to Jim Crow in the urban North and West, see Thomas Sugrue, *Sweet Land of Liberty: The Forgotten Struggle for Civil Rights in the North* (New York: Random House, 2008).

9. Ethnic groups in the South also had to navigate Jim Crow binaries. See Malinda Maynor Lowery, *Lumbee Indians in the Jim Crow South: Race, Identity, and the Making of a Nation* (Chapel Hill: University of North Carolina Press, 2010); Julie M. Weise, *Corazón de Dixie: Mexicanos in the U.S. South since 1910* (Chapel Hill: University of North Carolina Press, 2015); and Leslie Bow, *Partly Colored: Asian Americans and Racial Anomaly in the Segregated South* (New York: New York University Press, 2010).

10. The U.S. Supreme Court deemed the restrictive covenant unconstitutional in *Shelley v. Kraemer* (1948). Informally real estate agents and other individuals continued to discriminate against people of color.

11. The redlining maps, which have been digitized for cities across the country, are an excellent visual and interactive teaching tool for understanding the role of federal and private policies in racial discrimination. They are available at https://dsl.richmond.edu/panorama/redlining/.

12. On the migration of African Americans out of the South, see Isabel Wilkerson, *The Warmth of Other Suns: The Epic Story of America's Great Migration* (New York: Random House, 2010). On Jim Crow real estate practices in Chicago, see Beryl Satter, *Family Properties: Race, Real Estate, and the Exploitation of Black Urban America* (New York: Metropolitan Books, 2009). For a southern example, see N. D. B. Connolly, *A World More Concrete: Real Estate and the Remaking of Jim Crow South Florida* (Chicago: University of Chicago Press, 2014).

13. On segregation in spaces of leisure outside the South, see Victoria Wolcott, *Race, Riots, and Roller Coasters: The Struggle over Segregated Recreation in America* (Philadelphia: University of Pennsylvania Press, 2012).

14. Some of the most notorious murders of the era included fourteen-year-old Emmett Till (1955), four African American girls—Addie Mae Collins, Cynthia Wesley, Carole Robertson, and Denise McNair—at a Birmingham church (1963), civil rights leader Medgar Evers (1963), and civil rights workers James Chaney, Andrew Goodman, and Michael Schwerner (1964).

15. On television coverage, see Aniko Bodroghkozy, *Equal Time: Television and the Civil Rights Movement* (Urbana: University of Illinois Press, 2012).

Freedom Rights

Reconsidering the Movement's Goals
and Objectives

HASAN KWAME JEFFRIES

Freedom was the watchword during the civil rights movement. When African Americans gathered at mass meetings, they sang freedom songs. Whey they marched, they shouted "Freedom Now!" When they organized to participate in the political process, they formed freedom parties. When they attempted to desegregate interstate travel, they took freedom rides. And when they created alternative educational institutions, they called them freedom schools.

In the protest lexicon of African Americans, *freedom* was more popular than any other term or phrase. To be sure, there was no single definition of freedom. The term took on different meanings in different contexts. When African American housing activists in major northern cities such as Chicago talked about freedom, they meant helping black people gain access to decent housing on a nondiscriminatory basis. When their counterparts in rural Lowndes County, Alabama, spoke of freedom, they meant helping black people build modern homes on land that was their own.

But a general understanding of what freedom meant did permeate the movement. From Mississippi to Michigan, African Americans embraced the idea that freedom entailed enjoying the full range of civil and human rights afforded white Americans. The roots of this understanding ran deep, reaching as far back as slavery. And its hold on the people was strong.

Although African Americans always had freedom on their minds, the term *civil rights* began to dominate mainstream public discourse in the late 1950s. As the Cold War heated up, black moderates, such as NAACP Executive Director Roy Wilkins, whose approach to change revolved around political and moral appeals to liberal whites, favored framing the struggle solely as a pursuit of civil rights. At a time when red-baiting was rampant, civil rights sounded less un-American. It implied governmental reform, rather than communist revolution.

But rebranding the struggle as a pursuit of civil rights did much more than simply ease liberal white anxiety. It fundamentally changed how people outside of the African American community understood the movement. For them, the struggle became strictly about securing federal legislation to end segregation in public accommodations and to increase black political participation. Gone were the movement's much broader economic and political goals, from nondiscrimination in employment to control of local governments. The movement's core human rights objectives, including gaining access to decent housing and desperately needed healthcare services, also disappeared.

This narrow view of the movement's goals has reverberated through the years, influencing how people understand the movement today. Above all else, instead of seeing the struggle as an effort to secure a wide range of civil and human rights, most people think of it as being primarily concerned with passing antidiscrimination legislation. What's more, this mistaken notion distorts other rudimentary aspects of the movement. It truncates the movement's chronology by pointing to laws such as the 1964 Civil Rights Act and 1965 Voting Rights Act as marking the end of the movement. It obscures grassroots organizing by focusing mainly on those large-scale mobilizing events such as the 1965 Selma to Montgomery March that led directly to new legislation. It understates the gravity of white supremacy by presuming that changing a few laws could end racial discrimination and create equality of opportunity and outcome. And it marginalizes tactics such as armed self-defense and ideologies such as black nationalism that do not fit neatly into political reform frameworks.

Reconceptualizing the movement as a fight for freedom instead of as an effort designed principally to secure civil rights is a necessary first step toward fully comprehending the struggle. Thinking about the movement in this way acknowledges the centrality of slavery and emancipation to the effort to bring about racial justice and equality. It incorporates the long history of black protest dating back to the daybreak of freedom and extending beyond Black Power. It recognizes African Americans' civil and human rights goals. And it allows for regional and temporal differentiation, as well as moments of ideological radicalization.

Understanding the movement requires recognizing freedom as the movement's primary aim. Therefore, making sense of the movement's objectives necessitates tracing the origin of freedom as a goal back to slavery and grasping the concept of freedom rights—the combination of civil and human rights that newly emancipated African Americans sought as soon as slavery ended. It also requires examining the pursuit of freedom rights during the high point of black protest in the 1950s and 1960s.

Among the nation's founders, no one had a better grasp of the meaning of freedom than James Madison, the fourth president of the United States and the architect of the Bill of Rights. He knew that in order for the young republic to survive and thrive, its people had to be able to worship as they pleased, assemble when they wanted, speak what was on their mind, arm and protect themselves, and receive due process under the law. He gleaned this understanding in part from the four thousand books in his personal library at Montpelier, his plantation estate in the Virginia countryside, where he spent endless hours pouring over the writings of Greek philosophers and Enlightenment thinkers. But Madison need not let his mind wander far from his home to appreciate the importance of freedom. All he had to do was walk among the one hundred African American men, women, and children he held in bondage on his plantation. Enslaving so many for so long taught Madison all he needed to know about the meaning and importance of freedom.

But Madison was not the only person at Montpelier with a profound grasp of freedom. The members of Montpelier's enslaved community knew what freedom meant too. In fact, they had a much deeper understanding of it than Madison because they knew exactly what it was like to live without it. They did not need European sages to point out that freedom meant enjoying those fundamental civil and human rights that Madison, and his father before him, and his father's father before him, denied them. They need only wake up and reflect upon the entirety of their lives, which was spent toiling under the lash for the economic benefit of others; living in cramped quarters with few possessions and no privacy; worrying constantly about being separated from loved ones through sale; being prevented from learning to read and write; not being allowed to come and go as they pleased; and having no recourse for redress under the law.

For the enslaved at Montpelier and everywhere else, freedom was not an abstraction, but a concrete notion. By law, they were property, chattel that could be bought and sold. Freedom, therefore, had a single, clear meaning—emancipation, and the enslaved knew that the only way to bring it about was to sever the ties that bound them to their enslavers. Free blacks understood this too. They knew that as long as some black people wore the shackles of slaves, then all black people would be treated unequally.

Emancipation, however, was extremely hard to come by. It could happen through manumission, although most enslavers, like Madison, did not free a single soul, even upon their deaths. It could occur by court order, although judges rarely recognized an enslaved person's right to petition or sue. And it could take place as a result of escape, although self-emancipatory actions, such as Ellen Stewart's failed attempt to steal away from the Madisons aboard the schooner *The Pearl* in 1848, hardly ever succeeded. So it was that four million enslaved African Americans did not experience the freedom of emancipation until the Confederacy collapsed in 1865.

Emancipation did not change African Americans' deeply held desire for freedom, but it did cause them to refine their understanding of it. As soon as slavery ended, they reflected on their experiences in bondage and identified those fundamental civil and human rights that slaveholders had denied them. They viewed this assortment of government guarantees and birthrights as their freedom rights, and not only did they claim them as free people, but they also made securing them the basis of their post-emancipation agenda.

In the simplest terms, emancipated African Americans wanted the freedom not to be treated as slaves. In white, clapboard churches nestled quietly at the end of dusty dirt roads in places such as Claiborne County, Mississippi, they expressed this desire through spirituals. Together, they sang:

> Oh, freedom,
> Oh, freedom,
> Oh, freedom over me.
> And before I'd be a slave,
> I'd be buried in my grave,
> And go home to my Lord and be free.

Since slavery touched every aspect of black life, the pursuit of freedom rights did the same. To reap the reward of their own labor, African Americans refused to work in gangs, insisting instead on farming land they owned, and when this proved impossible, settling into rental and sharecropping arrangements. To preserve the integrity of their families, they flocked to county courthouses and recorded their marriages. To improve their living conditions, they abandoned the slave quarters and built single-family cabins away from prying white eyes. To ensure cultural autonomy, they withdrew from white churches and established black ones. To learn the basics of reading and writing, they petitioned the federal government to start elementary schools. To have a say in the political decisions that affected their lives, they registered to vote and cast ballots for candidates willing to stand against the plantocracy. And to protect themselves against white terrorists, they took up arms, defending themselves individually and collectively.

But as the new century dawned, freedom rights remained elusive. In fact, the gains that had been made immediately after emancipation were rapidly eroding. Sharecropping robbed African Americans of economic security. Segregated schools denied them quality education. Disenfranchisement silenced their political voice. Jim Crow accommodations stole their dignity. And lynching took their lives. Still, freedom rights remained African Americans' primary goal. W. E. B. Du Bois, one of black America's leading lights, gave voice to this idea in 1905 when explaining the aims of the newly formed Niagara Movement. "We claim for ourselves every single right that belongs to a freeborn American—political, civil and social." And he did not see the struggle abating anytime soon. "Until we get these rights," he said, "we will never cease to protest and assail the ears of America."[1]

As Du Bois predicted, African Americans continued to organize and raise their voices in dissent in the early decades of the twentieth century. Millions rallied to Marcus Garvey's "Back to Africa" clarion call, intrigued by the utopian dream of a mass exodus from the United States and inspired by the full-throated demand for freedom rights enumerated in the Universal Negro Improvement Association's (UNIA) "Declaration of the Rights of Negro Peoples of the World." Black migrants exercised their right of mobility, leaving the Jim Crow South behind in search of a better life in the industrial North. Black workers, in factories and fields, attempted to organize for better wages and nondiscriminatory employment practices. They found common cause with whites whenever possible, as some did in the tobacco warehouses of Winston-Salem, and they struck out on their own whenever necessary, as others did in the steel mills of Pittsburgh. Black educators demanded excellence in segregated public schools such as Dunbar High School in Washington, DC, which helped produce a cadre of black professionals committed to freedom rights, including attorney Charles Hamilton Houston, the architect of the NAACP's school desegregation campaign. Black artists reimagined black culture, asserting a new kind of autonomy of interpretation and integrity of expression, leading to a renaissance of art and spirit in Harlem and Chicago. And black homeowners such as Ossian Sweet, who was attacked by a lynch mob when he and his family moved into a white neighborhood in Detroit, picked up guns to defend their lives and property.

Although African Americans valued all of their freedom rights the same, they did not pursue them with equal vigor. Doing so would have been too dangerous. In Alabama, it made no sense to agitate for voting rights following the ratification of the 1901 state constitution, which expressly disenfranchised African Americans, since whites made it clear through word and deed that even attempting to register would be met with swift and severe violence. In Florida, however, where African Americans had a little more space to operate, they participated freely in the political process, registering, casting ballots, and even running candidates, at least until the Bloody Election of 1920. Keenly aware of the social and political environment in which they lived, African Americans made close and careful assessments of the risks and rewards of agitating for freedom rights, deciding when and where to pursue them depending on the likelihood of success and the probability of death.

At midcentury, African Americans continued to frame their struggle as a quest for freedom. As the nation raced headlong into World War II, the prominent black newspaper the *Pittsburgh Courier* introduced the

Double "V" campaign. "In our fight for freedom," the editors wrote, "we wage a two-pronged attack against our enslavers at home and those abroad who will enslave us."[2] The campaign resonated with African Americans, many of whom had been wrestling with the idea of fighting for freedom over there, while being denied freedom over here.

Pressing the issue at the highest levels, African Americans lobbied President Franklin D. Roosevelt for equal treatment in the military, an appeal he ignored, and for nondiscrimination in defense industry employment, a demand he eventually agreed to in order to keep labor activist A. Philip Randolph and a hundred thousand black folk from marching on Washington, DC. They also challenged the constitutionality of the all-white primary, restrictive covenants, and segregation in higher education, winning precedent-setting rulings that enabled black political activists to form an independent statewide third party in South Carolina, eliminating a major weapon in the arsenal of those who wanted to keep African Americans from buying homes in white neighborhoods, and paving the way for *Brown v. Board of Education.*

Closer to the ground, African Americans remained as committed as ever to freedom rights. Like the generation of black workers before them, they migrated to industrial centers outside the South in search of better life opportunities. They leapt at chances to move into new, modern, public housing, since decent private sector housing was rarely made available to them. They resisted the daily indignities of Jim Crow by quietly avoiding segregated five-and-dime stores and not so quietly confronting abusive municipal bus drivers. And they affirmed their humanity through recreation and leisure. In the Magic City, they found escape by going to historic Rickwood Field to watch the Birmingham Black Barons take on Negro League rivals such as the Kansas City Monarchs.

When the war ended, American victory abroad did not translate into African American victory at home. Indeed, Jim Crow persisted everywhere, effecting black life as profoundly in New York City as it did in New Orleans. There would be some notable firsts in the offing, such as Jackie Robinson breaking into Major League Baseball in 1947, making him the first African American to play white professional baseball in the twentieth century. But the goal of the movement was never simply creating an opportunity for a black first, but rather to clear the way for a second, a third, and a fourth. Having Robinson play for the Brooklyn

Dodgers was a milestone in the struggle to desegregate professional sports, a turning point, in fact. But it did not mark the end of this effort. Instead, it signaled the start of a new, and in many ways more militant, phase.

For a brief time after the Allied victory, space did open up for African Americans to agitate for freedom in the broadest possible terms. To help stave off future Nazi-like aggression, world leaders formed the United Nations and charged it with maintaining global peace and solving the economic, social, and cultural problems that plagued so many nations, including the United States. Seizing the moment, Du Bois made the case for the movement's human rights objectives and for UN intervention. In "An Appeal to the World," the founding editor of the NAACP's *The Crisis* magazine explained the systematic denial of African Americans' human rights and called on the world body to act. "Our treatment in America is not merely an internal question of the United States," he wrote. "It is a basic problem of humanity; of democracy; of discrimination because of race and color; and as such it demands your attention and action. No nation is so great that the world can afford to let it continue to be deliberately unjust, cruel and unfair toward its own citizens."[3]

But the Cold War soon collapsed the space that Du Bois and others had used to assert African Americans' human rights claims. And although black moderates increasingly shied away from framing the struggle as anything but a civil rights campaign, others in the movement did not. When the state of Alabama outlawed the NAACP in 1956, activists in Birmingham formed the Alabama Christian Movement for Human Rights, making sure the name of their new group reflected the people's core objective. And a decade later, activists in nearby Lowndes County did the same, forming the Lowndes County Christian Movement for Human Rights.

It is hardly surprising, then, that despite the Cold War crackdown, African Americans continued to agitate for freedom in the 1960s. This meant organizing for the full range of freedom rights, not just for civil rights. To secure quality education, they worked to desegregate white schools in New York City and improve segregated black schools in Hyde County, North Carolina. It did not matter whether black children sat next to white kids or black ones as long as they received the education they deserved. To bring about black political empowerment, they registered black voters in the Mississippi Delta and formed freedom parties in the Alabama Black Belt. If the Democratic Party would not let them have a say in the decisions that affected their lives, then they would form their own independent parties. To provide decent housing, they held fair housing demonstrations in Milwaukee at the same time as they launched a self-help housing construction program in Lowndes County. They could care less who their neighbors were as long as those neighbors did not discriminate against them. To change the behavior of violent white supremacists, they demonstrated nonviolently in St. Augustine, Florida, and formed the Deacons for Defense and Justice in Jonesboro, Louisiana. If stopping racial terrorism required the use of guns, then so be it. And to achieve economic justice, sanitation and hospital workers went on strike in Memphis and Charleston, while black autoworkers formed their own unions in Detroit. African Americans were willing to challenge both management and organized labor to ensure nondiscrimination in hiring and promotion, fair wages, and just treatment.

As Black Power gained momentum in the late 1960s, freedom remained the watchword, and freedom rights remained the goal. Indeed, there was tremendous continuity in the movement's aims after the 1960s, much like there was before. To be sure, the tenor and tone of black protest changed as African Americans lost patience with the pace of progress and grew less concerned with liberal white criticism of the struggle. Most importantly, though, the movement's goals had not been fully achieved. Schools had been desegregated, but integration and quality education remained elusive. Voting booths were accessible, but too few black elected officials had the power, and too few white ones had the will, to substantially improve black people's lives. Public sector jobs had opened up, but deindustrialization, agricultural mechanization, and racial discrimination made well-paying private sector ones hard to come by. Fair housing protections had been strengthened, but residential segregation had intensified, leaving African Americans trapped and isolated in decaying cities. And racial terror groups had been broken up, but very little had been done to stop police violence.

The civil rights movement was about a great deal more than enjoying a handful of government promises and protections. It was about securing the wide spectrum of civil and human rights that African Americans had been denied during slavery and that they claimed as free people immediately after emancipation. These were their freedom rights, and they fought vigorously for them for the next century. Thus, the starting point for fully comprehending the movement, and for teaching it effectively, is identifying and contextualizing its deeply rooted and broadly configured freedom rights objectives.

NOTES

1. W. E. B. Du Bois, "Battle for Humanity," in *In Our Own Words: Extraordinary Speeches of the American Century*, ed. Robert Torricelli and Andrew Carroll (New York: Kodansha America, 1999), 18.

2. "The Courier's Double 'V' for a Double Victory Campaign Gets Country-Wide Support," *Pittsburgh Courier*, February 14, 1942.

3. Jon E. Taylor, *Freedom to Serve: Truman, Civil Rights, and Executive Order 9981* (New York: Routledge, 2013), 81.

The Ballot *and* the Bullet

Rethinking the Violent/Nonviolent Dichotomy

CHRISTOPHER B. STRAIN

Dichotomies are useful, giving the brain a simple way to process information. Just as computer functions start with a one or a zero—the simplest of binaries—human cognition begins with "either-or" comparisons: on/off, light/dark, happy/sad, and so on. Categorization and compartmentalization are fundamentals of learning, and as with other forms of inquiry and analysis, dichotomies form the basic taxonomies of historical knowledge. For instance, a profusion of dichotomies tends to dominate understanding of the 1960s: love/hate, peace/war, liberal/conservative, mainstream/alternative, hip/square, JFK/LBJ, Beatles/Stones, Woodstock/Altamont, black/white, integration/separation, Martin/Malcolm, and violence/nonviolence. They offer a straightforward "this-way, that-way" lens through which to view this tumultuous period. There were those who fought patriotically in Vietnam, and there were those who grew out their hair and opposed the war. There were housewives and feminists, hardhats and hippies, "freaks" and "straights." There were those who observed the philosophy of nonviolence, and those who looked for freedom down the sights of a gun.

But as author James Thurber once wrote (using a dichotomy himself), "There are two kinds of light—the glow that illuminates, and the glare that obscures." Many of these 1960s dichotomies turn out to be, upon closer inspection, much less cut-and-dried than they initially appear—particularly the violent/nonviolent dichotomy, clearly delineated by Malcolm X in his famous 1964 speech "The Ballot or the Bullet." This chapter explains this bifurcation and shows why it is insufficient in studying the civil rights movement; discusses how the issue of armed self-defense complicates the violent/nonviolent dichotomy; and contends that the civil rights movement must be considered *contextually* (in a historical framework), *constitutionally* (in terms of rights and liberties), and *confrontationally* (as a gesture of protest) in order to be fully understood.

Consider the typical students of the civil rights movement. When first studying the movement, they learn about Dr. Martin Luther King Jr., Rosa Parks, Montgomery, Birmingham, sit-ins, freedom rides, and so forth. They may meet the towering ministers of the Southern Christian Leadership Conference—Rev. Ralph David Abernathy of Montgomery, Rev. Fred Shuttlesworth of Birmingham, Rev. Joseph Lowery of Mobile, Rev. C. K. Steele of Tallahassee—or the youthful idealists of the Student Nonviolent Coordinating Committee: Marion Berry Jr., John Lewis, Charles McDew, Bob Moses, Diane Nash, Julian Bond, James Forman, and others. Mention is made of the brave yet iconoclastic James Meredith, the lone crusader who desegregated Ole Miss in 1962. Digging a little deeper they meet Jo Ann Robinson, Bayard Rustin, Ella Baker, Jim Lawson, Stanley Levison—the theorists and tacticians who made nonviolent direct action so effective.

These students then learn about Malcolm X, Stokely Carmichael, Black Power, and the Black Panthers. They see the famous photo of the outspoken Nation of Islam minister, jabbing the air with his index finger, lower lip folded under his top teeth in a frozen "F" (as if to tell white America *exactly* what he thinks), or the one of him peering out from behind the living-room curtain with a rifle in his hand. They hear the story of SNCC's Carmichael riling a crowd in the Mississippi night, asking them what they want. "Black Power!" they roar ominously, encouraged by fellow activist Willie Ricks. These students see the video footage of the Panthers lining up mechanically in front of the Alameda County Courthouse in Oakland: stylin' and profilin,' ready for war. Often remembered as the appalling doppelgangers of the civil rights movement, these people, concepts, and organizations form a collective counterpoint to the dominant nonviolent narrative of civil rights. They complete the violent/nonviolent dichotomy.

Students' interest piqued, intrigued by these stories of heroes and anti-heroes, they then delve further into the historical record, studying civil rights memoirs and secondary texts written by historians. They begin to read critically, perhaps even doing their own research in primary sources. And in the course of their studies, the curious students stumble across Robert F. Williams, who organized armed resistance in 1957 against the Ku Klux Klan in Monroe, North Carolina, and wrote *Negroes with Guns* (1962), an affirmation of armed self-defense by African Americans. They learn the story of his exile to Cuba. They encounter the Deacons for Defense and Justice, an armed guard unit in Bogalusa, Louisiana, which also combated the Klan and provided protection for civil rights activists pledged to nonviolence. They meet Gloria Richardson: a forty-year-old divorcee and mother of two who led the civil rights campaign in Cambridge, Maryland. A graduate of Howard University and daughter of a prominent local family, Richardson in 1962 helped organize the Cambridge Nonviolent Action Committee; by the summer of 1963, she was carrying a gun, warning off government troops, and countering white aggressors who fired at the homes of black organizers. Students may even chance upon "The Ballad of Joan Little," a 1975 folksong that retells how the twenty-one-year-old Little, indicted for first-degree murder in Beaufort County, North Carolina, in 1974 for killing the jailor who attacked her, was found not guilty, becoming the first woman in U.S. history to be acquitted for using deadly force to resist sexual assault.

These characters have never quite seemed to fit the civil rights master narrative, and historians have until recently been unkind to these figures on the periphery. To illustrate, Fred Powledge—a journalist who covered the movement—called Robert Williams "a transitory phenomenon, a mere glitch in the chronology of those years—the exception to the rule." General histories of the civil rights movement have also tended to marginalize Williams. For example, Harvard Sitkoff has provided an accurate synopsis of Williams's activism, describing both his counterpoint to King and his fearful image in the media; however, Sitkoff's *The Struggle for Black Equality, 1954–1992* treats him as tangential to the larger movement. More recent studies such as Timothy Tyson's *Radio Free Dixie: Robert F. Williams and the Roots of Black Power* have corrected the historical record, moving Williams closer toward the center of civil rights historiography, but the perception still lingers that

Williams was, like James Meredith, a civil rights maverick, marching to the beat of his own drum.[1]

Martin Luther King Jr. and others, however, acknowledged Williams as a central figure in the movement, one who opposed King diametrically before Malcolm X filled that role. King and Williams sparred in print, taking jabs at each other in the press. In the summer of 1959, Williams began publishing his newsletter, the *Crusader*. That same year, Lawrence D. Reddick published an early biography of Dr. King, which he called, in a seeming nod to Williams, *Crusader without Violence*. The peerless scholar-activist W. E. B. Du Bois also respected Robert Williams, whom he admired as much as, if not more than, Dr. King. Du Bois, in fact, criticized both King and Reddick in a 1959 review of Reddick's *Crusader without Violence* published in the *National Guardian*, in which he described Reddick's portrayal of King as "interesting and appealing but a little disturbing." King's application of nonviolence in Montgomery was "well-known and deserves wide praise, but leaves me a little in doubt," he wrote. "I was sorry to see King lauded for his opposition to the young colored man in North Carolina who declared that in order to stop lynching and mob violence, Negroes must fight back."[2]

If civil rights leaders such as King and Du Bois treated Williams seriously, then shouldn't we? Were Williams and Richardson and the Deacons indeed aberrations, or did they represent an underlying ambiguity within the movement? How did these activists fit within the accepted nonviolent paradigm defined by mainstream civil rights activists? What is a "mainstream civil rights activist," anyway? Once such questions begin, it is difficult to know where to stop. In fact, the square pegs of the civil rights movement necessitate a reconsideration of the dichotomies themselves. Were the Panthers really monsters, with their Free Breakfast Program, courageous stand against police brutality, and pointed critiques of racism, classism, and sexism? Were Martin and Malcolm really so different? Were nonviolence and "violence," in the form of armed self-defense, mutually exclusive?

Furthermore, how many activists believed wholeheartedly and unabashedly in nonviolence, not simply as a tactic in civil rights reform but as a way of realigning human relations? Fifty years later it is still unclear, necessitating further inquiry. Nonviolence as a way of life ran afoul of traditional American notions of manhood that required in-kind response to aggression and incivility—particularly in the South—and those who study the civil rights movement do not have to read very deeply to find those activists who honored nonviolence in public but expressed doubt in private. That outlook was so common that it has become a familiar trope in civil rights studies, what I call the "OK-I'll-be-nonviolent-during-this-march-but-so-help-me-if-one-of-these-crackers-lays-a-hand-on-me-later" mindset.

By 1965, many black southerners, fed up with being persecuted, bombed, beaten, and murdered, had exhausted their stores of patience waiting for the federal government to intervene. None other than baseball great Jackie Robinson, writing in his regular column "Jackie Robinson Says" (distributed by the Associated Negro Press International for publication in a variety of black newspapers) hailed the Deacons as "an organization of Southern Negroes who have banded together to swap an eye for an eye and a tooth for a tooth with whites who seek to scare, hurt, or kill black and white civil rights demonstrators." Robinson wondered if the Deacons' willingness to take up arms would "awaken" the Justice Department into finding ways to protect black American citizens. "If it doesn't," he wrote in June 1965, "the black people will damn sure defend themselves."[3]

Outliers and counterexamples also complicate the violent/nonviolent dichotomy. Dr. King had a gun in 1956 in the early stages of the Montgomery Bus Boycott, when armed sentinels protected his parsonage; Malcolm X, on the other hand, did *not* carry a firearm or a weapon of any sort after his conversion to Islam until the days immediately before his death, and even then, he carried a nonlethal teargas pen. Malcolm X, along with Robert Williams and Deacons founder Charles Sims, all publicly praised nonviolent direct action at various points in their lives. The Black Panthers accepted white allies. There was even a white Deacon: Rev. William Howard Melish, an Episcopal priest ousted from Holy Trinity Church in downtown Brooklyn in 1957 for his "alleged left-wing views"![4]

The aberrations, outliers, and counterexamples only begin to make sense when one interrogates the Master Narrative itself. First, one must understand the civil rights movement *contextually*. Much like the Civil War—begun on the northern side as a struggle to preserve the Union, finished as a crusade to end slavery, and begun on the southern side as a secession to preserve slavery and "the southern way of life" and finished as a battle to preserve the Confederacy itself—the goals, aims, tactics, and strategies of the civil rights movement changed over time.

What began as a battle *for* civil rights, evolved into a war *against* white supremacy. In other words, the civil rights movement grew into something more than a movement for civil rights. Beginning as a quest to reform American polity—an effort to include African Americans in the body politic by dismantling Jim Crow and securing voting rights—it became an assault on institutionalized racism and white privilege.

Rather than destroying or "killing" the civil rights movement, as some observers charged at the time, this change actually aligned it with larger themes in African American history. In this framework, the civil rights movement elides into Black Power rather easily, less a staccato break than a predictable transition—a return to a long tradition of self-assertion and self-protection in the struggle for black equality. This transition, much subtler than the mainstream press could grasp in 1966, cannot be appreciated without studying how the movement evolved over time, without situating the movement into a broader historical context, and without considering it in relation to larger themes in African American history.

The latter, for example, abounds with instances of self-defense as a well-known and oft-utilized method of checking white aggression. In a wider historical framework, self-defense therefore becomes the norm and nonviolence the anomaly. Without studying black history, one might be unaware of Ida B. Wells's recommendation that a Winchester rifle have a "place of honor" in every black home; the bawdy folk ballad "Frankie and Johnny," which immortalized a famous 1899 self-defense case involving a woman seeking revenge against her violent, two-timing lover; the NAACP's first legal battle, a self-defense case that went all the way to the U.S. Supreme Court as *Pink Franklin v. South Carolina* (1910); or Claude McKay's 1919 poem "If We Must Die," which became a key writing of the Harlem Renaissance. Within the context of this longer view of the struggle for black equality, it is not Robert Williams or Gloria Richardson or the Black Panthers who were "glitches" (to borrow Powledge's phrasing), but rather Dr. King and others who faithfully adhered to the strict tenets of nonviolence. In other words, it was nonviolence that represented a break from the established tradition of armed self-defense, not the other way around.

When considering the civil rights movement contextually, it also becomes easier to understand Charles Sims's downplaying of the violent rhetoric of Black Power as well as his interpretation of it as simple self-determination. Visiting Boston on a fundraising tour in July 1966, the outspoken leader of the Deacons for Defense and Justice reiterated how Black Power was often misinterpreted as racism in reverse, a violent lurch away from nonviolent direct action:

> When Rev. M. L. King led the Montgomery bus boycott in 1957, that was nothing more than a display of Black Power. When Negroes in the South work in voter registration campaigns, that's nothing more than some Black Power. When Negroes press for passage of federal civil rights and voting rights bills, they're using that Black Power to get those bills through Congress. To say that we're in favor of increasing our Black Power does not mean that we won't use what white help we can get to aid us in our fight.[5]

Sims deliberately associated Black Power with nonviolent activism, voting reform, federal legislation, and white help—mainstays of 1960s civil rights reform up to that point—to desensationalize it and render it nonthreatening. Because it was compatible in his mind with "mainstream" activism, Sims logically viewed Black Power on a continuum with civil rights reform, not as a discontinuous break from it.

Relatedly, one must also understand the movement *constitutionally*, in terms of civil rights, civil liberties, and human rights: all different from one another, each speaking to different kinds of freedoms. Civil rights are rights guaranteed and protected by the U.S. Constitution and by federal laws enacted by Congress, such as the right to vote, due process of law, and protection from unlawful discrimination; civil liberties are individual rights protected by law from government interference, such as freedom of speech, freedom of assembly, or other freedoms protected in the Bill of Rights. If civil rights exist by virtue of one's relationship to the state, then civil liberties exist independent of that relationship: the former are "positive rights" requiring action, the latter are "negative rights" that do not (not unlike human rights, such as the right to self-protection). At heart, the question of tactics and strategies in the civil rights movement is a question belonging to political theory, with different individuals interpreting the struggle through different understandings of rights and liberties, with different emphases at different junctures. It may make sense, therefore, to move away from "civil rights" alone toward what Hasan Kwame Jeffries has termed "freedom rights"—an amalgam of civil rights, civil liberties, property rights, human rights, and assurances of safety and security—in describing the goals and aspirations of African Americans in the 1960s.[6]

Finally, conscientious students of history must appreciate the civil rights movement *confrontationally*, as a lever for full inclusion in American life. Malcolm X's "The Ballot or the Bullet" address is particularly illustrative here. In this rangy speech delivered on April 3, 1964, at Cory Methodist Church in Cleveland, Malcolm covered a variety of topics: Islam, Christianity, politics, Democrats, Dixiecrats, Republicans, civil rights, human rights, voting rights, black nationalism, economic power, guerrilla warfare, and the Cold War, among other issues. Notably, Malcolm actually spoke very little about the violent/nonviolent dichotomy, using it primarily as rhetorical punctuation after making other points. "By ballot I only mean freedom," he noted at one juncture. "I don't mean go out and get violent," he emphasized at another. But at a time when Senators Strom Thurmond (D-SC) and Richard Russell (D-GA), among others, were actively filibustering President Kennedy's civil rights bill for days on end on the floor of the U.S. Senate, where its passage was by no means assured, Malcolm's reminder that further delay could bring bloodshed made his rhetorical use of ballots and bullets quite literal to many listeners. He offered a choice: liberty or death—of blacks and whites alike. "Let your dying be reciprocal," he urged his audience. Focusing on 1964 as an election year, his main point was that white politicians clambered for the Negro vote but offered little in return—a "political con game" with black Americans in the middle. Black voters should recognize their own political power, refuse to give away their ballots when unearned, and hold elected officials accountable. "If the white man doesn't want the black man buying rifles and shotguns, then let the government do its job," he argued. "That's all."

> If he's not going to do his job in running the government and providing you and me with the protection that our taxes are supposed to be for, since he spends all those billions for his defense budget, he certainly can't begrudge you and me spending $12 or $15 for a single-shot or double-action.[7]

"The dark people are waking up," he announced, arguing here for *inclusion*, not separation. Less a call to arms than a demand for full citizenship, "The Ballot or the Bullet" still managed to couple a demand for political reform with an ominous, not-so-veiled threat. One wonders if the speaker's message would have been heard without the incorporation of *both* rhetorical elements.

Reconsidering the violent/nonviolent dichotomy also precipitates a new appreciation of nonviolence as a truly revolutionary approach to social change and human advancement. Dr. King learned that suffering unanswered violence to wear down an enemy—his own personal conviction—defied the logic and common sense of many black Americans. It was quite literally a foreign concept (borrowed from Hinduism), a most implausible proposition requiring extraordinary courage and willpower. Some, like Robert Williams, regarded it as debasing, as not so much a moral imperative but a political tactic. For him, self-defense carried reformist and socially conscious overtones. To others, the Hobson's choice of "nonviolence or violence" did not make sense on the front lines of the civil rights struggle. As SNCC activist Fred Brooks told an interviewer in 1967:

> Before we went into the South with nothing but prayers and love, and they burned our churches down, they burned our houses down. But when people decided that they no longer would accept the philosophy of nonviolence but would begin to protect themselves, things changed. They stopped burning down our churches, they stopped harassing us, they stopped beating us because they knew that if they hit us we were gonna hit back.
>
> So I think as far as the technique goes, violence versus nonviolence— in fact, I don't even like to look at it like that. I like to look at it "nonviolence versus self-protection," and I think that change . . . We have benefitted tremendously.[8]

There are a number of recent studies that engage this other dichotomy by examining the practice of armed self-defense.[9]

To adhere to the violent/nonviolent dichotomy is to impose a false binary on the thoughts and actions of black folks; it is to find contradiction where none necessarily existed. "It is incomprehensible to most white Americans that deep in the heart of every black adult lives some of Malcolm and some of King, side by side," explained CORE founder James Farmer in his 1985 autobiography. "The same audience that showered Martin with 'amens' could punctuate Malcolm's rhetoric with emphatic shouts of 'right'!"[10] James H. Cone, founder of black

Martin Luther King Jr. and Malcolm X meet face to face while waiting for the start of a press conference on March 26, 1964. (Library of Congress, Prints & Photographs Division, USN&WR Collection, Job no. 11695, Frame 27 [digital file from original neg.] LC-USZ6-1847 [b&w film copy neg.])

liberation theology, recognized as much in 1991 when he wrote, "Popular images of Martin and Malcolm seldom acknowledge their movement toward each other and their break with earlier deeply held convictions about America."[11]

All of these nuances and subtleties round out deeper understanding of the civil rights movement even as they raise new questions and compel reconsideration of basic assumptions. What was it all about anyway? Civil rights? Justice? Peace and love? Dignity and respect? Civil rights scholars continue to unravel what was a complicated, multivalent social movement, one "bigger than a hamburger"—and one bigger than violence versus nonviolence, too, as activists such as Malcolm X intuitively recognized. "When a man is on a hot stove, he says, 'I'm coming up, I'm getting up,'" he asserted in a 1962 debate with Bayard Rustin. "Violently or nonviolently doesn't even enter the picture—I'm coming up, do you understand?"[12]

Our brains are binary-seeking machines, finding dichotomies even where none exist. But they are capable of nuance and finesse, too. What psychologists refer to as cognitive dissonance—the ability to hold two contradictory thoughts at the same time—is what novelist F. Scott Fitzgerald called "the test of a first-rate intelligence." Perhaps history is best understood in this realm, where blurred boundaries are more instructive than brightened ones—that is, in the grey areas between black and white, in the liminal spaces between extremes and dichotomies. It is here—where people think nonlinearly and contradict inherited wisdom and contemplate both the ballot *and* the bullet—that dichotomies fade into truer comprehension and understanding.

Notes

1. Fred Powledge, *Free at Last? The Civil Rights Movement and the People Who Made It* (New York: Harper Perennial, 1991), 311; Harvard Sitkoff, *The Struggle for Black Equality, 1954–1992* (New York: Hill & Wang, 1993), 141, 143; see also Timothy Tyson's *Radio Free Dixie: Robert F. Williams and the Roots of Black Power* (Chapel Hill: University of North Carolina Press, 1999).

2. W. E. B. Du Bois, "Martin Luther King's Life: Crusader without Violence," *National Guardian* 12, no. 4 (November 9, 1959): 8.

3. Jackie Robinson, "Bus Driver Learns Not to Call Negro Man 'Boy,'" *Pittsburgh Courier*, June 19, 1965, 8, New York edition; Robinson, "Deacons Will Stay Unless U.S. Moves," *Pittsburgh Courier*, July 31, 1965, 8, New York edition.

4. "White 'Deacon' Supports Need of Firearms," *Pittsburgh Courier*, November 2, 1965, 21; see also Christopher Strain, *Pure Fire: Self-Defense as Activism in the Civil Rights Era* (Athens: University of Georgia Press, 2005).

5. "Sims Defends Black Power," *Bay State Banner*, July 16, 1966, 2.

6. See Hasan Kwame Jeffries, *Bloody Lowndes: Civil Rights and Black Power in Alabama's Black Belt* (New York: New York University Press, 2009).

7. Malcolm X, "The Ballot or the Bullet," in George Breitman, ed., *Malcolm X Speaks: Selected Speeches and Statements* (New York: Panthfinder, 1965), 43.

8. Fred Brooks, interviewed November 29, 1967, by John Britton in Nashville, TN; Ralph J. Bunche Oral History Collection (Civil Rights Documentation Project), Moorland-Spingarn Archives, Howard University, Washington, DC.

9. For example, see Strain, *Pure Fire*; Jeffries, *Bloody Lowndes*; Tyson, *Radio Free Dixie*; Simon Wendt, *The Spirit and the Shotgun: Armed Resistance and the Civil Rights Movement* (Gainesville: University Press of Florida, 2007); Lance Hill, *The Deacons for Defense and Justice: Armed Resistance and the Civil Rights Movement* (Chapel Hill: University of North Carolina Press, 2006); Akinyele Umoja, *We Will Shoot Back: Armed Resistance in the Mississippi Freedom Movement* (New York: New York University Press, 2013); and Charles Cobb, *This*

Nonviolent Stuff'll Get You Killed: How Guns Made the Civil Rights Movement Possible (Durham, NC: Duke University Press, 2015).

10. James Farmer, *Lay Bare the Heart: An Autobiography of the Civil Rights Movement* (New York: Plume, 1985), 224.

11. James H. Cone, *Martin and Malcolm and America: A Dream or a Nightmare* (Maryknoll, NY: Orbis, 1991), ix–x.

12. Malcolm X, quoted in "Malcolm X: Witness for the Prosecution" in *Black Leaders of the Twentieth Century*, ed. John Hope Franklin and August Meier (Urbana: University of Illinois Press, 1982), 315.

Place Matters

*The Indispensable Story of Civil Rights
Activism beyond Dixie*

Patrick D. Jones

When I started graduate school in 1993 at the University of Wisconsin–Madison, the history of the civil rights era was undergoing a dramatic and exciting transformation. A host of scholars were in the process of dismantling the Master Narrative, which privileged the South, exalted nonviolence, and focused overwhelmingly on heroic leaders, national politics, and legislative achievements. Collectively, their work challenged the idea that the southern movement was a clear and triumphant story about redemptive American democracy, suggesting instead a much murkier and complex history of both achievement and failure. It was an energizing time to be a movement scholar.

Yet, as important as these and subsequent historiographical developments have been, movement histories have remained stubbornly and overwhelmingly focused on the South. Wittingly or not, they have reinforced the notion that racism was primarily a regional affliction in the United States and that the movement was most significantly a function of "southern exceptionalism." From my own experience growing up in Cleveland, Ohio, I knew that there was a whole other landscape of racial struggle during the postwar era waiting to be rediscovered, explored, and added to the narrative of the civil rights movement.

Despite this persistent bias, each year compelling new work emerges on the black freedom struggle outside the South, further adding to our still-evolving understanding of the northern movement for racial justice and bringing greater clarity to the full measure of its importance. In an era of renewed racial crisis and the #BlackLivesMatter movement, these stories of racial activism "beyond Dixie" have become even more significant as many Americans try to make sense of a tragic stream of police killings of unarmed black men and women, urban uprisings in Ferguson, Baltimore, and Milwaukee, and the persistent racial inequalities that plague every medium and large U.S. city more than fifty years after the landmark legislative achievements of the civil rights era.

As with all academic work, when we looked in new ways at old topics, we began to see new things. So, what do we see when we look at the movement "beyond Dixie"? What are some of the broad contours of this important emerging area of civil rights scholarship? What key insights do we gain by exploring northern movement stories? And why is it imperative that we teach this aspect of the broader postwar struggle for racial justice?

To make sense of northern struggles for racial justice in the post–WWII era, we have to first understand the unique terrain of race relations in the urban North out of which these struggles emerged. While northern activists often shared a consciousness with those in the South, their campaigns took place within and responded to a distinctive context. The industrial base of the economy, with its strong labor movement, the presence of white ethnic groups, the dominance of the Catholic Church, the strong link between race, ethnicity, and urban geography, the relatively secure, if limited, right to vote, and the diffuse nature of discrimination—all of which set it apart from the South—critically affected the development of race relations and civil rights activism in the urban North, Midwest, and West.

While there is a deeper history of racial struggle in the northern cities, the Great Migration played a pivotal role in transforming race relations outside of the South, calcifying northern-style Jim Crow, catalyzing white reaction to racial change, spurring black community building within the bounds of segregation, and, ultimately, propelling civil rights activism. During that period, millions of rural, southern African Americans moved to industrial cities in the East, Midwest, and West, seeking safety, equality, and new opportunities in what they hoped would be the "Promised Land." Yet, despite a modicum of freedom and opportunity not found in the Jim Crow South, in reality most black people did not find liberated terrain or full autonomy, but a new and distinct system of white supremacy, discrimination, and racial subordination. Pervasive employment and housing discrimination, segregation, dilapidation, inferior public schools, social isolation, limited political and civic representation, and police brutality were all typical features of northern cities, defining the conditions under which most African Americans lived, played, worked, and struggled.

In the late 1910s and 1920s, the "New Negro" movement brought forth a more assertive generation of black political leadership and a flowering of cultural politics in Harlem, Chicago, Washington, DC, and elsewhere. On street corners and in the pages of the *Crisis, Opportunity,* the *Messenger,* the *Crusader,* the *Chicago Defender,* and similar smaller publications, progressive and radical African American thinkers, including W. E. B. Du Bois, A. Philip Randolph, Marcus Garvey, and Hubert Harrison, vociferously (and sometimes viciously) debated political ideology and strategies for racial uplift. More moderate organizations, such as the NAACP and National Urban League, both headquartered in New York City, chose institutional approaches and quiet, behind-the-scenes negotiation over radical ideology and protest politics to open up new opportunities in employment and housing for African Americans. Young artists, including Langston Hughes, Zora Neale Hurston, and Aaron Douglas, created works of art that articulated a more complex and uncompromising view of the black experience that challenged degrading stereotypes of African Americans and often pushed back explicitly against various forms of racial injustice in the North, as well as in the South.

During the 1930s and 1940s, economic issues dominated black political activism in the urban North. A wave of "Don't Buy Where You Can't Work" campaigns in several large and medium-sized cities targeted local businesses that discriminated against African Americans. Black industrial workers joined with white labor organizers, socialists, communists, and other radical organizations, such as the National Negro Congress, to protest unfair labor practices and demand jobs, better wages, and benefits. These groups often fought against war and fascism, as well as racial discrimination. The March On Washington Movement, an all-black effort spearheaded by socialist labor leader A. Philip Randolph, drew thousands of African Americans in dozens of cities in an effort to utilize nonviolent direct action to open up wartime industries to black workers and establish a permanent Fair Employment Practices

Commission (FEPC). In 1942, an interracial coalition of pacifists and civil rights activists, influenced deeply by Gandhian nonviolence, formed the Congress of Racial Equality (CORE). In May 1943, the group organized sit-ins at the Jack Spratt Restaurant and White City Roller Skating Rink in Chicago, followed by similar protests in Washington, DC. In 1947, CORE sent sixteen members to participate in the "Journey of Reconciliation" through Virginia, North Carolina, Kentucky, and Tennessee in an effort to end segregation in interstate travel. The protest was the precursor to the more famous Freedom Rides in 1961. During the 1930s and 1940s as well, the NAACP, which had chapters in dozens of northern cities and a growing number of southern locales, established its Legal Defense Fund, led by Charles Hamilton Houston, and began the slow march through the courts to challenge the formal system of segregation in the South, which culminated in the 1954 *Brown v. Board of Education* decision.[1] Of particular import in the urban North, the Supreme Court's 1948 decision in *Shelley v. Kraemer*, a case also brought by NAACP lawyers, outlawed racially restrictive housing covenants, a key tool used by white property owners to bar African Americans from purchasing homes in white neighborhoods. And in a more dramatic display of African American resistance to the northern Jim Crow system, 1943 saw major urban rebellions in Detroit and Harlem, two of the largest and most significant black communities outside of the South.

In the postwar period, between the late 1940s and early 1960s, African American activists continued to focus on the intersections of race and economic equality, while also mounting numerous nonviolent campaigns in northern cities, including picketing, boycotts, sit-ins, "wade-ins," "call-ins," and "stall-ins," to challenge segregation and outright exclusion from a wide array of public accommodations, from restaurants and hotels to movie houses and theaters, libraries and public parks, beaches, swimming pools, amusement parks, and public transportation, all with varying degrees of success. Early sit-ins broke out in Baltimore (1955), Wichita (1958), and Oklahoma City (1958) to challenge segregation in local retail stores. Between 1952 and 1954, prior to the Montgomery Bus Boycott, members of the Omaha DePorres Club, an interracial civil rights group that started at Creighton University, mounted a successful boycott against the Omaha and Council Bluffs Street Railway Company's policy of not hiring African American bus drivers. Another notable action took place in 1960 at Chicago's Rainbow Beach, where thirty members of the NAACP Youth Council, led by Velma Hill, staged a water protest against the long-standing custom of racial segregation at the beach, as well as a recent mob attack on a black family there. White onlookers met the demonstrators with a hail of rocks, one of which clunked Hill on the head. During this same period, northern civil rights advocates pushed for increased political and civic representation, as well as public housing to address broad housing shortages in urban America for poor and working-class African Americans. While public housing had been embraced by the white working class during the 1940s and early 1950s, when they were the primary beneficiaries, many of these same voters opposed new public housing development in the mid- and late 1950s, particularly in white neighborhoods, as black residents pushed for inclusion and large numbers of whites increasingly saw public housing as a dangerous social experiment in integration. At the same time, growing frustration in deteriorating black and brown central city neighborhoods led to rising tensions and periodic clashes between local African Americans and the overwhelmingly white, working-class police forces that patrolled the color line in urban America.

As the national struggle for racial justice reached a crescendo during the 1960s, African American civil rights activism in the North accelerated on a number of fronts. In terms of economic justice, African Americans continued to push for expanded employment opportunities within the industrial and service economies, construction and building sectors, skilled trades, clerical workforce, public transportation, and a variety of white-collar professions. "Selective patronage" campaigns in a number of cities, which entailed targeted boycotts of employers who hired few or no African Americans, carried on the legacy of the "Don't Buy Where You Can't Work" movement from the previous generation. And it is important to remember that the historic 1963 March on Washington for Jobs and Freedom accentuated economic demands and was supported by thousands of northern African American workers and union members. Once hired, black workers fought for equal treatment from white coworkers and bosses, fair pay, honest assessment based on merit, and, ultimately, advancement through the ranks into management and ownership positions. In the 1970s, affirmative action became an important, if hotly contested, tool for black workers to press for further change.

Similarly, African American laborers struggled to gain access to exclusionary labor unions, which were often the gateway to secure and well-paying industrial jobs. Even when union leaders endorsed civil rights and nondiscrimination, white rank-and-file workers often rebelled, sometimes refusing to work with black workers, harassing them on the job, or, in extreme cases, engaging in wildcat strikes.

African Americans also fought to build and maintain black-owned businesses and to press for greater access to financing and credit from the banking industry, as well as reinvestment of their dollars from local businesses and banks back into their communities. And from the mid-1960s on, as automation, deindustrialization, white flight to the suburbs, and the broader abandonment of central city neighborhoods took a devastating toll on "ghettoized" communities of color, locking shameful numbers of black and brown working-class Americans in structural impoverishment, civil rights activists and organizations across the country pressed for increased government relief and urban revitalization programs, as well as full employment and, later, a basic minimum income.

Public education was another important area of civil rights activism outside of the South. Many black parents and community members viewed a quality education as the most significant vehicle to improve access and opportunity for their children and a way out of the increasingly dire circumstances confronting African American residents in many segregated inner-city neighborhoods. Broad patterns of racial imbalance plagued urban public schools, the result of segregated housing patterns, but also specific decisions and policies by overwhelmingly (and sometimes exclusively) white school boards regarding, among other things, district lines, allocation of resources, the construction of new schools, and biased pupil placement programs.

During the early postwar period, African Americans and their allies in the northern cities pressed for educational reform in a number of ways: increased hiring, as well as equitable pay, evaluation, assignment, and advancement processes for black teachers; greater funding for predominately African American schools and improved curriculum; compensatory programming for the children of southern migrants; relief from overcrowding in central city schools; and the construction of new buildings and other educational infrastructure. Following the Supreme Court's historic *Brown* decision, a generation of civil rights lawyers and activists debated whether the ruling might extend to the de facto segregation of public education in the northern cities. By 1963, the NAACP had filed eighteen legal suits against segregated urban school systems. The mounting courtroom challenges provided a seedbed for civil rights activism around the issue of education throughout the urban North and West during the mid-1960s.

As early as the late 1950s, a group of African American mothers in New York, led by Mae Mallory, protested the inferior and discriminatory conditions in segregated local public schools. Inspired by a report by black psychologists Kenneth and Mamie Clark, and supported by legendary figures such as Ella Baker and Adam Clayton Powell Jr., as well as the *New York Amsterdam News*, the group sought permission to transfer their children into superior local white schools. The NAACP filed suit on their behalf, and in 1958 and 1960 the women led effective school boycotts, the first lasting 162 days and involving an estimated 10,000 parents and the second featuring alternative "freedom schools," some of the first of the civil rights era. When New York officials (unsuccessfully) attempted to prosecute the women for "negligence," their case became a cause célèbre among northern civil rights activists who dubbed them the "Harlem 9." In 1960, the women won their court case, resulting in more than a thousand African American parents gaining the right to transfer their children to integrated schools over the next five years. In the wake of their legal victory, between 1963 and 1965 a wave of school boycotts swept the urban North, drawing support and participation from hundreds of thousands of students, parents, teachers, and other community members. In another boycott in New York City in 1964, an astonishing 464,361 students withdrew from schools across the city to demand a comprehensive plan for desegregation, making it the largest civil rights demonstration in U.S. history to that point. Many of these northern school boycott campaigns also established "freedom schools" as alternative learning spaces for boycotting students.

Educational activism took many other forms in northern cities during this period, including lobbying, administrative maneuvering, electoral advocacy, writing campaigns, picketing, sit-ins, and other creative forms of protest. In Milwaukee, civil rights activists in the Milwaukee United School Integration Committee (MUSIC), led by NAACP lawyer Lloyd Barbee, formed "human chains" to block school busses from transferring black students to segregated receiving schools while their regular buildings were under construction, a move that resulted in numerous arrests. In Cleveland in 1964, members of the United Freedom

Movement, an interracial civil rights coalition, used their bodies to block heavy construction equipment that was being used to dig holes for new segregated public schools. In a tragic episode, Rev. Bruce Klunder, a young Presbyterian minister who led the local CORE chapter, was run over and killed by a bulldozer while protesting. As the struggle for racial justice moved into the Black Power era, education reformers increasingly pulled back from demands for integration, emphasizing instead "community control" of local schools and school boards and demanding curricular reforms to include African American history and culture.

The challenges to educational reform in northern cities during the civil rights era were significant. White school board officials and other civic leaders were often recalcitrant in the face of demands for desegregation. White parents frequently reacted angrily to the prospect of integration or simply fled traditional urban neighborhoods for the lily-white suburbs, undermining a variety of potential remedies for inner-city school segregation. In 1957, white parents in New York rallied to block a proposal to send four hundred African American and Puerto Rican students from Brooklyn to Queens schools. In Detroit in 1960, white residents organized a school boycott to halt the busing of three hundred black students to a less crowded white school. And in a particularly ominous episode, white antibusing activists in Boston during the early 1970s attacked busing advocates outside a courthouse and pelted school buses carrying African American children with eggs, bricks, bottles, and racist slogans, as police in riot gear struggled to regain order. Legal challenges to northern school inequality were required not only to establish a pattern of racial segregation in public schools but also prove that the imbalance was intentional, the result of conscious, or purposeful, action on the part of school administrators.

Formal politics was another important site of civil rights struggle in the urban North. Unlike their counterparts in the Jim Crow South, African American residents of northern cities had access to the ballot box prior to passage of the 1965 Voting Rights Act. As the African American population grew dramatically beyond Dixie in the post–WWII period, so too did black political potential and opportunity. Part of the political focus of the civil rights era had to do with representation, getting black people elected to office or appointed to other civic boards and commissions. Many believed that increased political representation would lead to more responsiveness to black interests and, ideally and ultimately, better solutions to persistent problems facing African American communities. And it is true, during this period, pioneering black elected officials at the state and local level, such as congressional representatives Charles Diggs in Detroit and Shirley Chisholm in New York and mayors Carl Stokes in Cleveland, Ohio, and Richard Hatcher in Gary, Indiana, used their positions to push for civil rights legislation, as well as a range of other programmatic solutions to various problems confronting African Americans in the urban North. The black political movement reached its zenith in 1972, when eight to ten thousand African American men and women—elected officials, activists and revolutionaries, integrationists and black nationalists, Christians and Muslims—met in Gary for the First National Black Political Convention. Delegates gave speeches, debated issues, sometimes fought and protested one another, and tried to pound out a National Black Political Agenda. It was a heady time for black political empowerment.

But a closer look at African American politics during the civil rights era reveals a more complicated picture. The struggle for black political representation took place within the context of segregation, systematic impoverishment, large urban machines, and the sharp and often divisive ethnic and class politics of the urban North. Pervasive urban segregation conceded some black representation on city councils, school boards, and state legislatures by concentrating black votes, but it also severely limited black political representation overall, ensuring continuing white political dominance in many cities. Traditional white Democratic Party elites did not give up or share their political power easily and often fought to maintain their advantage. Mobilizing, let alone unifying, black voters was a major obstacle as well. Coalition politics were essential in urban America, but fraught with significant pitfalls that made them hard to achieve and maintain. Politics easily surfaced a host of divisions within African American communities around class and color, gender, ideology, and partisan affiliation. By the 1970s, many progressive, left, and nationalist leaders claimed a new black political elite had emerged, more beholden to self-interest, corporate power, or Democratic Party allegiance than the interests and needs of the black community more broadly. Some feared inclusion and incorporation into the broader urban political system could easily evolve into institutionalization or cooptation. And even as white flight increased the power of black voters in urban America during this era, putting more and more black elected officials into office, most inherited deep and profound problems in a context of increasing urban abandonment, deindustrialization, globalization, and the rise of a new conservative politic, which made their work tremendously difficult.

Beyond formal electoral politics, northern movement history also expands our conception of black politics and civil rights activism in other directions. This is particularly true when we focus on African American women. For instance, poor black women in Philadelphia struggled for increased welfare benefits and expanded services, while poor black women in Baltimore organized for public housing, stories that challenge a host of stereotypes about impoverished African American mothers and the public housing system itself. Meanwhile, the National Welfare Rights Organization (NWRO) protested consumer giant Sears for refusing to grant credit to welfare recipients, thereby expanding civil rights activism to the realm of consumerism.

Northern movement stories also add new dimensions to our thinking about the politics of armed self-defense and violence within struggles for racial justice. Beyond the Black Panther Party, the northern movement is replete with stories of activists who embraced armed self-defense. For example, Malcolm X delivered his famous "Ballot or the Bullet" speech first at Cory Methodist Church in Cleveland, Ohio. His words became influential nationally and also spurred one local activist, Lewis Robinson, to start a gun club at the Jomo Freedom Kenyatta (JFK) House. The surge in urban rebellions that rocked dozens of U.S. cities between 1964 and 1968 also offers challenging new opportunities to confront what Dr. King called "the language of the unheard" and to consider civil disturbance as a form of political action. Furthermore, during the Black Power era, a variety of radical activists suggested that "revolutionary violence" was necessary to break through white supremacy in the United States. In his book *Blood in My Eye*, for instance, George Jackson explained the ways urban revolutionaries might outfit cars and vans with guns and heavy armor as a part of a race war with law enforcement.

No other issue in the urban North, save police brutality, was more explosive than housing in the civil rights era. During the first half of the twentieth century, racially restrictive covenants, redlining, discriminatory real estate practices such as blockbusting and steering, pervasive discrimination within the financial industry, and economic inaccessibility helped establish and maintain fairly rigid housing segregation in northern cities. When these mechanisms failed, suburban flight and strong white resistance—in the form of "closed housing" groups, anti-black petitions and propaganda, threats and intimidation, vandalism, and even violence—held the line. When Ossian Sweet, a black physician in Detroit, purchased a home in a previously all-white neighborhood in 1925, a mob of white neighbors violently attacked the home. Such incidents were commonplace outside of the South throughout the first two-thirds of the twentieth century.

Systematically locked out of the new postwar suburban "American Dream" in the post–WWII era, the vast majority of African Americans in the urban North rented property, rather than owned it, most often from a white landlord who lived outside of the neighborhood. Rents were usually higher in segregated black communities. White "slumlords," as they were derisively labeled, split single-family homes into small, cramped apartments to maximize profits. Plumbing and sanitation problems, lead paint, rats, and general dilapidation were common, while upkeep was usually slow, shoddy, or nonexistent. Highway construction often cut through black neighborhoods, destroying thousands of low-income houses and apartments, displacing their inhabitants, and exacerbating the housing crisis. Slum clearance and urban renewal programs, pitched initially as "urban revitalization" projects, came to be seen by many as "Negro removal" programs meant to clear the way for more affluent white "gentrifiers."

As northern campaigns for racial justice accelerated during the mid-1960s, open housing emerged as a particularly divisive, and often violent, issue in city after city. The upsurge in popular agitation pushed housing onto the national civil rights agenda. By 1965, President Johnson was convinced that racial discrimination in housing was so invidious and pervasive that legislation was required to root it out. He sought to capitalize on his hard-won legislative victories in the 1964 Civil Rights Act and 1965 Voting Rights Act, as well as growing urban unrest, to push for a federal open housing law as the centerpiece of a 1966 Civil Rights Act. But legislators backed by powerful housing, construction, and real estate interests, as well as a host of far-right organizations, such as the John Birch Society, and bolstered by widespread popular opposition to open housing legislation among whites, defeated the measure.

The failure of federal legislators to come up with a strong bill spurred dozens of local open housing campaigns across the urban North between 1966 and 1968. The most well-known of these campaigns took place in Chicago. There, in 1965 and 1966, a fractious alliance between local civil rights activists and the SCLC led a series of open housing marches through white working-class neighborhoods. The demonstrations symbolized Dr. King's attempt to prove that his brand of nonviolent direct action could work outside of the South. The campaign attracted national media attention when thousands of angry white counterdemonstrators pelted nonviolent marchers with bottles, rocks, cherry bombs, and racist epithets. Ultimately, the Chicago open housing campaign failed. But the following year, farther up the shores of Lake Michigan, in Milwaukee, militant nonviolence made a more successful stand for fair housing. There, the local NAACP Youth Council and their adviser, a white Catholic priest named Fr. James Groppi, led more than two hundred consecutive nights of often contentious marches to demand an open housing ordinance from the city's Common Council. When the marchers were met with "massive resistance" by thousands of local whites on the city's white working-class South Side, the campaign drew national media attention and played a catalytic role in passage of the 1968 Fair Housing Act, the often-forgotten third major piece of 1960s-era federal civil rights legislation.

Despite the legislative achievement of the 1968 Fair Housing Act, housing segregation in the urban North has persisted all the way to the present. Uneven enforcement of nondiscrimination laws, difficulty regulating the real estate market, persistent bias against black borrowers by banks, racialized economic inequality, pervasive stereotyping of black residents as precursors to and carriers of community decline, white flight, and a general unwillingness of large numbers of white Americans to welcome black and brown neighbors have all undermined housing desegregation in American cities.

By far the most incendiary issue confronting northern civil rights activists during the long 1960s was police brutality. Urban rebellions in Watts, Cleveland, Detroit, Philadelphia, Newark, Rochester, New York, Omaha, and elsewhere were either directly precipitated or indirectly fueled by the clash between local law enforcement and black community members. It had long been the duty of urban police forces to patrol the class and color line in American cities, and they often did so through force and brutality. During the civil rights era, urban police forces were regularly deployed to harass, intimidate, undermine, and suppress civil rights activism. So-called Red Squads, special police units tasked with infiltrating, gathering intelligence on, and counteracting political radicalism, labor organizing, and organized crime during the first half of the twentieth century, were redirected toward civil rights, Black Power, and antiwar demonstrators in the 1960s. Not surprisingly, a growing proportion of inner-city African Americans came to view the local police—which were made up almost exclusively of white, working-class men who did not live in the neighborhoods they patrolled and who often brought racist ideas to the job—in adversarial terms, as "the enemy." More and more, civil rights activists discussed the nexus between poverty, crime, and law enforcement and organized to "defend" their communities. Most famously, the Black Panther Party for Self-Defense emerged initially in Oakland in 1966 to combat pervasive police violence against local black community residents. Their willingness to defend black people against police brutality was central to their appeal and quick rise nationally.

The emergence of Black Power in the second half of the 1960s dramatically altered the terrain of racial struggle in northern cities. While the Black Power movement was born in the rural South and had deep roots stretching back decades, it found its most forceful articulation during the 1960s and 1970s in segregated urban ghetto communities beyond Dixie.

Black Power represented a reassessment of the goals, tactics, and strategies within the struggle for racial justice and was rooted in the successes, but more importantly the failures, of the liberal, nonviolent, and integrationist voices that had dominated the movement, in the North and South, in the late 1950s and early 1960s. According to Stokely Carmichael, Black Power was "a call for Black people in this country to unite, to recognize their heritage, to build a sense of community. It is a call for Black people to define their own goals, to lead their own organizations . . . to resist the racist institutions and values of this society." Black Power, he wrote, "calls for black people to consolidate behind their own, so that they can bargain from a position of strength."[2] Increasingly, circumstances on the ground in urban black communities demanded new ways of thinking about the black experience and racial struggle, as well as the development of new tools for both "survival" and "liberation."

Black Power signaled the rise of a militant consciousness that centered black experience and race pride, reclaimed African and African American history, rejected moderate black leadership, repudiated nonviolent direct action for armed self-defense, or even revolutionary violence, and challenged integration as the goal of racial struggle, emphasizing instead self-determination, autonomy and the cultivation of independent African American leadership, as well as "community control" of local institutions.

This assertive black consciousness fueled a new cultural flowering across African America. Evidence of it could be heard in the decidedly urban sounds of James Brown, singing "Say It Loud, I'm Black and I'm Proud," or in the "soul power" aesthetic, which emphasized the collective identity of black people in America. Dashikis, natural hair, African artwork, the iconic raised fist, militant rhetoric, and a deep and profound love of "blackness" were all indicators of this Black Power consciousness. The Black Arts Movement in literature, theater, poetry, music, and the visual arts stood on the shoulders of the New Negro era cultural movements, utilizing various cultural forms as weapons in the struggle for liberation and as powerful vehicles to communicate and spread the new ideology and posture of Black Power. The cultural outpouring of the Black Power era also importantly pointed the way toward hip-hop culture, which would emerge out of the dire urban circumstances facing African Americans trapped in the post–civil rights urban landscape of the late 1970s and early 1980s.

Black Power was largely misunderstood (and feared) by the white majority and was often defined pejoratively by the mainstream press, prompting a new wave of white resistance and massive governmental repression against movement activists in the urban North, particularly against the Black Panther Party, which FBI Director J. Edgar Hoover infamously labeled "the greatest threat to internal security of the country."

Northern struggles for racial justice were clearly distinct, but they also interacted with the southern movement in myriad ways. Campaigns in the South were a never-ending source of inspiration for northern activists. They learned tactics and strategies from southern organizations and leaders and debated their applicability in their own local contexts. Civil rights activists in dozens of northern cities engaged in sympathy pickets following the murders of Emmett Till and Medgar Evers and in support of the southern sit-in movement. They also established solidarity groups, such as Friends of SNCC, to provide material support to their counterparts in the South. Northerners traveled South to join Freedom Summer, the Selma voting rights campaign, and to participate in southern efforts for racial justice more generally. They often came home transformed, ready to work in their own backyards with a dramatically altered consciousness and commitment. Similarly, Dr. King and SCLC mounted important campaigns outside of the South in Chicago, Cleveland, and Philadelphia in the late 1960s. And the Poor People's Campaign was a national, not regional, effort to build an interracial movement of the poor. The NAACP and CORE were active in both regions as well. Conversely, southern-based organizations such as SNCC came north to publicize their struggles, marshal support, and raise much-needed resources. So, while it has been necessary to focus on the North in this essay to trace out some of the broad contours of civil rights activism beyond Dixie, it is equally important to remember that the struggle for racial justice was and is, in the end, a national phenomenon.

Foregrounding northern struggles for racial justice complicates a number of debates that southern movement historians have been grappling with for the past couple of decades. It explodes the popular narrative's chronology, which has the movement starting in 1954 and ending in 1968. It highlights the interactivity between formal politics, legal action, social movement activism, and cultural politics. It also underscores the fact that local struggles were critical to national change. In the North, as in the South, we can discern some broader patterns in civil rights activism but must also remain mindful of the distinctiveness of local contexts and campaigns, as well as regional variation. Northern movement stories contribute to discussions over black political leadership, ideology, tactics, and strategies, including black radicalism, and add significantly to our thinking about the roles of nonviolence, armed self-defense, and violence in postwar struggles for racial justice. Similarly, they expand our understanding of religion and faith in the movement. Additionally, the civil rights movement beyond Dixie powerfully adds to debates over the possibility and limitations of political liberalism to address the nation's racial failings. Moreover, northern campaigns highlight the sometimes maddeningly complex internal dynamics of black community diversity and open up new possibilities to explore the intersection of black freedom struggles with other justice movements, such as the antiwar movement, second wave feminism, gay liberation, the American Indian Movement, the Chicano Movement, environmentalism, and more. And they raise new questions about coalition building, white allyship, reaction, and "massive resistance."

Including northern movement history in the overall narrative of the civil rights era is about "getting it right," offering a more accurate, complex, and inclusive portrait of racial struggle in post–WWII America. Too often, we tell the southern story as a tidy narrative of regional exceptionalism that mystifies white supremacy, discrimination, and racial subordination outside of the South, sidesteps the rich history of civil rights activism in the North, and thereby lets the rest of the country off the hook for racial injustice. In this telling, the mythic southern civil rights story plays as a redemptive story of American democracy. It may have taken a while, but ultimately American democratic institutions acknowledged the obvious injustice of the Jim Crow South and overcame it. That story is not fully accurate, but it has great power as a national narrative, particularly among white folks looking to be redeemed and forgiven for a long history of white supremacy.

Conversely, we do not tell northern movement stories because they compel a reckoning with contemporary racial issues—the ongoing urban crisis—that historians and the public have been reluctant to entertain. Yet, in a new era of racial reaction and rekindled mass protest, this is precisely the reason that these northern movement histories are so urgent. This relevancy holds out the prospect of helping students and the broader public better understand the deeper contexts for our current national ruckus over race. And if we are serious about solving these enduring problems, then northern movement history is not optional—it is indispensable.

NOTES

1. In *Murray v. Maryland* (1936) and *Missouri ex rel. Gaines v. Canada* (1938), the NAACP scored two important early educational victories, while in *Smith v. Allwright* (1946) they were successful in getting the U.S. Supreme Court to outlaw the all-white primary.

2. Stokely Carmichael and Charles Hamilton, *Black Power* (New York: Random House, Vintage Press, 1967), 44.

must discover new and thoughtful ways to provide our students with an understanding of King that better conforms to what we know to be true about him. Most crucially, we have to make him human again.

King in Context

It is important to identify the set of assumptions and conclusions with which we have been operating since before the first King Day celebration. King's role in the Master Narrative—drained of possibility and contingency—reads as the fulfillment of a struggle whose success was a foregone conclusion: Martin led Negroes to freedom; then he died. Additionally, a King-centric narrative reinforces powerful and problematic notions about the composition and contours of the movement. This rendering of the movement would have us believe that leadership structures were exclusively top down and hierarchical, bureaucratic, and driven by charismatic individuals; that the movement was primarily occupied with black folks in urban spaces; that it was *totally* nonviolent; that marches and mass mobilizations formed the centerpiece of movement activity; that unity and conformity of thought and action defined the struggle; that women played no significant roles in the liberation struggle; and that the passage of legislation was the movement's central aim.

There are many challenges to teaching about the life and work of Dr. King. One of the ways we complicate the effort is by conceding a critical point to the Master Narrative: that King, even during his lifetime, operated *outside of history*. If we think of King as the Alpha and Omega of civil rights struggle, we turn him into a perpetual soloist on any and all issues with which he contended. If our narratives begin and end with King, we don't learn from the fact that he constantly engaged in the back and forth of dialogue, debate, and refinement when it came to strategies, tactics, and philosophies. King grew as a thinker and a leader; the Martin King of 1955 was *not* the Martin King of 1963, or 1968. I can think of no more effective means of countering the many problematic notions related to King than by simply *placing him back within his historical context*. When we return him to the cauldron of history, we are better able to help our students connect with his passion, choices, missteps, and triumphs. We are able to render him, in the words of the singer Jill Scott, "beautifully human." Over the years, I have found that the best way to achieve this is by situating King's sermons and writings alongside other easily accessible primary source materials, readings that remind our students that King was both influencing and influenced by the moments in which he lived.[3]

Montgomery

In his excellent book *Becoming King: Martin Luther King, Jr and the Making of a Leader,* Troy Jackson recounts the musings of a parishioner at King's Dexter Avenue Baptist Church in Montgomery, Alabama, on the eve of King's departure from the city: "The history books may write that Rev. King was born in Atlanta, and then came to Montgomery, but we feel that he was born in Montgomery in the struggle here."[4] Indeed, the historical King was, in a very real way, "born" in the struggle that began in Montgomery in the winter of 1955. The Master Narrative of the movement regards King's activities in Montgomery as something of an inevitable confirmation of his participation in the emerging black freedom struggle. Primary source material, used alongside King's sermons, can render a much more complex (and interesting) story. By the time King arrived in Montgomery in 1953, black folks had been engaged in an extended effort to reshape the political terrain of the city. In the wake of the 1944 U.S. Supreme Court ruling in *Smith v. Allwright,* which outlawed the all-white primary, black voter mobilization in Montgomery began yielding small, yet noticeable, gains in city politics. These efforts were also coupled with the increasing mobilization of all classes of black folk in the city.[5]

By the time city police officers arrested Rosa Parks in December 1955, significant segments of the city's black protest infrastructure had already been energized. In oral histories, E. D. Nixon, the head of the city's NAACP chapter and head of the Brotherhood of Sleeping Car Porters, and Jo Ann Gibson Robinson, who led the Women's Political Council (WPC), a political action committee composed of black professional women in the city, reveal the inner workings of a community ready to spring into action when the right opportunity presented itself. Both Nixon and Robinson immediately saw Parks's arrest for what it turned out to be: a chance to mobilize a citywide boycott of the bus system that routinely denigrated black citizens, particularly black women. We now have access to the interviews conducted for the historic series "Eyes on the Prize," archived at Washington University. The interviews of Parks, Nixon, and Robinson provide much-needed context to the boycott and can give students a glimpse of black life in the city.[6]

Placing King's first address to the Montgomery Improvement Association (MIA) in dialogue with documents produced by the WPC and interviews with Parks accomplishes at least two important things. First, the pairing underscores King's eloquence and clarity during his initial foray into protest politics. It is important to point out to our students that King deftly ties the boycott to larger issues of legal freedom, a global struggle for liberation, and an insurgent religious activism— threads that are often overlooked by students and teachers in his earlier sermons and speeches. Also, it is always important to note to our students that King did not *initiate* the boycott. Rather, he was brought into an ongoing struggle between black and white Montgomery.

The second, and more profound, accomplishment of this pairing is that it highlights the silences regarding the role of women in the boycott. Parks, for instance, was a dedicated activist and longtime member of the NAACP. She had spent time at the Highlander Folk School in Monteagle, Tennessee, one of the epicenters of activist training in the middle of the twentieth century. By the beginning of the boycott, Parks was no stranger to the freedom struggle in Montgomery. We are now the beneficiaries of some excellent scholarship on Parks and her activist roots. Danielle McGuire's book, *At the Dark End of the Street: Black Women, Rape and Resistance—A New History of the Civil Rights Movement from Rosa Parks to the Rise of Black Power*, reveals a truly brave activist and advocate whose work for black equality was anchored in efforts to bring justice to black victims of sexual assault in the 1940s. Jeanne Theoharis's book *The Rebellious Life of Rosa Parks* is a political biography that also illuminates Parks' decades-long dedication to black equality. Simply put, Rosa Parks did not begin her political life as a "tired" black woman on a bus in 1955. Imagine how much this moment can shift in the minds of our students once they realize that, between King and Parks, it was Parks who brought a decade of frontline freedom work to the boycott. An introduction to Parks also enables us to better explicate the gender dynamics within the movement; as King becomes the focal point of the movement, Parks is relegated to a secondary role.[7]

The WPC stood at the forefront of efforts to mobilize black folk in Montgomery around the problem of harassment perpetrated by bus drivers. Jo Ann Gibson Robinson and the WPC were quite clear about the action they would take if the harassment and denigration of black riders—especially women—persisted. In a letter to the mayor of Montgomery sent a year and a half before the boycott, Robinson observed: "Mayor Gayle, three-fourths of the riders of these public conveyances are Negroes. If Negroes did not patronize them, they could not possibly operate." The inclusion of Robinson in the story of the boycott shows us how black women were not new to the tensions regarding segregated seating on public transportation. To be clear, when we highlight the role of political organizing done by women prior to the boycott, we can see how their actions were foundational to the forward momentum of the boycott. Robinson tells her own story forcefully in her memoir, *The Montgomery Bus Boycott and the Women Who Started It: The Memoir of Jo Ann Gibson Robinson,* an accessible volume that teachers from late elementary through high school will find quite useful. Stewart Burns' book, *Daybreak of Freedom: The Montgomery Bus Boycott,* also provides a wealth of primary source documents, so teachers and students can immerse themselves in the decisions, tactics, and perspectives that comprised this emerging movement.[8]

Properly situating King's role in the movement provides a crucial understanding of this moment for students: at the time of the boycott, King is only twenty-six years old and is working in concert with experienced activists who had been struggling for greater freedom for years. Montgomery represented his first foray into the thicket of the mass-based social movement that would dominate the rest of his tragically short life. King was a brilliant young man—one who had a lot to learn about the calculus of social change and who discovered he was part of a larger network of black activists in the region, many of whom had been laboring for years. By shifting the narrative regarding King—from an all-knowing prophet to a curious, cautious, and passionate young man—we also open up the possibility of treating King *as a student of social protest.* This shift can shed light on some of the most basic facets of King's life and work, facets that our students often take for granted. King, and most other movement figures in Montgomery, were learning how to build a nonviolent social movement in real time. Other activists across the nation observed this struggle and lent their considerable expertise to the boycott. In New York in 1956, Ella Baker, Bayard Rustin, and Stanley Levison formed an organization called In Friendship designed to grant financial and technical assistance to black folks across the South battling segregation. When news of the boycott reached them, they responded vigorously. To say that Baker and Rustin are important to the movement would be a severe understatement. Each of them would play a major role in King's life after their initial encounter with him at the height of the boycott and would—quite literally—design the organizations and mobilizations that came to define the movement. Baker, a master strategist and organizer who in the 1940s and 1950s worked across the South building grassroots leadership, would become the first executive director of the Southern Christian Leadership Conference and would be a guiding force for SNCC. Levison became one of King's most trusted confidants. Rustin would also become one of King's close associates. Documents produced by Baker and Rustin during the late fifties and early sixties provide a glimpse of the high level of expertise each of them brought to their relationship with King; by the time of the boycott, both of them had been deeply involved in the work of cultivating leadership, movement building, and creating permanent organizations.[9]

Students are routinely surprised that King actually had to *learn* how to utilize nonviolence in the pursuit of racial justice. Documents in *Daybreak of Freedom* showing the relationship between King and veteran activist Bayard Rustin are great for bringing this point to light. After racial terrorists in the city bombed his house, King and his lieutenants packed his residence with guards and guns. Any why wouldn't they? When I ask my students what they would do after local terrorists tried to murder their spouses and children (Yolanda King was ten weeks old at the time of the bombing) I hardly ever get a response based in "nonviolence." Rather, I get a variety of responses firmly rooted in Second Amendment–based notions of self-defense. Then I ask: Why do you think King's answer to that question would be any different from yours? This opens up a space to discuss King's growth in this area. How did the shift from self-defense (the default mode for most Americans regardless of race or region) take place for King? How did Rustin and others shape his thinking in the midst of this violent moment? The critical inquiry regarding nonviolence can then progress to other salient issues. What is he learning during the boycott? What did movement veterans have to teach him? How does this moment push him to grow, and in what ways? How is he limited by his worldview? Is he afraid, and if so, what does he do with his fear? How many different versions of leadership can you identify in this moment? How do leaders support the collective will of the community?

Dr. Martin Luther King Jr. speaks at the Freedom Rally in Memphis, Tennessee, on July 31, 1959, on behalf of African American candidates running for public office. (Memphis and Shelby County Room, Memphis Public Library)

Letter from Birmingham Jail

King's iconic "Letter from Birmingham Jail" stands as one of the great pieces of protest literature in American history. Written while King was jailed at the height of the movement in Birmingham, its crisp, clear, powerful prose reverberates through time. There is a lot of ground a teacher can cover with the "Letter." When I use it in my classes, I pair it with the letter that spurred King to write it in the first place—the "Letter to Martin Luther King" penned by eight racially moderate white religious leaders in which they ask King *not* to protest in Birmingham. Positioning themselves between racial segregationists on their political right and liberal integrationists on their left, the white clergy members call on African Americans in Birmingham to refrain from direct action protests, to respect the rule of law, and to press for change in the courts. It is a window into the (increasingly) perilous position of white moderates across the South. At a time when even the most tepid support of integration could lead to anything—from social ostracism to a bombing—white moderates clung to the principles of racial diplomacy and the hope that social change could be brought to the region by way of dialogue, patience, and prayer. It is also a compelling window into how segregation and racial subordination constituted the status quo in the South and across the nation, and how whites of all political stripes made peace with a system of violent, state-sanctioned dehumanization, the maintenance of which outweighed any call for justice and equality under the law.

King's "Letter" is a brilliant response to these eight clergymen. Using their letter, he positions himself (and the movement he increasingly represents) in opposition to both violent segregationists, such as the city's Police Commissioner Eugene "Bull" Connor, and white moderates who sought to discourage nonviolent direct action. He lays bare the increasingly untenable position held by white southern moderates, who, in King's words, treasured "order" over "justice." King's "Letter," when juxtaposed with the letter from local clergy, gives students a sense of how the gap between white moderates and black activists had widened considerably in the years after the *Brown v. Board of Education* decision. King's point about "order" is particularly salient. As always, context is crucial. In Alabama, "order" was shaped by a sustained resistance to federal law in the area of integration. The state *outlawed* the NAACP in 1956. The state's congressional delegation unanimously supported the "Southern Manifesto" of 1957. In Birmingham, the "iron aristocracy," entrenched iron executives who avidly supported segregation and the low wages that accompanied the regime, vigorously opposed moderate political and economic leaders. In response to a court order to desegregate city parks and municipal facilities, the city simply closed them. Segregationists in Birmingham used "order" to remain as far away from "justice" as possible.[10]

King's letter helped crystalize the philosophy of nonviolence in the national imagination. It is a disquisition on the law, religion, and the role of nonviolence in the freedom struggle raging in Birmingham and, increasingly, across the country. Written three years after sit-ins revolutionized the struggle for freedom, two years after the Freedom Rides rocked the region, and a year after James Meredith's integration of Ole Miss, King's "Letter" helped white America interpret the images and stories streaming out of the South and other parts of the nation. His advocacy of nonviolence is unsurpassed here, and his argument for the movement's *moral* center is also quite compelling. In fact, it is in King's "Letter" that we see his most thoroughgoing exposition of the moral underpinnings of the nonviolent direct action phase of the movement. King raises another crucial point in here—that the moral, political, and tactical forces the movement brings to bear in Birmingham are illuminating and countering the systemic failure of the American tradition with regard to African Americans.

In my civil rights course, I remind my students that, when we think of the movement, we have to remember the truly national scope of the moment; people were acting up all across the country. To that end, it is instructive to pair King's musings on these weighty issues with other on-the-ground activists who were also grappling with how to confront and dismantle legal segregation. In Cambridge, Maryland, Gloria Richardson led a protest movement that also garnered national attention. As leader of the Cambridge Maryland Nonviolent Action Committee (CNAC), Richardson—who'd been trained by SNCC—helped sustain protests that brought both the enmity of the federal government and many national civil rights leaders. While Richardson led a nonviolent movement, she openly advocated self-defense, particularly after racial terrorists began shooting into homes in the black community. In "Focus on Cambridge," Richardson asks the question "What is the meaning of the Negro revolt for American democracy?" Though there are many overlaps with King's thinking, Richardson's experiences, and the conclusions she draws from them, make for a thoughtful companion to King's musings on Birmingham.[11]

There is another interesting juxtaposition in the "Letter"—when King chastises the clergymen for considering him to be "extreme." He takes issue with this characterization, claiming that he stood "in the middle of two opposing forces in the Negro community": a "force of complacency" composed of Negroes too beaten down to object to the dehumanization of segregation, and the force of "bitterness and hatred," represented by those who come "perilously close to advocating violence." As with the juxtaposition with white segregationists and moderates, King skillfully establishes an effective, viable "third way." Within the civil rights movement, King cultivated the ability to both explicate and flow between different ideological positions. Indeed, his ability to do so was one of his greatest strengths as a leader. However, we would be remiss if we did not challenge King's triangulation with regard to "violence." Both Robert Williams and Malcolm X have a lot to offer our students when we juxtapose their words with King's. SNCC activist Charlie Cobb and others have written forcefully about the fluid nature of the nonviolence/self-defense debate and moved us away from the "this vs. that" formulation that has come to dominate this (and other) debates within the movement.

The perils and prospects of King's centrist sensibilities are on full display when students read documents featuring Rev. Fred Shuttlesworth, who was dubbed by his peers in Birmingham as "The Courage of the Movement." The stories of Shuttlesworth's bravery are legion. Indeed, it is a singular act of God that he lived past 1963. Anchored by a bedrock faith in a God that called him to action in the service of racial justice and human dignity, Shuttlesworth began confronting segregation in the wake of the 1954 *Brown* decision and quickly earned the enmity of the city's white leaders. Racial terrorists bombed his home on Christmas Day in 1956. The presence of SCLC in Birmingham in 1963 rested largely on the foundation created by the decade's worth of mass meetings that Shuttlesworth facilitated. In fact, he was the one who encouraged King's organization to come to town and take on Birmingham's medieval racial practices.

Shuttlesworth provides a vital complement to King's charismatic centrism. When officials in the Kennedy administration insisted that King halt the protests taking place downtown during the desegregation negotiation process, King agreed to stop. This decision, made without Shuttlesworth's input, sent the fiery preacher into a rage, a dispute that provides vital insight into King's high-wire act with regard to navigating the many big, local personalities with whom he contended across the country as the SCLC mobilized mass demonstrations. Shuttlesworth and other movement leaders produced two documents that also shed light on the conditions in Birmingham at the time of the protests. "The Birmingham Manifesto" of April 1963 was the opening salvo of the campaign. Sixty protesters, members of the Alabama Christian Movement for Human Rights, began what would become a nationally regarded local movement.[12] The other document, "Birmingham: People in Motion," chronicles the movement beginning with the state outlawing the NAACP in 1956.[13] These documents, coupled with a series of interviews in Howell Raines's important book *My Soul Is Rested: Movement Days in the Deep South Remembered*, the "Eyes on the Prize" interview collection, and other places, show us—in a powerful way—why

Shuttlesworth and others were so reluctant to heed Kennedy and King's call for a cessation of the protests. They were deeply invested in their hard-fought forward momentum and were determined not to jeopardize it.[14]

Documents on the Birmingham movement also serve another crucial function: they highlight the casual and pervasive nature of violence in the city. Black folk nicknamed the city "Bombingham" because of the vast amounts of dynamite utilized in the service of racial terror and white supremacy. Documents that bring people such as Shuttlesworth to life help students understand that navigating racial violence was not simply a religious or philosophical exercise. Rather, it shaped every corner of life for black folk in Birmingham—particularly black folks involved in the freedom struggle. Angela Davis, the philosopher and activist, is a native of Birmingham. Her autobiography, *Angela Davis: An Autobiography*, lays bare the nature of violence in Birmingham and shows that everyone—from iconic activists to small children—lived in the shadow of sanctioned, ceaseless violence.[15]

Dreams

No text of King's is more used, and misused, than his "I Have a Dream" speech. Delivered on the steps of the Lincoln Memorial during the 1963 March on Washington for Jobs and Freedom, the aspirational tones set in the second part of the sermon point the way toward the fulfillment of the "Dream"—a time when African Americans can enjoy the full privileges of citizenship and equality. To be sure, this is powerful oratory. However, when I use this text, I am drawn to the first portion of the speech, because it foregrounds the soaring hope exhibited at the end of the speech in some very specific and important ways. King is clear about the fact that the nation has *failed* its black citizens. America wrote her Negroes a "bad check," he says. He then goes on to inform his fellow Americans that should the nation continue its "business as usual" in terms of denying black people their full citizenship, "there will be neither rest nor tranquility in America [and] the whirlwinds of revolt will continue to shake the foundations of our nation until the bright day of justice emerges." It is important to point out to our students that in this portion of his speech, King essentially promises to maintain and, potentially, *increase* the volume of protest and insurgency if political leaders fail to strike down segregation. These are not the words of a man who is ambivalent about the usage of mass-based direct action methods to achieve political ends.

In the next paragraph, King anchors his comments with his now unwavering commitment to nonviolence, encouraging black folks to avoid "drinking from the cup of bitterness and hatred." But then he pivots quickly back to the systemic inequality that plagues the lives of black folks from sea to shining sea. In response to the rhetorical question, "When will you be satisfied?" King responds "We can never be satisfied as long as the Negro is the victim of the *unspeakable horrors of police brutality.*" The violence of police brutality is then juxtaposed with the violence of legal segregation, with specific reference to the kind imposed on the minds and attitudes of young black children forced to contend with state-sanctioned apartheid. To be clear, what King is doing is laying out the justification and blueprint for *a sustained nationwide revolt.*

It is the stark nature of the first portion of the speech that gives the second portion its lilt and prophetic vision. King's belief in the ability of the nation to shift (in response to pressure) its ancient racial habits is on full display when he begins his riff on the "Dream." King's dream, which, as he tells us, is "deeply rooted in the American dream," entails the eventual inclusion of black folks into the mainstream of American life, as evidenced by the transformation of "jangling discords" into a "beautiful symphony of brotherhood." It is in this speech that King, the pragmatic radical, shows the reader a determination to disrupt the nation in the pursuit of black equality, thereby revealing the dynamic relationship between protest and progress.

On March 3, 1968, King delivered his final sermon at Ebenezer Baptist Church in Atlanta titled "Unfulfilled Dreams." The scriptural basis for the sermon was the eighth chapter of the book of Kings. The center of the story is Solomon's reflection on his father David's unsuccessful effort to build a temple to honor God. The passage from 1 Kings 8: 17–19 reads: "And it was in the heart of David my father to build a house for the name of the Lord God of Israel. And the Lord said unto David my father, 'Whereas it was in thine heart to build a house unto my name, thou didst well that it was within thine heart.'" Whereas "I Have a Dream" explored the stony road that America trod in order to fulfill its dream of racial equality, this sermon explores the implications of one of life's great realities—that life, King tells us, "is a continual story of shattered dreams."

The juxtaposition of these two sermons is stunning. In 1963, King's oratory reflected a searing commitment to the possibility of hard-fought social change. King, that most elusive of public figures, could exhibit an optimism that bordered on the romantic while also displaying a hard-nosed political realism. After leaving the steps of the nation's Capitol and commiserating with the president of the United States, King would make his way back to Birmingham to lead a massive protest in the nation's most segregated city. "Unfulfilled Dreams" provides a glimpse of King's political and spiritual evolution. It also reveals an understanding of the increasing intractability of the federal government in the area of civil rights. King's recognition that engaging in the effort to move the government and the nation to the side of justice may itself be the ultimate reward in life reveals the emergence of what can be called prophetic pessimism. In this text, he eschews any references to completion and victory. Rather, he takes solace in the *effort* to make change. As the philosopher Paul Taylor writes in a discussion of the sermon, for King, "the key is not that success is ensured; it is that one makes the effort."[16] After grappling with this text, students often ask, "Is he giving up?" The answer: no, he is not. Rather, he is coming more fully into the notion that the work of political, social, economic, ethical, and racial transformation will continue through the generations—down to now. This realization provides a great opportunity to reflect on the contemporary struggles that King would recognize and to connect the movement for freedom in his time to contemporary efforts for liberation.

"The Fierce Urgency of Now": King in the Contemporary Moment

If we as teachers take the life and legacy of Martin Luther King Jr. seriously in our classrooms, we will have to move him from a state-sanctioned position of political neutrality and harmlessness toward something approaching the fierce social critic he actually came to be during the middle of the last century. To be sure, we cannot project with certainty where King would stand on any number of issues, but history is a powerful guide in this regard. We do not know if King, a Baptist preacher from a middle-class enclave in Atlanta, Georgia, would march with the supporters of the #BlackLivesMatter movement. I'm inclined to believe that he would. We do know that he spoke out forcefully against the "unspeakable horror" of police brutality for the entirety of his public life. We do know that he stood opposed to the state-sanctioned killing of black people, and that he was expert at navigating an expansive notion of political change that encompassed the ballot box as well as the boycott and mass march. We do know that he would embrace a critical mass of the agenda set forth in the Movement for Black Lives. We know that he believed in the need for a wholesale restructuring of American life—a restructuring that forcefully confronted the evils of racism, militarism, and poverty. We also know that he excelled at reaching across ideological differences to build relationships with those with whom he may have disagreed. After all, the ideological differences between King and Stokely Carmichael, one of King's biggest critics from 1966 until his assassination in 1968, did not keep Carmichael from having Sunday dinner at the King residence anytime he found himself in Atlanta.

We face a number of other challenges that, sadly, King would find all too familiar. He would recognize churches dotting the nation that are nothing more than "irrelevant social clubs without moral or spiritual authority." He would recognize that "the giant triplets of racism, materialism, and militarism" have yet to be conquered. He would recognize the racially inscribed pockets of poverty found from coast to coast. In the wake of the gutting of the Voting Rights Act by the Supreme Court in *Shelby County, Alabama vs. Holder* in 2013, King would view, with weary recognition, the systematic efforts of state legislatures to disenfranchise minority voters. He most certainly would utter full-throated condemnation of the resurgent nature of white nationalism in the nation, an ideology nurtured in the toxic racial climate that defines the Trump era.

In numerous respects, justice has not rolled down like waters upon many of the people in our nation. We live in a society still buffeted by pervasive racial divisions. But King would also recognize, and appreciate, the value in our attempts to make sense of our past, especially the effort to grapple with its complexity and possibility. Assessing King in his fullness provides us an opportunity to reinvigorate our understanding of both the man and the movement he joined. For teachers, there are myriad rewards for guiding our students in an enhanced exploration of King's words and actions. When we render "Brother Martin" fully human and place him back in his time, we open our students to the possibility of achieving significant insights into history, language, race, and politics. We also expose them to the essential elements of what King once called "the beautiful struggle to make a new world."

RESOURCES

A Group of Clergymen. "Letter to Martin Luther King." http://teachingameri
canhistory.org/library/document/letter-to-martin-luther-king/.
King, Martin Luther, Jr. "Letter from Birmingham Jail." April 16, 1963, Martin
Luther King, Jr. Research and Education Institute, Stanford University,
https://kinginstitute.stanford.edu/king-papers/documents/letter-bir
mingham-jail.
Robinson, Jo Ann Gibson. "Don't Ride the Bus." Leaflet, December 2, 1955.
Martin Luther King, Jr. Research and Education Institute, Stanford University, https://kinginstitute.stanford.edu/king-papers/documents/dont
-ride-bus.
Shuttlesworth, Fred. Interview, October 27 and 28, 1988. Birmingham Public
Library Digital Collections, http://bplonline.cdmhost.com/cdm/ref/col
lection/p15099coll2/id/83.

NOTES

1. Timothy B. Tyson, *Blood Done Sign My Name: A True Story* (New York: Three Rivers Press, 2004), 107.

2. For thoughtful work on the relationship between history, memory, and memorialization, see Jeanne Theoharis, *A More Beautiful and Terrible History: The Uses and Misuses of Civil Rights History* (New York: Beacon Press, 2018), and Renee Romano and Leigh Raiford, eds., *The Civil Rights Movement in American Memory* (Athens: University of Georgia Press, 2006).

3. For this essay, I've decided to focus on the main "stops" of King's life and career. There are, of course, countless ways to teach and contend with King. But, in many cases, we simply don't have the time to really dive into the many facets of his work. With any luck, this essay points the way toward one viable approach.

4. Troy Jackson, *Becoming King: Martin Luther King, Jr and the Making of a Leader* (Lexington: University Press of Kentucky, 2011), 1. The most essential book on King's life remains Taylor Branch's trilogy, which begins with *Parting the Waters: America in the King Years, 1954–1963* (New York: Simon and Schuster, 1989).

5. On the political terrain of Montgomery in the decades leading up to the boycott, see J. Mills Thornton, *Dividing Lines: Municipal Politics in Montgomery, Birmingham and Selma* (Tuscaloosa: University of Alabama Press, 2006).

6. "Eyes on the Prize Interviews: The Complete Series," http://digital
.wustl.edu/eyesontheprize/browse.html#n (accessed April 30, 2019).

7. Danielle McGuire, *At the Dark End of the Street: Black Women, Rape, and
Resistance—A New History of the Civil Rights Movement from Rosa Parks to the Rise
of Black Power* (New York: Knopf, 2010); Jeanne Theoharis, *The Rebellious Life of
Mrs. Rosa Parks* (Boston: Beacon Press, 2015).

8. Jo Ann Gibson Robinson, *The Montgomery Bus Boycott and the Women
Who Started It: The Memoir of Jo Ann Gibson Robinson* (Knoxville: University of
Tennessee Press, 2011); Stewart Burns, *Daybreak of Freedom: The Montgomery Bus
Boycott* (Chapel Hill: University of North Carolina Press, 2012).

9. On Ella Baker, see Barbara Ransby, *Ella Baker and the Black Freedom Move-
ment: A Radical Democratic Vision* (Chapel Hill: University of North Carolina
Press, 2003); J. Todd Moye, *Ella Baker: Community Organizer of the Civil Rights
Movement* (New York: Rowman and Littlefield, 2013). On Bayard Rustin, see
John D'Emilio, *Lost Prophet: The Life and Times of Bayard Rustin* (New York: Free
Press, 2003). Rustin's writings have been collected in the excellent volume edited
by Devon Carbado, Doe Weise, and Barney Frank, *Time on Two Crosses: The Col-
lected Writings of Bayard Rustin* (New York: Cleis Press, 2015). See *Daybreak of
Freedom* for documents relating to Baker and Rustin during the boycott.

10. Numan Bartley, *The New South: 1945–1980* (New Orleans: Louisiana
State University Press, 1995), 334. On the political orientation of black working-
class people in the state during this period, see Robin D. G. Kelley, "The Black
Poor and the Politics of Opposition in a New South City, 1929–1970," in *The
"Underclass" Debate: Views from History*, ed. Michael Katz, 293–333 (Princeton:
Princeton University Press, 1992).

11. Gloria Richardson, "Focus on Cambridge," originally published in
Freedomways, 1964, https://www.crmvet.org/info/cambridg.htm (accessed
May 1, 2019). Documents on what came to be known as the "Treaty of Cam-
bridge" can be accessed at https://snccdigital.org/events/treaty-of-cambridge/.
See also Faith Holsaert et al., eds., *Hands on the Freedom Plow: Personal Accounts
by Women in SNCC* (Urbana: University of Illinois Press).

12. "The Birmingham Manifesto," https://www.crmvet.org/docs/bham
manf.htm (accessed May 1, 2019).

13. "Birmingham: People in Motion," https://www.crmvet.org/info/bham
_pim.pdf (accessed May 1, 2019).

14. Howell Raines, *My Soul Is Rested: Movement Days in the Deep South Remembered* (New York: Viking, 1983).

15. Angela Davis, *Angela Davis: An Autobiography* (New York: International,
1995).

16. Paul Taylor, "Moral Perfectionism," in *To Shape a New World: Essays on
the Political Philosophy of Martin Luther King, Jr.*, ed. Tommie Shelby and Brandon
Terry, 33–57 (Cambridge: Harvard University Press, 2018). A bit later in the

essay, Taylor continues: "To pretend that there are guarantees, or that the experiences of despair and disappointment have no place in the ethical life, is to fail to take the burdens of ethical life seriously." Special thanks to Paul Taylor for pointing me to this compelling sermon. Martin Luther King Jr., "Unfulfilled Dreams," sermon, March 3, 1968, https://kinginstitute.stanford.edu/king -papers/documents/unfulfilled-dreams (accessed May 1, 2019).

Not That Kind of Tired

*Rosa Parks and Organizing
the Montgomery Bus Boycott*

Emilye Crosby

Rosa L. Parks is one of the best-known figures of the civil rights movement; she is also one of the most misunderstood. My students, almost all of them educated in New York State, which received an A ranking from the Southern Poverty Law Center for movement education, have been taught an almost identical, very superficial story of the movement that very much revolves around Rosa Parks.[1] In the wake of Barack Obama's presidential victory, some of his supporters popularized a version that goes like this: "Rosa sat so that Martin could walk; Martin walked so that Obama could run; Obama ran so that our children could fly." Most students, most people, see Parks as a symbol and project onto her (and onto King and the Montgomery bus boycott) a version of Julian Bond's Master Narrative—a story focused on integration, top-down leadership, and government action. In this telling, Parks is a physically tired, accidental activist, someone whose sole importance rests in giving rise to King's leadership. People tend to think of her as sweet, even grandmotherly. Simultaneously, the bus boycott is primarily seen as the launching pad for King and nonviolence, while giving the nation an opportunity to affirm and extend a commitment to integration (expressed less than two years earlier in the *Brown v. Board of Education* decision).

Among other things, this myth of Montgomery obscures Rosa Parks's extensive and determined activist history. She was neither accidental nor, as some have suggested, an NAACP plant. Rather, she was a life-long activist who refused to passively accept abuse and was more committed to dignity and self-determination than integration. The boycott itself was initially focused on better treatment; the decision to file suit challenging bus segregation came only after white leaders remained intransigent and initiated a "get tough" policy aimed at destroying the boycott. Most importantly, as I emphasize to my students, the bus boycott was an extraordinary example of determined grassroots leadership, effective organization, and resolute mass action. Women, in particular, played a crucial role. Teaching the real history of Rosa Parks and the Montgomery bus boycott is an effective way to help students confront and move beyond superficial movement myths to grapple with the reality of Jim Crow and how African Americans organized to challenge it.

Students are very receptive to replacing their mythologies with real history, to learning, for example, that the movement was fueled by ordinary people, including students like themselves. I find this works especially well with Parks and the bus boycott because the mythology is so widely known and accepted and because what actually happened is so much more compelling. I usually introduce the bus boycott, and sometimes even the civil rights movement as a whole, by asking my students to analyze a document that the Women's Political Council (WPC) of Montgomery sent to the mayor of Montgomery the year before the boycott. I typically do not provide students with much context, preferring to see what they can figure out on their own. The letter reads:

May 21, 1954
Honorable Mayor W. A. Gayle
City Hall
Montgomery, Alabama

Dear Sir:
    The Women's Political Council is very grateful to you and the City Commissioners for the hearing you allowed our representative during the month of March, 1954, when the "city-bus-fare-increase case" was being reviewed. There were several things the [Women's Political] Council asked for:

1. A city law that would make it possible for Negroes to sit from back toward front, and whites from front toward back until the seats are taken.

2. That Negroes not be asked or forced to pay fare at front and go to the rear of the bus to enter.

3. That buses stop at every corner in residential sections occupied by Negroes as they do in communities where whites reside.

We are happy to report that busses have begun stopping at more corners now in some sections where Negroes live than previously. However, the same practices in seating and boarding the bus continue.

Mayor Gayle, three-fourths of the riders of these public conveyances are Negroes. If Negroes did not patronize them, they could not possibly operate. More and more of our people are arranging with neighbors and friends to ride to keep from being insulted and humiliated by bus drivers.

There has been talk from twenty-five or more local organizations of planning a city-wide boycott of busses. We, sir, do not feel that forceful measures are necessary in bargaining for a convenience which is right for all bus passengers. We, the Council, believe that when this matter has been put before you and the Commissioners, that agreeable terms can be met in a quiet and unostensible manner to the satisfaction of all concerned.

Many of our Southern cities in neighboring states have practiced the policies we seek without incident whatsoever. Atlanta, Macon and Savannah in Georgia have done this for years. Even Mobile, in our own state, does this and all the passengers are satisfied.

Please consider this plea, and if possible, act favorably on it, for even now plans are being made to ride less, or not at all, on our buses. We do not want this.

Respectfully yours,
The Women's Political Council
Jo Ann Robinson, President[2]

Sometimes I go from a collective reading of this document to open-ended questions such as what do you think? or what's important about this? Other times, I give the students a set of questions and ask them to discuss the questions in small groups before coming back together and either going through the questions or jumping right to one question: what's important? Though I do little to set this up, depending on what students know, it can be helpful to provide them with this basic chronology:

- *Brown v. Board of Education* decision, May 17, 1954;
- Rosa Parks arrested, Thursday, December 1, 1955;
- Montgomery bus boycott begins, Monday, December 5, 1955;
- *Browder v. Gayle* Supreme Court case from Montgomery that ruled bus segregation unconstitutional, filed February 1, 1956; decided November 13, 1956; implementation goes into effect December 20, 1956; boycotters return to buses, December 21, 1956.

The questions I use are very basic and are simply intended to help students engage with the text.

1. When was this letter written in relation to the Montgomery bus boycott?
2. Who wrote this letter (was it Martin Luther King)?
3. What is the letter about?
4. What does the WPC say about the conditions on the buses?
5. What does the WPC want? What support do they offer for their position?
6. What does the WPC say might happen if the mayor and City Commission don't address the concerns of Montgomery African Americans?

My students tend to embrace this exercise, and by the time we are done, they will have identified a number of important details and broad themes related to the bus boycott. And while they are using the close reading to generate these important points, I also use our discussion to fill in some of what they cannot learn from the document.

I want my students to come away from this exercise with an understanding that Dr. King did not start the boycott, that there was broad African American dissatisfaction with the Montgomery buses at least eighteen months before the boycott started, and that, for the WPC at least, the primary issue was not segregation, but mistreatment. Some of my students have been sure, and quite vocal about their certainty, that King was behind this letter. That there is no evidence to support this view apparently cannot compete with the strength of the mythology. It is always interesting to watch them grapple with the fact that King was in graduate school in Boston when the letter was written; he did not move to Montgomery until September 1954. From this letter, students should also begin to suspect that the boycott was not quite as spontaneous as the mythology would suggest. Though it does not provide direct information about Parks, it makes it clear that the idea of boycotting was in play well before Parks made her stand. According to the WPC, "twenty-five or more local organizations" were "planning a city-wide boycott of the buses." This detail offers a hint about how African Americans in Montgomery managed to get an almost 100 percent successful boycott launched just a few days after Parks's arrest. Finally, the WPC letter provides a helpful opening for exploring the role of women and gender in the boycott.

As useful as the WPC letter is for introducing students to the boycott, it actually underplays the extent of the harassment that African Americans faced on the buses. Depending on the situation, I either fill in some of those details or, if it is possible, assign some additional documents for students to analyze. There is useful testimony about bus conditions from two major court cases that emerged during the bus boycott. Women, especially, recount violent harassment by drivers who regularly used racist insults, assaulted passengers, forced African Americans to pay at the front and board through the back (sometimes driving away and leaving them behind even though they had paid their fare). Montgomery bus drivers had police authority and claimed the right to regulate African American behavior, at times, ironically, violating the local segregation ordinances themselves. This was actually true in Parks's case. She was sitting in what was considered to be "no man's land" and was ordered to move, even though there was not an empty seat for her as the law required.

Tensions over the treatment of blacks on the buses were escalating in the months before Parks was arrested. Students are often particularly interested to learn about Claudette Colvin, a high school student who, like Parks, refused to give up her seat for a white patron. Colvin, who later testified that "our leaders is just we ourself," refused to give up her seat because she was "just as good as any white person."[3]

It is critically important for students to understand that tens of thousands of black Montgomery citizens did not boycott the buses because they wanted to sit next to whites. They boycotted because they refused to accept the brutal Jim Crow system that gave white bus drivers arbitrary authority that they, and police officers, too often used to abuse and attack African Americans. Eventually bus boycotters challenged legal segregation, but that was only one aspect of the much more fundamental goal of decent treatment. Historian Danielle McGuire argues compellingly that the bus boycott should be understood as "more than a movement for civil rights. It was also a women's movement for dignity, respect, and bodily integrity."[4] The best source for the court testimony that works so well to introduce students to this brutal system, and women's resistance, is Stewart Burns's edited book, *Daybreak of Freedom*, which combines a helpful introduction to the boycott with a useful chronology and an extensive collection of documents, including many that can be used effectively in the classroom.

While it is useful for students to understand that the boycott went beyond both King and Parks, Parks was an important activist, and knowing more about her will help students understand the movement. "People always say that I didn't give up my seat because I was tired, but that isn't true," explained Parks. "I was not tired physically, or no more tired than I usually was at the end of a working day. I was not old, although some people have an image of me as being old then. I was forty-two. No, the only tired I was, was tired of giving in."[5] I often ask students: If you were tired, would you do something that meant you were likely to be thrown off the bus you were riding home? or be arrested? I wouldn't, I say, because there's nothing appealing about jail. What's more, Parks knew the potential for violence and abuse from bus drivers and police officers.

I begin teaching Parks by sharing with my students some key biographical details, especially about her pre-boycott history, and supplement that by assigning short excerpts from oral histories with Parks.[6] I make sure students know that Parks was a lifelong activist who had served as NAACP secretary at the local and state levels. I explain that in the early days of her marriage to Raymond Parks, she joined him in working to free the Scottsboro Boys. Her own militancy was nurtured at a young age by her grandfather, a follower of Marcus Garvey, who believed in armed self-defense. Parks also worked closely with E. D. Nixon, who, among other things, was an organizer for A. Philip Randolph's Brotherhood of Sleeping Car Porters, as well as a local and state NAACP leader. He aggressively encouraged African Americans to register to vote and was, without question, one of the most important African American leader-activists in Montgomery.

In the years before her bus stand, Parks attended an NAACP leadership workshop led by veteran organizer Ella Baker and spent two weeks at Highlander Folk School as part of an integrated group of southern activists discussing ways to implement the *Brown* decision. When Claudette Colvin was arrested, Parks recruited her to join the NAACP Youth Branch. Parks empathized with the teenager and likely recognized a fellow fighter. Before her arrest in December 1955, Parks had had her own conflicts with drivers, refusing to let them push her around. She explained later that if she had been paying attention, she never would have boarded *that* bus, driven by James Blake, who had thrown her off his bus years before. At its most fundamental, students should know that Parks "spent her adult life looking for a way to make a difference." While her defiance and arrest were not planned, they also were not surprising.[7]

Given Parks's long history of activism, how did she come to be defined in such passive terms? The answer lies in the crucial intersection of race, class, and gender, and the conscious desire of male leaders, such as E. D. Nixon and King, to use her as a symbol. As African Americans in Montgomery, including the women who led the WPC, grew increasingly angry about their treatment on buses, Nixon believed that any serious challenge would require a person around whom others could rally and someone who could withstand everything white supremacists would throw at her. When others wanted to use the teen-aged Claudette Colvin's arrest to launch a boycott and court case, he felt she might not stand up to scrutiny. Parks, by contrast, was the perfect person. Not only was she a fierce and seasoned freedom fighter, she also personified respectability. She was well spoken, a conservative dresser, and a dedicated churchgoer. Thus, even as Parks's activist history positioned her as the spark and symbol of the boycott, others stepped into the spotlight and justified the protest around her respectability.

What happened after Parks was arrested on Thursday, December 1, 1955? What else should students know about how the boycott was organized? When police officers took Parks off the bus, word spread quickly through Montgomery's black community, and planning for a boycott began immediately. E. D. Nixon, Parks's friend and ally from the NAACP, the Brotherhood of Sleeping Car Porters, and other racial justice campaigns, moved quickly to bail her out and asked her for permission to fight her case in court. At the same time, he began reaching out to ministers and other community leaders—the people who would ultimately become the public face of the boycott. Meanwhile, Jo Ann Gibson Robinson decided that the time had come for the WPC to call for a boycott. She and a colleague spent most of Thursday night mimeographing fliers calling for a one-day boycott on Monday, December 5, 1955, the day Parks was due to appear in court. "Another Negro woman has been arrested and thrown into jail because she refused to get up out of her seat on the bus for a white person to sit down," read the flier. "If we don't do something to stop these arrests, they will continue. The next time it may be you, or your daughter, or mother." Explaining that "This woman's case will come up on Monday," the flier called for "every Negro to stay off the buses" that day "in protest of the arrest and trial." The WPC distributed the fliers all over Montgomery, and Nixon convinced ministers to publicize the boycott during their Sunday services and call for a mass meeting to be held Monday night.[8]

The Monday boycott was virtually 100 percent effective. Parks, meanwhile, appeared in court where she pleaded not guilty, was convicted, and entered an appeal. That afternoon, Nixon led a meeting of community leaders, most of them ministers, who hesitatingly formed the Montgomery Improvement Association (MIA) and elected Dr. King president. King was chosen in part because he was relatively new and was not aligned with any particular faction in the community. He was also a member of the NAACP and was developing a reputation as a good speaker. The ministers were unsure of the next step, but when they arrived at Holt Street Baptist Church for the mass meeting that night and saw thousands of people surrounding the church and packed inside, they knew they had to continue the boycott. While Nixon and Parks hoped to use her arrest and conviction to challenge segregation, the MIA's initial demands called for whites to be seated from front to back and African Americans from back to front, the amended form of segregation the WPC had asked for in its letter to the mayor eighteen months earlier. The MIA also demanded more courteous treatment and the hiring of black drivers for routes in black neighborhoods.

Organizing an effective one-day boycott of tens of thousands of people was a major accomplishment. But it would take quite a bit more to sustain the boycott for more than a year. Boycott organizers had to contend with a massive array of issues and problems. To help keep people off the buses, they immediately began coordinating a car pool system, asking those who owned vehicles to drive friends as well as strangers. Over time, they raised the money and created the infrastructure needed for a mass transportation alternative. The new system included full-time dispatchers, paid drivers, and a motor pool for repairs. It helped that virtually everyone in the black community had experienced or knew someone who had experienced harassment on the buses. But organization and leadership were essential to the boycott's success.

When time permits, I show my students the Montgomery segment of the television series *Eyes on the Prize*, which introduces them to some of the key leaders and participants.[9] The HBO film *Boycott* is even more effective at exposing students to the overlapping leaders and participants who made the boycott successful.[10] Based on Stewart Burns's *Daybreak of Freedom*, it is good history, and my students love it as a movie. One of the most important things you can use these films to teach students about is the three types of overlapping leadership that built and sustained the boycott. There were the visible, charismatic leaders, led by King and mostly other ministers, who mobilized the community. There were the organizers who generally worked behind-the-scenes, but they were also important strategists who were essential to making things happen. This layer included Parks, Nixon, and Robinson. In addition, "as many as several thousand activists led at the micro-level of extended family, neighborhood, church, and workplace." And finally, another twenty thousand or so people stayed off the buses, even if they did nothing else. While the most visible leaders tended to be middle class, they simultaneously led and were pushed forward by the "foot soldiers from the class of working poor."[11]

Women were central to this. While very few women made it into the visible leadership structure that spoke at mass meetings, Jo Ann Gibson Robinson made sure that she, Parks, and Mrs. Irene West, who also belonged to the WPC, were on the MIA executive committee; another four WPC members were ultimately hired in essential MIA staff positions. In addition to launching the boycott, Robinson was a key member of the negotiating team that met with white officials, edited a newsletter, drove in the car pool, and served as the "chief strategist." These organizers and other women were also central to fundraising and establishing and maintaining the alternate transportation system. For example, Georgia Gilmore and then Inez Ricks set up rival supper clubs, cooking and selling food to raise money for the boycott; their weekly competition became a highlight of mass meetings. So, too, were the testimonies of the women who worked as domestics and maids. As the majority of the bus riders, with considerable firsthand experience with abuse, they became the backbone of the movement. And when the MIA decided to shift strategy and launch a legal challenge to the segregated bus system, all of the plaintiffs were women, including Claudette Colvin, even though King begged the all-male ministers on the MIA executive committee to join the suit. It was this case, *Browder v. Gayle*, that ultimately took down segregation and was the impetus for ending the boycott.[12]

Regarding King, the movement may have made him, but once he was thrust into the spotlight, he rose to the occasion and quickly became the public face of the boycott. Charismatic and a good listener, he was effective at motivating people and delegating tasks to a close group of ministers. Robinson praised his ability to "foster moral courage," while many working-class women were captivated by his preaching. His involvement was important for "nurturing people's morale, commitment, courage, endurance, solidarity and faith," suggests historian Stewart Burns, "but not essential for strategizing, policy making, managing, fund-raising, and community organizing."[13] King was also essential to the development of the nonviolent philosophy that has become so closely associated with the boycott and the movement. Students should know that there was nothing automatic about nonviolence. King was still forming his opinion of nonviolence when the boycott began. Indeed, in Montgomery and elsewhere, most movement participants understood nonviolence as a potentially useful tactic rather than an essential way of life. Many people were prepared to use weapons in self-defense, and when King's home was bombed it took all of his powers of persuasion to dissuade an angry crowd from retaliating violently.

Nonviolence or nonretaliation were challenging concepts for people to embrace, especially because white supremacists used violence freely. In addition to bombing King's house while his wife and young daughter were home with a friend, segregationists bombed the homes of other movement leaders, including E. D. Nixon and Ralph David Abernathy. The white city fathers also formed a Citizens' Council to harness their power to maintain segregation; manipulated the legal system by indicting King, Robinson, Parks, Abernathy, Nixon, and dozens of other leaders on trumped-up conspiracy charges; abused carpool drivers and issued tickets for everything and nothing; used economic intimidation by firing people, withdrawing credit, and denying insurance; and generally harassed boycott participants and leaders. Though there were a few close calls, white resistance generally failed to undermine the boycott. In fact, whites' refusal to negotiate a different form of segregated seating led the MIA to challenge segregation itself, while the bombing of King's home made people angrier and more committed.

Students who know only the myth about Parks and the boycott think that the civil rights movement was initiated by accident and needed the larger-than-life leadership of King. The real history teaches them that the movement happened because people made it happen. Once Parks's defiance acted as a spark, the boycott was successful because hundreds of ordinary people exerted leadership and thousands committed themselves to the boycott, no matter the cost. Students also need to see through the myth that our country was moving toward justice and white citizens only needed a little nudge in order to do right. In terms of Montgomery, the Supreme Court's decision in *Browder v. Gayle* arced toward freedom, but a critical and often untold part of the story is that of white resistance. White supremacists, many of them with considerable political and economic clout, used everything from violence to their influence over the southern legal system to try to stop the boycott, to halt the movement, and to control African Americans. White Americans did not suddenly come to their senses and decide racism was wrong. African Americans and their allies won victories through determined and sustained action.

While segregation was part of the problem, it was not *the* problem. Students need to understand that Jim Crow was not really about keeping African Americans and whites apart; it was a hierarchical system that was built around the abuse and exploitation of black workers. The boycott and the larger movement, then, were always about essential human and civil rights, what Hasan Kwame Jeffries calls "freedom rights." Students should also learn from Parks's lifelong activism that the movement had deep roots going back in time, and the struggle extended well beyond the 1960s. Parks's post-boycott life in Detroit included fighting against segregated and substandard housing, police brutality, job discrimination, and many other aspects of structural inequality, problems that persist today.

The bus boycott was a victory, but it was just one small step in a larger struggle. It may have been most important in serving notice that African Americans were going to assertively and persistently challenge oppression. And through their collective stand, black people in Montgomery inspired others, including some of the young people who, five years later, put their bodies on the line to launch the sit-ins and kick off waves of direct action and community organizing that propelled the struggle forward.

NOTES

1. For an example, see Alex Waldauer quoted in Emilye Crosby, *A Little Taste of Freedom: The Black Freedom Struggle in Claiborne County, Mississippi* (Chapel Hill: University of North Carolina Press, 2005), xiii; "SPLC Study Finds That More than Half of States Fail at Teaching the Civil Rights Movement," September 27, 2011, Southern Poverty Law Center, https://www.splcenter .org/news/2011/09/28/splc-study-finds-more-half-states-fail-teaching-civil -rights-movement, accessed August 10, 2016.

2. Women's Political Council and [Jo Ann Gibson Robinson], "A Letter from the Women's Political Council to the Mayor of Montgomery, Alabama," in Jo Ann Gibson Robinson, *The Montgomery Bus Boycott and the Women Who Started It: The Memoir of Jo Ann Gibson Robinson*, ed. David J. Garrow (Knoxville: University of Tennessee Press, 1987). An excerpt can be found at the National Humanities Center Resource Toolbox, http://nationalhumanitiescenter.org /pds/maai3/protest/text5/robinsonbusboycott.pdf.

3. Danielle McGuire, *At the Dark End of the Street: Black Women, Rape, and Resistance—A New History of the Civil Rights Movement from Rosa Parks to the Rise of Black Power* (New York: Knopf, 2010), 70; Stewart Burns, ed., *Daybreak of Freedom: The Montgomery Bus Boycott* (Chapel Hill: University of North Carolina Press, 1997), 5, 73–77.

4. McGuire, *At the Dark End of the Street*, 43.

5. Rosa Parks, "'Tired of Giving In': The Launching of the Montgomery Bus Boycott," in *Sisters in the Struggle: African American Women in the Civil Rights-Black Power Movement*, ed. Bettye Collier-Thomas and V. P. Franklin, 61–74 (New York: New York University Press, 2001).

6. Two good oral history options are the Montgomery chapter in Howell Raines, *My Soul Is Rested* (New York: Putnam, 1977), and Rosa Parks, "'Tired of Giving In.'"

7. Charles Payne, "Debating the Civil Rights Movement: The View from the Trenches," in *Debating the Civil Rights Movement, 1945–1968*, by Steven F. Lawson and Charles Payne (Lanham, MD: Rowman and Littlefield, 2006), 127. For more about Parks, teachers and students should consult Jeanne Theoharis's recent biography, *The Rebellious Life of Mrs. Rosa Parks* (Boston: Beacon Press,

2013). See also "The Rebellious Life of Mrs. Rosa Parks," https://rosaparks biography.org/bio/. Among other things, Theoharis makes clear that Parks was anything but meek. She was a radical freedom fighter who embraced Black Power as readily as civil rights. Parks considered Malcolm X a personal hero and spoke at the funeral of Robert F. Williams, notorious for his commitment to armed self-defense. Parks was a militant woman with a strong feeling of race pride who remained committed to struggle throughout her life.

8. Burns, *Daybreak of Freedom*, 87.

9. Henry Hampton, prod., "Awakenings (1954–1956)," directed by Judith Vecchione, *Eyes on the Prize* (PBS, January 21, 1987).

10. Clark Johnson, dir., *Boycott* (HBO, 2001).

11. Burns, *Daybreak of Freedom*, 11, 4.

12. For more information on Gilmore or a short reading for students, see Premilla Nadesen, "How One Courageous Black Household Worker Changed the Outcome of the Montgomery Bus Boycott," August 14, 2015, https://www.alternet.org/2015/08/how-one-courageous-black-household-worker-changed-outcome-montgomery-bus-boycott/.

13. Burns, *Daybreak of Freedom*, 12, 18.

Freedom Is a Constant Struggle

Teaching the 1964 Mississippi Freedom Project

NICOLE A. BURROWES AND
LA TASHA B. LEVY

In August 2014, armored vehicles encroached upon Ferguson, Missouri, in response to African American protesters raising their voices against the police murder of an unarmed teenager, Michael Brown. The tanks were part of the 1033 Program, designed to give domestic police forces access to surplus military supplies.[1] Images of African American citizens facing police officers with high-powered military weaponry struck a chord that ignited a national movement against police killings of unarmed African American men, women, and children.

The visual parallel between military combat tanks in Ferguson and police repression in the 1960s was not lost on our students. They had just completed our course called "Freedom Summer," a multimedia exploration of the 1964 Mississippi Freedom Project. During the uprising in Ferguson, which transpired just two weeks after the conclusion of our course, students filled our inboxes with emails drawing upon their knowledge of the civil rights movement to critically analyze the present crises stemming from the intersections of racial injustice, economic exploitation, police surveillance, and the criminalization of blackness.

As resistance in Ferguson unfolded, our students grappled with what Amiri Baraka has referred to as the "changing same"—a concept that aptly characterizes the protracted struggle for black freedom in the United States. Little did we know, activists Patrisse Cullors and Darnell Moore would subsequently organize "Freedom Rides" to Ferguson, firmly planting a burgeoning movement for black lives within an African American protest tradition.

In many ways, our class on the 1964 Mississippi Project was a "civil rights movement remix" that upended conventional iconography favoring male leadership, integration, and middle-class respectability. One of our primary goals was to disrupt what students think they already know about the civil rights movement. Beyond Dr. Martin Luther King Jr.'s "dream," most students have a dearth of knowledge of social movement history despite their feelings of civil rights fatigue due to the constant cooptation and commodification of 1960s social protests— especially the sanitized representations of Dr. King. Rather than reproduce uncritical narratives of civil rights progressivism, as if we have already overcome, our course highlighted competing ideologies and strategies for black liberation as well as continuity and change over time. Our charge was to place present challenges in education, politics, economics, and social justice within historical context, but through the lens of a radical, yet often neglected, moment in civil rights history— the 1964 Mississippi Freedom Summer Project.

Why Freedom Summer?

The 1964 Freedom Summer Project represents a critical moment in the history of the black freedom struggle. Despite the relative success of the sit-in movement that swept across the South after the founding of the Student Nonviolent Coordinating Committee (SNCC) in 1960, Mississippi remained a brutal battleground in the fight for racial equality and one of the most extreme cases of racial terror and economic deprivation. In other southern states, such as Tennessee, South Carolina, and Georgia, African American voter registration had increased between 30 and 60 percent as a result of social protests. In the Magnolia State, however, African American registration had declined over the course of the 1950s, stagnating at a mere 2 percent in the early 1960s. White domination in Mississippi only intensified as local African

Americans, who constituted the vast majority of the population (more than 80 percent in the Delta region), attempted to exercise their rights as US citizens. But access to voting booths and lunch counters was the least of white domination in Mississippi. The economic exploitation that black Mississippians suffered was astounding. For all of the expressions of white supremacy, vigilante violence, and government corruption and complicity, it was singer Nina Simone who triggered national outrage when she belted out the lyrics, "Alabama's gotten me so upset / Tennessee made me lose my rest / And everybody knows about Mississippi Goddam!"

When SNCC field secretary Bob Moses traveled to Mississippi in 1961 to launch a voter registration drive, he learned, rather quickly, that the social, political, and economic dynamics in Mississippi required different strategies than what had been practiced in other areas in the South. For decades, local black Mississippians fought white domination. And they paid a high price with their bodies, which were bloodied, jailed, threatened, and lynched. Unrelenting black death and white intransigence pushed organizers to strategize about how to place a national and international spotlight on racial terror and oppression in Mississippi. Given the severity of white resistance, which included the threat of economic sanctions against a people mostly living in abject poverty, some black Mississippians balked at demonstrations and voting rights campaigns, chastising neighbors for getting involved in "that civil rights mess." The landscape of white domination in Mississippi, and the federal government's refusal to intervene, created the conditions for a radical local movement to eventually emerge.

SNCC collaborated with local organizers and other organizations, including the Congress of Racial Equality (CORE) and the NAACP to form an umbrella organization—the Council of Federated Organizations (COFO)—which would become the backbone of the 1964 Mississippi Freedom Summer Project. Designed to "open up Mississippi to the country" and attract international scrutiny of civil rights violations and human rights abuses in the United States, Freedom Summer was a ten-week campaign that included mass voter registration drives, the creation of Freedom Schools, community centers, research programs, and the development of a progressive, independent political party— the Mississippi Freedom Democratic Party (MFDP). All of this was life-threatening work, and it challenged a system that was bent on instituting and enforcing African American subservience and second-class citizenship. Remembered perhaps most readily for the hundreds of white student volunteers from the nation's elite colleges and universities and the infamous murders of three civil rights workers—James Chaney, Andrew Goodman, and Michael Schwerner—Freedom Summer was a deadly period. Yet, it was also a transformative experience for participants, and it continues to inspire social justice movements all over the world.

What makes Freedom Summer essential to teaching the civil rights movement is its comprehensive vision of African American freedom. Freedom was not only about the right to vote or integration. Freedom Summer embodied a movement for deep societal transformation and human dignity, a movement whose goals were "bigger than a hamburger," a phrase freedom fighter Ella Baker used in the title of her speech at SNCC's inaugural conference.[2] Baker's quiet, yet pervasive, influence cultivated what scholar-activist Barbara Ransby refers to as a "radical democratic vision," which continues to inspire African American activists in the contemporary Movement for Black Lives against state violence and antiblack racism.[3]

Freedom Summer 1964 also challenges the Master Narrative of the civil rights movement, which focuses almost exclusively on charismatic male leadership; integration and voting; uncomplicated notions of American democracy; and nonviolence. How do movement narratives change when we center women like Fannie Lou Hamer, Anne Moody, Vera Pigee, Anne Braden, and Ella Baker? What happens to the civil rights agenda when we study the efforts to create parallel institutions such as the Freedom Schools and the Mississippi Freedom Democratic Party rather than programs that focus exclusively on integration? How do we come to understand American democracy through the fight for human rights in Mississippi, particularly the MFDP's brilliant challenge to the lily-white racist delegation at the Democratic National Convention? Certainly, the intense ideological debates over the merits of nonviolence as a strategy also complicate narratives of the movement and act as a corrective to the sanitized representation of passive resistance that veil a longstanding tradition of armed self-defense among black southerners.

Since these aspects of the civil rights movement have been muted, mischaracterized, or understudied, young activists today may assert that the current Black Lives Matter movement is not "your grandmother's civil rights movement." Such an assertion reflects a narrow understanding of the diverse strategies, campaigns, and perspectives emanating from 1960s black protest traditions. Freedom Summer 1964 provides an opportunity to complicate civil rights iconography and dig deeper into the fight for the "least of these." Educators can draw from the history of Freedom Summer 1964 to explore state violence, collective leadership, the legacy of Ella Baker, and ideological debates within the movement, all of which are especially relevant to the contemporary Movement for Black Lives.

Teaching Freedom Summer

To commemorate the fiftieth anniversary of landmark federal legislation and civil rights activism, we decided to co-teach a summer session course called "Freedom Summer" as part of the "50/5: Remembering the Modern Movement for Civil Rights," a multiyear initiative led by Dr. Deborah E. McDowell, director of the Carter G. Woodson Institute for African-American and African Studies at the University of Virginia. The philosophy and curriculum of the 1964 Freedom Schools, one of the most successful yet underrated outcomes of the civil rights movement, provided the inspiration for our course. Borrowing directly from the 1964 Freedom Schools, our course objectives were threefold: (1) to engage students in radical questioning; (2) to challenge myths that shape attitudes, beliefs, policy, and historical narratives; and (3) to link the past to present realities. Freedom Schools were designed to provide a blueprint for a transformative educational experience based on a dynamic and collaborative classroom culture, one that countered generations of miseducation and educational apartheid in the Jim Crow South. At the heart of the Freedom Schools was a mission to engage students, who ranged in age from five to eighty, in "radical questioning" as articulated by SNCC activists and Freedom School visionary Charles Cobb Jr., who described segregated schools in Mississippi as "intellectual wastelands" that were "committed to a policy of non-think, and students to an attitude of no questions."[4] Liz Fusco, coordinator of COFO Freedom Schools, wrote: "The staff in Mississippi understood what Charlie [Cobb] was dreaming because, they, too, were daring to dream that what could be done in Mississippi could be deeper, more fundamental, and in a sense more far-reaching, more revolutionary than voter registration alone: more personal, and in a sense more transforming, than a political program."[5] Freedom Schools were the foundation of this transformational process—they were designed to build leadership by connecting learning to political action.

From the 1964 Freedom School curriculum,[6] we contemplated the following:

Basic set of questions:
1. Why are we (students and teachers) in Freedom Schools?
2. What is the freedom movement?
3. What alternatives does the freedom movement offer us?

Secondary set of questions:
1. What does the majority culture have that we want?
2. What does the majority culture have that we don't want?
3. What do we have that we want to keep?

The very nature of these questions alone is enough to immerse students in an examination of power and resistance. In our course, we explored a different set of questions that would speak to the study of the civil rights movement as well as contemporary issues. One example posed the following:

Basic set of questions:
1. Why do we study the civil rights movement?
2. What was the goal of the civil rights movement?
3. How is the movement usually framed?

Next set of questions:
1. What do students think about racial equity and the concept of freedom today?
2. What were the strategies of the civil rights movement that we want to keep?
3. What goals, ideas or practices would we want to change?

Another important aspect of the Freedom Schools that guided our course was a critical examination of the "myths of society." Freedom School coordinators sought to combat the myths of white supremacy and black inferiority, which legitimized white domination and economic repression. Challenging the "myths of society" was a powerful tool that sharpened our students' critical thinking and critical reading skills. Not only did we facilitate discussions about the myths of the civil rights movement, but we also encouraged our students to unpack the myths underlining treasured concepts like democracy, equality, individualism, and merit that fuel American exceptionalism and legitimize unequal power relations.

Just as we challenged students to rethink key concepts that are often taken for granted, we also pushed students to rethink what counts as intellectual space. We employed what Deborah McDowell refers to as the "moving classroom," a concept borrowed from the Freedom Schools, which functioned wherever the people were, "in churches, basements or under shaded trees." We held class at different locations in an effort to reflect the experience of Freedom Summer 1964 and to expose students to various community sites in Charlottesville, Virginia. As part of our moving classroom, we went to Mel's Café, a local soul food restaurant, where we held an energetic discussion on Ta-Nehisi Coates's award-winning article, "The Case for Reparations," which begins with a discussion of the racist regime in Mississippi. We paired this article with a two-part critique written by historian Nathan Connolly entitled "The Case for Repair."[7] The owner of the restaurant, a Charlottesville native named Mel, chimed in with history about the Vinegar Hill neighborhood, a once-vibrant black commercial district destroyed by "urban renewal." We also held a class at a popular barbershop to discuss Stokely Carmichael's 1966 article, "Power and Racism: What We Want."[8] The barber, a young man from Charlottesville, also named Mel, facilitated a conversation about the freedom vision implied in Carmichael's piece and our freedom visions for today.

Because the Summer Project of 1964 was designed with an emphasis on the importance of teaching in the community, the "Freedom Summer" class venues included those able to accommodate larger audiences, including the historic First Baptist Church, where we screened Stanley Nelson's film *Freedom Summer*. Led by Pastor Hodari Hamilton, the church was originally built by the congregation of the Charlottesville African Church shortly after the Civil War and continues to have a strong local membership and activist stance in the community. The multiracial audience included members of the church's congregation, local government officials, and teachers and students from the University of Virginia—not all enrolled in the course. On evaluations, students cited the "moving classroom" as the most enjoyable aspect of the class

University of Virginia Freedom Summer Class participants gather at Mel's Café and Lunch Diner in Charlottesville, Virginia, to enjoy a traditional soul food meal and discuss Ta-Nehisi Coates's essay "The Case for Reparations" alongside Nathan Connolly's critique, "The Case for Repair." (courtesy of *UVA Today*)

and suggested that we add more opportunities in future courses to visit and engage the local community.

Local Connections: The Service-Learning Project

In the spirit of linking the past to present realities and identifying patterns of racial injustice, our course required a service project that addressed two core issues that were central to Freedom Summer: voter registration and education. We divided students into two groups and set aside class time, one day each week, for students to meet with community leaders and brainstorm strategies and action items. One group worked in consultation with the local chapter of the NAACP, led by Dr. M. Rick Turner, president of the Charlottesville/Albemarle branch, and vice president Janet Martin. Drawing from the struggle for the right to vote in Mississippi, students researched the controversy surrounding the recent voter ID laws and the potential impact of the Supreme Court's decision to strike down Section 5 of the Voting Rights Act. They brainstormed strategies to register voters, raise awareness about new laws and the Voting Rights Act, and address skepticism within the community among those who have lost faith in the power of the vote to make change.

The second group worked with a municipal program called City of Promise, a Department of Education Promise Neighborhood initiative modeled after the Harlem Children's Zone. City of Promise is designed to harness resources and to create a "pathway" for all children in the poorest neighborhoods to attend college. Students met with the executive director, Sarad Davenport, a Charlottesville native, to learn about the challenges facing young people locally and the need to give children and youth comprehensive programming to support them in obtaining a high-quality and culturally relevant education. Students organized two workshops, modeled after the Freedom School curriculum, to teach elementary, middle, and high school youth enrolled in City of Promise about the 1964 Freedom Summer Project. They worked to incorporate reading and writing using an interactive multimedia approach, similar to the approach of our course, but geared toward younger students.

Given the short amount of time allotted for summer session, the service project did not allow students to develop strong relationships with community members, which is necessary for meaningful community action, as the 1964 Freedom Summer Project demonstrates. Nevertheless, the service component served as an invitation to students to think about themselves as part of a broad local community beyond the university.

Course Materials

There is a wealth of primary sources and revisionist histories of the civil rights movement that provide opportunities for a rich and innovative engagement with students. For this course, we assigned one textbook, Charles M. Payne's *I've Got the Light of Freedom: The Organizing Tradition and the Mississippi Freedom Struggle*, which remains exemplar in its narrative, insights, and accessibility.[9] We also assigned Anne Moody's autobiography, *Coming of Age in Mississippi*, as well as several chapters from John Dittmer's *Local People: The Struggle for Civil Rights in Mississippi*, both of which offer invaluable insight into the lives of black Mississippians, the culture of fear, the looming threat of white violence and black death, and the challenges of movement building.[10]

In choosing course material, we wanted the readings to underscore the fact that the civil rights movement was not organized to rid the nation of "whites only" signs in public spaces, a popular view among our students. Jim Crow segregation was a vicious system in which physical violence was routine and the psychological and economic impact of white supremacy was no less traumatic.

In selecting our course readings, we were mindful of histories that offer an intersectional analysis, and we introduced the black feminist theory, *intersectionality*, as a lens through which to analyze course material. Intersectionality was foundational to the course as we continuously pushed students to consider the entanglements of race, class, and gender in the study of Mississippi freedom. One of the reading assignments that posed an intersectional and complex analysis of the black freedom movement was chapter 6 from Danielle L. McGuire's *At the Dark End of the Street: Black Women, Rape and Resistance — A New History of the Civil Rights Movement from Rosa Parks to the Rise of Black Power*. We placed this chapter in conversation with excerpts from the documentary film *Freedom on My Mind*, directed by Connie Field and Marilyn Mulford, in order to explore sexual predation among white men who constantly harassed and raped African American women and girls with impunity.[11]

In addition, we assigned revisionist texts that offer competing interpretations of the civil rights movement. For example, *Crossroads at Clarksdale: The Black Freedom Struggle in the Mississippi Delta after World War II* by Françoise N. Hamlin unearths several less-known local activists such as Vera Pigee and includes a section on Freedom Summer that is a cautionary tale regarding the organizational tensions within the movement, tactical mistakes, and the disintegration of the COFO coalition.[12] Similarly, we read excerpts from Akinyele Omowale Umoja's *We Will Shoot Back: Armed Resistance in the Mississippi Freedom Movement*, which navigates the ideological tensions and debates over guns, nonviolence, and self-defense.[13] Umoja, a long-time scholar-activist, native of Mississippi, and chair of the Department of African American Studies at Georgia State University, joined one class via Skype, giving students a valuable opportunity to dialogue with him about his work and scholarship.

The Civil Rights Movement Veterans website was also invaluable to the course due to its rich repository of primary source documents related to Freedom Summer and beyond. Students had the opportunity to study the actual materials distributed during Freedom Summer 1964, including brochures and volunteer forms. For example, the application of Andrew Goodman, a Freedom Summer volunteer who was killed alongside CORE activists James Chaney and Michael Schwerner, brought a human dimension to the often-told story behind their murder.[14] Similarly, the "Declaration of Independence," drafted by the Freedom School at St. John's Methodist Church in Palmer's Crossing, Hattiesburg, Mississippi, provided an opportunity to examine how young Black Mississippians outlined their grievances and framed their pursuit of "total freedom" within and beyond the framework of American ideals.[15] These primary sources also encouraged students to talk about the connections that activists were making, at that time, to independence movements in Africa and the larger world, arguing that the situation of black people in Mississippi was a colonial one tied to an illegitimate state government. Finally, firsthand accounts from movement veterans such as Victoria Gray Adams, Stokely Carmichael, James Forman, and others provided rich texture and historical context for our students and pushed them to think critically about movement participants as complicated individuals with their own circumstances, motivations, challenges, political agendas, and sacrifices.[16]

Sounds of the Movement and Visual History: Using Music and Film in the Classroom

As the lifeblood of the black freedom movement, music stirred a sense of unity and fellowship among activists, but it also empowered them to overcome their fears. Celebrity artists used music as a form of protest, raising the national profile of the movement and expanding its circle of allies. Folk singers such as Bob Dylan, Pete Seeger, and Joan Baez expressed solidarity with the black freedom struggle by singing protest songs at concerts and at Freedom Summer workshops and schools. Jazz artists John Coltrane and Nina Simone released "Alabama" and "Mississippi Goddamn," respectively, chronicling violence and white supremacy in the South. Just before every class, our students listened to freedom songs from the 1960s, and on a few occasions they had the opportunity to analyze lyrics and compositions.

In one activity, we asked students to compare Nina Simone's rendition of "Strange Fruit," which many had never heard before, to hip-hop artist Kanye West's sampled version on his critically acclaimed 2013 album, *Yeezus*. Students juxtaposed Simone and West's compositions and debated the merits of West's use of "lynching" as a metaphor for contemporary ills in society. Although students expressed conflicted reactions to West's invocation of racial violence in a song about materialism and relationship woes, most students appreciated his sample as a way to introduce a new generation to the work and power of Nina Simone.

On another occasion, students listened to the harrowing song "Triptych: Prayer/Protest/Peace," by jazz musician Max Roach featuring vocalist Abbey Lincoln. The song, in which Lincoln screams for approximately seventy seconds, appeared on the 1961 album *We Insist! Max Roach's Freedom Now Suite*, which paid homage to the sit-in movement spreading across the South. After defining *triptych* and withholding the song's subtitle, we asked students to listen to the song's three parts carefully and choose three words to describe each part of the triptych. Their discussions were as powerful as the song itself. Subtitles included "haunted/rumble/melancholy" and "stagnant/struggle/hope." Students also described the discomfort the song induced in their bodies, confirming the power of music to have a physical effect, making clear its potential to enlighten, strengthen, comfort, or threaten.

In the same ways that we encouraged students to think critically about primary sources, music, and secondary texts, we wanted them to utilize similar processes to conduct visual analysis and to begin to understand the politics behind visuals, art, storytelling, accuracy, and documentation. Often students believe documentaries are statements of ultimate truth, missing the interpretive gestures made by filmmakers as they construct historical narratives.

After students gained foundational knowledge of the history, we designed a quiz that required students to write a storyline for a documentary on Freedom Summer 1964 in order to jumpstart a discussion on the politics of film production. We asked them to identify which elements they would include, the political actors they would feature, and the organizations they would highlight, and to give a rationale for their choices. This assignment tested students' knowledge and comprehension, but it also opened up a discussion about how all filmmakers make a series of key choices when developing their projects. These choices are often constrained by the availability and pricing of archival footage, stills, and music; funding; interview subjects; and what actually works visually during the editing process. But ultimately, the choices filmmakers make can tell us much about their perspective, their priorities, and their interpretations of history. After writing their own scripts, students watched the first feature-length film on Freedom Summer, the 1994 film *Freedom on My Mind*. They later compared this film to the most recent film on the topic, produced twenty years later in 2014, *Freedom Summer*.[17] These comparisons led to cogent observations and evaluations about the ways filmmakers' choices shape historical narratives.

Conclusion

The historical account of Freedom Summer 1964 facilitates a number of disruptions that are absolutely necessary for students today. First, it disrupts narrow representations of Black leadership. Students have been inundated with images of Dr. King and Malcolm X as the charismatic leaders of the civil rights movement. Freedom Summer underscores that black leadership is not inherently male and that collective leadership is possible. Breaking down what leadership looks like, and challenging its individualistic and gendered dimensions, created space for students to see themselves as potential leaders and to reconsider their own ideas about their role in developing the leadership of others.

The 1964 Mississippi Summer Project also encourages students to think deeply about what it means to be free. Freedom was not only about voting rights and integration; it was predicated on quality education, economic opportunity, the preservation of culture, the development of institutions, and the ability to live without fear. From the very beginning of the Freedom Summer campaign, ideas about voting went beyond an individual's right to participate in the political process. Freedom Summer was about a fundamental transformation of the society, and it required creating parallel and alternative institutions. Political education and building leadership—the purpose of the Freedom Schools—and political independence, as embodied by the MFDP, were the hallmarks of a radical democratic vision that deserves greater attention in our studies of the civil rights movement and our quest for freedom.

NOTES

1. For more information about this program, see American Civil Liberties Union, *War Comes Home: The Excessive Militarization of American Policing* (New

York: ACLU Foundation, 2014). The 1033 Program provided military equipment to state and local law enforcement agencies free of charge, sanctioned by the 1990 National Defense Authorization Act (updated in 1996). "1033 Program FAQs," Defense Logistics Agency, accessed April 29, 2019, https://www.dla.mil/DispositionServices/Offers/Reutilization/LawEnforcement/Program FAQs.aspx. In 2015, the Obama administration banned certain equipment and enacted restrictions on others, after widespread protests in response to images of a militarized Ferguson, Missouri, following the police shooting of Michael Brown. However, the policy was revisited in 2016. See Julia Edwards, "White House to Review Ban on Military Gear for Police," July 21, 2016, http://www.reuters.com/article/us-usa-police-gear-exclusive-idUSKCN1012KW. In August 2017, the Trump administration lifted the restrictions on surplus military gear for law enforcement by executive order. Tom Jackman, "Trump to Restore Program Sending Surplus Military Weapons, Equipment to Police," August 27, 2017, https://www.washingtonpost.com/news/true-crime/wp/2017/08/27/trump-restores-program-sending-surplus-military-weapons-equipment-to-police/?utm_term=.f28776afe55b.

2. Ella J. Baker, "Bigger than a Hamburger," *Southern Patriot* 18 (1960). Excerpted in Manning Marable and Leith Mullings, eds., *Let Nobody Turn Us Around: Voices of Resistance, Reform, and Renewal* (Oxford: Rowman & Littlefield, 1999).

3. Barbara Ransby, *Ella Baker and the Black Freedom Movement: A Radical Democratic Vision* (Chapel Hill: University of North Carolina Press, 2003).

4. Charles Cobb, "Some Notes on Education," http://www.crmvet.org/info/cobb_education.pdf, accessed July 30, 2016.

5. Liz Fusco, "Freedom Schools in Mississippi, 1964," http://www.educationanddemocracy.org/FSCfiles/B_16_FSchoolsInMSFusco.htm, accessed July 30, 2016.

6. The Freedom School curriculum is accessible at http://www.educationanddemocracy.org/ED_FSC.html.

7. See Ta-Nehisi Coates, "The Case for Reparations," *Atlantic Monthly*, June 2014, 54–71; and Nathan Connolly, "The Case for Repair, Part 1 and Part 2," Urban History Association, May 24, 2014, https://urbanhistorians.wordpress.com/2014/05/24/the-case-for-repair/.

8. Stokely Carmichael, "Power and Racism: What We Want," *New York Review of Books*, September 22, 1966, 5–8, reprinted in *Black Scholar* 27, no. 3/4 (1997): 52–57.

9. Charles M. Payne, *I've Got the Light of Freedom: The Organizing Tradition and the Mississippi Freedom Struggle* (Berkeley: University of California Press, 2007).

10. Anne Moody, *Coming of Age in Mississippi* (New York: Dell, 1968); John Dittmer, *Local People: The Struggle for Civil Rights in Mississippi* (Urbana: University of Illinois Press, 1995).

11. Danielle L. McGuire, "A Black Woman's Body Was Never Hers Alone," in *At the Dark End of the Street: Black Women, Rape and Resistance—A New History of the Civil Rights Movement from Rosa Parks to the Rise of Black Power* (New York: Alfred A. Knopf, 2010); Connie Field and Marilyn Mulford, dirs., *Freedom on My Mind* (1994, 105 min.).

12. We assigned chapter 4, "Fires of Frustration: Summers of 1963 to 1965," in Françoise N. Hamlin, *Crossroads at Clarksdale: The Black Freedom Struggle in the Mississippi Delta after World War II* (Chapel Hill: University of North Carolina Press, 2012).

13. We assigned chapter 4, "'Local People Carry the Day': Freedom Summer and Challenges to Nonviolence in Mississippi," in Akinyele Omowale Umoja, *We Will Shoot Back: Armed Resistance in the Mississippi Freedom Movement* (New York: New York University Press, 2013), 36–48.

14. "Andrew Goodman Freedom Summer Application, April 15, 1964," http://www.crmvet.org/docs/64_cofo-goodman_application.pdf, accessed July 30, 2016.

15. "Declaration of Independence, 1964," http://www.crmvet.org/docs/64_doi_hattiesburg.pdf, accessed July 30, 2016.

16. Stokely Carmichael and Michael Thelwell, *Ready for Revolution: The Life and Struggles of Stokely Carmichael (Kwame Ture)* (New York: Scribner, 2003); James Foreman, *The Making of Black Revolutionaries: A Personal Account* (New York: Macmillan, 1972); Faith S. Holsaert et al., *Hands on the Freedom Plow: Personal Accounts by Women in SNCC* (Urbana: University of Illinois Press, 2010).

17. Stanley Nelson Jr., dir., *Freedom Summer* (Firelight Media, 2014).

Teaching Malcolm X beyond the Mythology— By Any Means Necessary

CLARENCE LANG

More than fifty years after his assassination, Malcolm X (El-Hajj Malik El-Shabazz) remains a compelling figure of post–World War II black freedom struggles. This is in large measure because he was one of the more singularly uncompromising voices of African American defiance in the twentieth century, making him both a galvanizing and polarizing figure in conversations about racial justice and the means through which black people should pursue this goal. Like his most noted contemporary, Martin Luther King Jr., Malcolm also was a martyred leader who died young and in spectacular fashion during a moment of major social upheaval. Indeed, Malcolm endures in large measure because of a persistent fascination in US popular culture with the period of the 1960s—which, for better or worse, continues to shape attitudes about contemporary protest politics and cultures of dissent. Consequently, he looms large among those today whose imagination relies on the epic 1960s for framing transcripts of activism and resistance.

Yet, Malcolm's stature as an icon can obscure the historical and social circumstances that made his leadership possible, as well as minimize the actual substance of his political thought. This is an acute problem in light of a recent scholarly trend asserting that by the end of their lives, Malcolm and King had reached a similar, or even the same, outlook. Although this may be a well-intentioned effort to reconcile the differences between two activists who have been situated in direct opposition to each other, this interpretation flattens the legacies of both men. This error makes it difficult to determine what concrete lessons, if any, contemporary activists might harvest from either of their careers. In Malcolm's case, viewing him as virtually indistinguishable from King effectively silences the rich and complex black nationalist tradition that buoyed Malcolm's activism, reducing him to little more than a militant reformist whose goals fell within the boundaries of US liberal democracy.

Given the vile resurgence of white nationalism that occurred during the tenure of the nation's first black president, Barack Obama, and that became vigorously renewed in the White House under Donald Trump, the task of defending black nationalism, and differentiating it from white nationalism's appeals to racialized subordination, exploitation, and legally armed terror, is critical. Considering, too, that state-sanctioned white violence has ignited grassroots campaigns among students and other young adults to make "Black Lives Matter," the moment is ripe for a pronounced black nationalist thrust to supply greater depth, organization, and vision to protesters' demands.

Based on a small seminar about Malcolm X that I taught in the spring of 2017 to a self-selected group of undergraduate and graduate students at the University of Kansas, this chapter posits an approach to teaching Malcolm that avoids the mistake of portraying him as sui generis—a unique, timeless, and dislocated symbol of black militancy without reference to the broad and multiple circumstances that molded him equally as much as he responded to them. To the contrary, I argue that a worthy treatment of Malcolm in the classroom should place his individual biography against the backdrop of the key social developments that prevailed among African Americans during his lifetime. This environment included mass black migrations fueled by two world wars; the expansion of black urban communities limited externally by new forms of white racial control and characterized internally by new forms of class stratification among African Americans; the added hardships of the Great Depression and the glimmer of economic recovery that the federal New Deal signaled; a proliferation of black work cultures, including paid labor in the mass-production industries and service sectors, as well as "clean" and "dirty" hustles on the economic margins; and the flowering of black civic, economic, cultural, and political organizations mirroring African Americans' diverse ideological responses to racial oppression among colonized people of color globally.

This course—which I cross-listed between the Departments of American Studies, and African and African-American Studies—used mini-lectures, audio materials and documentary film, structured classroom discussion of assigned readings, and short weekly writing assignments (at a minimum of three to four pages) to facilitate student learning. Additionally, I welcomed students to freely draw from and share the accumulated knowledge and perspectives about the subject matter that they brought to the class themselves. The class enrollment was equally mixed between black and white students, with all of them expressing a desire not only to learn about Malcolm, Black America, and the social movements of the 1960s but also to think about black communities' current challenges and opportunities amid Black Lives Matter organizing, the end of the second administration of President Obama, and the rabidly racist landscape of the Trump presidency. In a similar spirit, I drew from my own experiences as a black male who had come of age in the late 1980s, an era in which the 1960s were transformed from history to myth, and Malcolm X enjoyed a revival of interest in black nationalist-oriented hip-hop music and videos by such recording acts as Public Enemy and X Clan, culminating in the release of Spike Lee's 1992 biographical film *Malcolm X* starring actor Denzel Washington.

For teachers interested in this era, the goal of placing Malcolm in broader historical perspective should be to contextualize his experiences, exposing his limited, imperfect humanity as well as his insights and strengths, while also attacking the mythology that has hardened around him since his death. As the instructor of such a course, I wished to see if the class could discover Malcolm X the flesh-and-blood human being constrained by the specific historical moment that he occupied, and distinguish him from Malcolm X the infallible Great Man. The objectives of such a course, further, should be to use Malcolm creatively to expose students to emergent developments in the interdisciplinary field of "black freedom studies," including the scholarship's emphases on identities of gender, class, sexuality, and nationality alongside race.

Laying a Foundation with Malcolm's *Autobiography*

At the outset of the course, I sought to determine what students knew about Malcolm X upon entering the class. Overall, their familiarity was limited to standard depictions of him as either an unapologetic advocate of black pride or a hate-filled prophet of separatism and bloodshed. Some of them knew more details about his life than others, including his origins as Malcolm Little, the suspicious death of his politically active father, and the state harassment of his equally outspoken mother that led to her institutionalization and the forced split of Malcolm and his siblings. Other students were aware of Malcolm's later criminal exploits as the hustler "Detroit Red," his incarceration and subsequent conversion to the Lost-Found Nation of Islam (NOI), and his ascent from minister of Harlem's Temple No. 7 to the position of national spokesman for the NOI's Honorable Elijah Muhammad. Most students knew something about his split from Muhammad and his international travels and disavowal of NOI doctrines. Some were familiar with the Organization of Afro-American Unity (OAAU) that he created after departing the NOI, though all of them knew generic details about his assassination at New York City's Audubon Ballroom in February 1965.

Remarkably few students, however, had actually read Malcolm's *Autobiography*, which suggested how far his life narrative has spread beyond reading audiences. Fortunately, *The Autobiography of Malcolm X: As Told to Alex Haley* was the course's initial major assignment, which students read and discussed over the first few weeks of class. To frame their reading, I provided a brief overview of the overarching features of twentieth-century African American history, the most important of which was the black mass migration that unfolded before, during, and between US involvement in two world wars. On this point, I highlighted that while much of this Great Migration flowed to major urban centers such as New York, Chicago, and Detroit (with West Coast cities such as Los Angeles becoming destinations in the 1940s), sizable populations of black migrants also relocated to smaller and midsized communities in the Midwest, such as Omaha, Nebraska, and Lansing, Michigan, where the Little family made its home during the 1920s and 1930s. In this sense, theirs was a common narrative of black migration, and an instructor here might encourage students to further explore the networks, economic opportunities, and transportation circuits that brought black migrants to regional outposts of the North.

Particularly with regard to white racism, the *Autobiography* provided several opportunities for students in the class to see the multiple forms it has assumed historically. First and foremost, many black families like Malcolm's encountered racism in the guise of raw terror, as when his childhood home was destroyed by fire-wielding night riders. It is significant that this episode opens the *Autobiography* and, as Malcolm recounts, constituted his first vivid memory. As I noted in class, Malcolm was born during an early twentieth-century period marked by recurrent white mob violence against black bodies and property, including bloody race riots in cities such as Atlanta; Springfield, Illinois; Tulsa; East St. Louis, Illinois; and Chicago.

On the other hand, Malcolm detailed how he experienced a more paternalistic, though equally damaging, form of white supremacy as the only black student in his junior high school. His white classmates and teachers treated him kindly, even anointing him class president, but he existed as something of a mascot, his presence accepted only insofar as his racially subordinate status remained intact. This point was hammered home when one of Malcolm's teachers politely scoffed at his ambition to become a lawyer, gently admonishing him to choose a more "realistic goal for a nigger" like manual labor. It is notable that such painfully alienating experiences occurred in a racially integrated northern school environment rather than in the legally sanctioned segregation of the South. Ironically, this dubious "integration" not only accounted for why Malcolm ended his formal education after the eighth grade but also conditioned his later disavowal of white society as an adult.

Further, Malcolm's relationship with a white girlfriend, "Sophia," relied on ruthlessly exploiting her for money, but it was also premised on her own fetishes for, and appropriations of, black urban culture—sentiments that anchored the underground interracial sex economies that Malcolm navigated during that period. The peculiar role that black cultural appropriation and exploitation play in reinforcing white racism was a topic that easily resonated among millennials who had seen Jordan Peele's popular 2017 thriller, *Get Out*. References to the film gave students an additional, contemporary context for a textured conversation about racialized violence that went beyond obvious phenomena such as lynching, police abuse, and antiblack massacres.

In a similar spirit, I led students in vigorous conversations about the slow, systemic racial violence of US housing discrimination during the twentieth century. Referring to the work of scholars such as Richard Rothstein (whose 2017 book *The Color of Law: A Forgotten History of How Our Government Segregated America* is an excellent primer for students), I explained how post–World War II racial apartheid in housing had buttressed and even expanded deep racial disparities in employment, education, wealth, safety from environmental hazards, and access to social amenities such as grocery stores and recreational facilities.

Along with foregrounding the pervasive role of white racism in black life, I centered attention on the simultaneous importance of black people's own agency in determining their conditions. Consequently, I took the opportunity in a subsequent class session to sketch a number of parallel, interrelated breakthroughs in black protest, most prominently the New Negro movement that included the meteoric rise of Marcus Garvey's Universal Negro Improvement Association (UNIA). Suitably, I paired chapters of Malcolm's *Autobiography* with Ted Vincent's article "The Garveyite Parents of Malcolm X," published in the *Black Scholar* in 1989.

I also gave close attention to the ways that the *Autobiography* illustrated the varied types of legal and illicit labor that Malcolm performed during his late teens and early adult years, his mastery of the cutting-edge jazz culture that shaped black America during the 1940s, and his intimacy with the cadences of everyday life among the black working-class majority who cleaned homes, bussed tables, shined shoes, stood behind soda fountain counters, cooked meals, tended bar, worked the railroads, peddled marijuana and bootleg liquor, sold sandwiches, and did other "slaves" in the service industries. As I suggested in the course, this period of Malcolm's life is key to understanding the sensibilities he exhibited as a minister of the Nation of Islam, as signified by the differences he popularly ascribed to present-day "house slaves" and "field slaves" on the imagined plantation of North America. This particular analogy, embryonic in Malcolm's perspectives as a youth, spoke to more general class conflicts that fragmented black political agendas in the twentieth century.

Contrary to standard depictions of collective American sacrifice and national unity to defeat European fascism and Japanese militarism during World War II, many disaffected black working-class youth during the war remained unimpressed by President Franklin D. Roosevelt's "Four Freedoms"—of speech and worship, and from want and fear—that did not apply to them. I highlighted many of these themes in an assigned supplementary reading—Robin D. G. Kelley's "The Riddle of the Zoot: Malcolm Little and Black Cultural Politics During World War II." One early exercise in the course was to engage students in conversation about the wide array of jobs that Malcolm held, and how these diverse, formative experiences of work factored heavily into his later ability to voice the perspectives, grievances, aspirations, and social norms of a growing black urban working class. Early in his ministry even, Malcolm continued his stints as an itinerant laborer, first in a furniture store and then on automobile and truck assembly lines.

These mundane details matter because they help to shift the overall weight of classroom conversations away from assumptions about charismatic personality, iron self-discipline, or fierce oratory skills as the hallmarks of his leadership. While he indeed possessed all of these qualities, Malcolm more importantly was a tireless street corner canvasser who recruited new members to the NOI's ranks and an energetic organizer who helped erect NOI temples in blue-collar black communities in the decade following his parole from prison in 1952 and suspension by Elijah Muhammad in 1963. As his former assistant minister, Benjamin Karim, reminisces in his short, readable book, *Remembering Malcolm*, the "Brother Minister" of Harlem's Temple No. 7 gained respect and a loyal following not simply because he electrified mass rallies, skillfully parried with white journalists on television, or enthralled the college students who attended his campus lectures. Rather, he also spent time with smaller, intimate groups in working-class living rooms and storefronts, frequented black community spaces teeming with activity, and—notwithstanding his criticisms of mainline black leaders—built cross-class relationships with a variety of African American professionals, intellectuals, elected officials, business owners, churchgoers, and assorted public figures.

Because recordings of Malcolm are abundant, a course about him lends itself to sources other than readings to help students more fully plot the basic facts of this biography and career. Aside from the grainy film and audio clips available on the web, I recommend screening "The Time Has Come (1964–66)," an episode of the *Eyes on the Prize* documentary series that first aired in 1990, which profiles Malcolm and establishes his significance to the modern civil rights movement after his murder. In addition, at least three feature-length documentary films cover the major phases of Malcolm's origins and activism: *Malcolm X: His Own Story as It Really Happened*, directed by Arnold Perl and released in 1972; *Malcolm X: Make It Plain*, produced by the Public Broadcasting Service for its American Experience series in 1994; and A&E's 1997 "Biography" series feature, *Malcolm X: A Search for Identity*. As an extension of Malcolm's *Autobiography*, I selected Ilyasah Shabazz's *Growing Up X: A Memoir by the Daughter of Malcolm X* as a reading, though I suspect that Russell J. Rickford's biography of Malcolm's widow, *Betty Shabazz, Surviving Malcolm X: A Journey of Strength from Wife to Widow to Heroine*, might have been the more appropriate selection. In either case, I propose reserving it toward the end of the course to bring Malcolm's story full circle and round out the term.

At the same time, I considered it essential to disrupt the very idea of a cogent narrative of Malcolm's life. As my students and I approached the conclusion of his *Autobiography*, I began raising the possibility of omissions in this work, highlighting Alex Haley's role in structuring the book and completing the editing on his own after Malcolm's death. Rather than casting doubts on Haley's reliability as the curator of Malcolm's narrative, my aim was to call into question the fundamental "truth" of the biography and autobiography as a genre of writing. To be sure, Malcolm's original aim in working with Haley was to champion the teachings of Elijah Muhammad, whom he praised for rescuing him from a life of crime and moral degradation. As I asserted to my students, the literary form of autobiography lends itself to linearity and destiny in explaining the role of the individual in history, overlooking or even suppressing the messy contradictions, unruliness, multiple outcomes, and unachieved possibilities that make individuals who they are. This began my first attempts as instructor at decentering Malcolm in a course designed explicitly to be about him.

Recovering the Black Nationalist Tradition

The second part of the course switched the lens from Malcolm to a robust treatment of black nationalism as a major component of African American modernity. Centering on E. U. Essien-Udom's 1962 classic, *Black Nationalism: A Search for an Identity in America*, I asked students to historicize organizations such as the Nation of Islam, the Moorish Science Temple, and the National Movement for the Establishment of the Forty-Ninth State in a longstanding tradition of thought anchored in a consciousness of black "peoplehood" and linked fate; a recognition of white racial oppression as a defining central feature of black life; an affirmation of culture and self-knowledge, and the solidarity of African and African–descended peoples; and the advocacy of black self-determination and land-based claims to independence and political sovereignty.

One colorful means of rendering these ideas might be screening and discussing portions of the 2018 Marvel Studios film, *Black Panther*, depicting the fictional republic of Wakanda, a technologically advanced African utopia hidden from outsiders. This offers a chance to probe several questions: Why is this republic secluded, and how might we imagine the relationship between its seclusion, its invisibility to the West, and its technologically superior state? What accounts for the exuberant reaction this film garnered among black audiences, many of whom attended screenings in large groups wearing Wakanda-inspired ensembles? Was this simply fandom, or did this film capture something profound in the black imaginary (as reflected in the multimedia phenomenon known as Afrofuturism)? Suitably, a film such as *Black Panther* might aid this section of the course exploring how *black* has constituted not only a racial identity, but also more importantly a nationality.

In the classroom conversations about the NOI, I pointed out the organization's essentially apolitical nature, as evident in its appeals to withdraw from US political affairs, separate from the white majority, and pursue group advancement through cultural improvement and redemption through Islam and collective economic development. My purposes for doing this were twofold. First, I wanted to dispel notions of the Nation of Islam as a black terrorist group by revealing that NOI teachings of moral uplift, obedience to law, and business ownership have been entirely consistent with idealized white Protestant mores and practices. This was the case even notwithstanding the Nation's religious cosmology, which held that black people were the progeny of the "Original Man" and whites were a race of "devils" created by a renegade scientist. According to this schema, Allah would dispense justice directly to the white "devils" without the need for human intervention. Second, it is critical to note that the NOI's political inaction was a major factor in the eventual schism between the Nation's Chicago headquarters and Malcolm, who had no use for mainstream civil rights activists' vision but admired their willingness to directly contest white supremacy and yearned to join the frontline of battle.

Examining these multiple facets of black nationalism paved the way for the class to return to Malcolm. That is, we were able to more fully value his importance as someone who not only left a legacy of memorable speeches but who also transmitted core black nationalist tenets from the past to younger contemporary black activists in mainline civil rights organizations such as the Student Nonviolent Coordinating Committee (SNCC). The best single work on this topic is William W. Sales Jr.'s *From Civil Rights to Black Liberation: Malcolm X and the Organization of Afro-American Unity*, with chapter 4 as the one I would recommend most highly for students to read and discuss. Specifically, Malcolm's challenge to liberal integrationism signified a shift in the movement's discursive framing from "Freedom Now" to "Black Power," which materialized as the clarion call among activists he prompted to rediscover black nationalism in the mid- to late twentieth century.

Building on his complex relationships with diverse communities of activists in Harlem and elsewhere, Malcolm attempted through the OAAU to fuse the dominant civil rights movement strategy of mass direct action to black nationalist goals for liberation, independence, and sovereignty. Freed from the constraints of the NOI, he also became more revolutionary pan-Africanist and internationalist in his aims, daring secular rivals and allies alike to globalize the larger black freedom movement by linking it to anticolonialist and anti-imperialist solidarities in Africa, Asia, Latin America, and the Caribbean.

Martin and Malcolm Redux

My secondary purpose for introducing students to black nationalism was to expose them more generally to the presence of multiple black ideological traditions and their influences across time. By *ideology* I generally mean the coherent set of beliefs that give order to one's understanding of the world, or the lens through which one comprehends society and how it changes. With Malcolm as a point of departure, I wanted to urge students to contemplate the fact that *how* black people have theorized their collective past and present and visualized the routes to possible futures has mattered every bit as much as the practical steps that they have taken toward freedom and liberation. In fact, these ideological perspectives have conditioned the diverse ways that black activist publics have envisaged how *freedom* or *liberation* should look concretely. I found that this opened the door to more critically assessing the relationship between Malcolm X and Martin Luther King Jr., which students initially either wanted to view in normatively dichotomous terms of "evil/violent" versus "good/peaceful," as siblings who merely proposed different solutions to the same problem, or as fraternal twins who were moving in remarkably identical directions when they were killed.

For better or worse, common popular depictions of 1960s black protest situate Martin and Malcolm in comparison to each other, making it awkward in the classroom not to deal with them in tandem, at least at some point in the course. To flesh out classroom discussion on this theme, I assigned select chapters from Britta Waldschmidt-Nelson's short monograph, *Dreams and Nightmares: Martin Luther King, Jr., Malcolm X, and the Struggle for Black Equality in America.* For the sake of discussion, I conceded mildly that King and Malcolm may have pursued a common goal of "freedom, equality, and social justice for people in America regardless of their skin color, race, or religion," as she argues. However, I redirected students to the previous readings about black nationalism and other ideologies, suggesting that the social transformations they imagined were far more distinct than similar. King envisioned an interracial "beloved community," achieved through the power of Christian love and nonviolent confrontation. Malcolm, schooled in the style of a self-taught street corner orator, championed separation and self-reliance for African Americans—a demand that he anchored in an unrelenting indictment of white crimes against black humanity. To be clear, it would have been wrong for me to have perpetuated the idea that Martin and Malcolm represented the movement's polar opposites with regard to integration versus separation, or nonviolence versus self-defense. King, for instance, was raised in an environment in which black institutions of higher education, churches, civic organizations, and other African American institutions were central features, and he embraced the need for black self-organization and community self-reliance. Still, *integrationism* and *separatism*, rather than representing discrete ideologies, have been strategies used by black activists to achieve varying group-based freedoms.

In due time, I stressed that the major point of division between Martin and Malcolm was *ideological*. In Malcolm's case, he may have cast aside the racial doctrines of the Nation of Islam and amended his views about the possibilities of cooperation with white allies, but he nevertheless remained a steadfast black nationalist. In this imagining, I argue, there are no realistic long-term prospects for black equality in America. This is dramatically different from a liberal-integrationist worldview. As for King, while he began to fundamentally question the structures of domestic and foreign policy in the last two years of his life, he did not depart significantly from a belief in the core principles of US liberalism that had emerged during the Great Depression of the 1930s and the Second World War of the 1940s. Although he criticized white liberal complacency as a barrier to progress, he clung to the idea that the United States could realize equality through racial, social, and economic reforms.

What changed in King's final years was the *extent* of reform that he believed was necessary. Since the passage of the 1964 Civil Rights and 1965 Voting Rights acts, he had reached the conclusion that the nation and its citizenry needed a far-reaching and systemic redistribution of wealth with measures like full employment or guaranteed incomes. Although this demanded a new radical reconstruction of US society, it did not entail an end to the basic hierarchies of US society that had created these inequalities in the first place. Indeed, Martin maintained hope in the possibility of redeeming the soul of America, which implied that racial democracy was inherent to the nation's character, and that America had merely strayed from its founding creed. These were all assumptions that would have been inconceivable to the revolutionary black nationalist Malcolm had become by the end of his life.

Malcolm in the Changing Field of "Black Freedom Studies"

The final section of the course embedded all of our preceding inquiries about Malcolm within the field of "Black Freedom Studies." We surveyed current areas of concentration in this literature, most especially the agency of the working class and poor, and women; histories of black activism before 1954 and after 1965; the cross-regional scope and local particularities of 1960s civil rights and Black Power campaigns; struggles across the global black diaspora; and the multiple gender and sexual identities that were incorporated, or not, into black social movement agendas.[1]

Notwithstanding his admiration for individual women such as Gloria Richardson, Maya Angelou, and SNCC organizer Fannie Lou Hamer, Malcolm's problematic gender politics came under close scrutiny during this portion of the course, with references to passages from his own *Autobiography*. While shedding light on the misogynistic fear and disdain that characterized Malcolm's view of women for most of his life, Farah Jasmine Griffin's chapter in Collier-Thomas and Franklin's *Sisters in the Struggle* ("'Ironies of the Saint': Malcolm X, Black Women, and the Price of Protection") does a particularly illuminating job of analyzing the contradictory appeal of protection that he offered black women in exchange for their subordination and compliance to black patriarchal authority.

If confronting Malcolm's sexism generated some unease among students predisposed to worshipping Malcolm, the very act of considering the complexities of his sexual identity made them absolutely uncomfortable. This discomfort spoke to the ways that black politics, and particularly nationalism, can envision black sovereignty in ways that promote hierarchies of gender and sexuality internally while opposing white supremacy externally.

By far the toughest reading to discuss in class was "The Sexuality of Malcolm X," a paper published by Christopher Phelps in *Journal of American Studies*. The article is part of a surge of scholarly works that have responded to controversies surrounding Manning Marable's Pulitzer Prize–winning book, *Malcolm X: A Life of Reinvention*, which claims that as the hustler "Detroit Red," Malcolm engaged in paid sex with other men. A number of black students regarded the claim as a threat to Malcolm's infallibility as a "man," which is precisely why Phelps's article was a good choice as an assigned reading. Unlike most of the written rejoinders to Marable, which vigorously questioned his sources and his intentions, Phelps indicated distinctions among sexual activity, sexual orientation, and gendered social roles and identities. From this standpoint, any sexual encounters that Malcolm may have had with other men would have had no direct bearing on whether he was gay or straight. Given the mores of the time, in fact, the manner in which he may have received or performed sexual acts with other men could be taken as indications of a hypermasculine heterosexual identity premised on the mastery, derision, and exploitation of both male and female others.

To be clear, the point of this discursive classroom exercise was not to use less defensive and reactionary means to achieve the same goal as outraged, homophobic scholars—that is, proving that Malcolm was a straight male. Rather, my goal was to use sexuality and gender as methods for probing how black identities are multiple and simultaneous and pivot on more than just race. Via changing gender and sexual norms in black urban working-class communities during the twentieth century, I also wanted to offer additional historical context to one of the many "lives" that Malcolm constructed over the course of his thirty-nine years.[2]

In my view, the final portion of the Malcolm course also should give attention to the movement efforts that took wing after his death, inspired by his example. Richard D. Benson's *"Fighting for Our Place in the Sun": Malcolm X and the Radicalization of the Black Student Movement, 1960–1973*, focusing on the creation of Malcolm X Liberation University, is a good option. The proliferation of books and autobiographies about the Oakland, California, Black Panther Party for Self-Defense, formed in 1966, provide many more choices. Because Malcolm helped popularize interpretations of Islam among African Americans (who currently comprise the majority of practicing Muslims in the United States), and given the current pervasiveness of Islamophobia directed at Arabs and Asians in US culture, I assigned Manning Marable and Hishaam D. Aidi's edited work, *Black Routes to Islam*.

Notwithstanding Malcolm's analogy of "house slaves" and "field slaves," the combined schisms of race and class were not developments that he could have fully predicted, and neither his generic pronouncements nor his political career offer guidance to contemporaries who lived through the two-term American presidency of a black man. Even Malcolm's time in prison could not be regarded as foreshadowing a late twentieth-century development that neither he nor others of his generation could have anticipated: the rise of mass incarceration as the defining feature of black working-class existence, with long-term consequences rivaling the impact of mass black migration between the 1910s and 1960s. From this standpoint, Keeanga-Yamahtta Taylor's *From #BlackLivesMatter to Black Liberation* furnishes a comprehensive survey of the changing forms of black racial oppression, and prospects for resistance, in the twenty-first century. As a supplement to this, I similarly endorse reading the Movement for Black Lives' 2016 "A Vision for Black Lives: Policy Demands for Black Power, Freedom & Justice," which the instructor might pair with the OAAU's "Basic Unity Program" or the Panthers' "Ten-Point Program" to compare and contrast both continuities and changes in black liberation agendas since the 1960s.

Final Thoughts about Malcolm X in the Classroom

I do not presume that the way in which I organized this course on Malcolm X is the best possible approach, nor do I presume that the readings I assigned or cited here are exhaustive. It was not my expectation that the students I taught would have reached vast judgments about Malcolm by the end of the course. At best, I expected that they would exit the course with deeper knowledge about the contexts of African American history in the twentieth century that shaped Malcolm, and how he in turn made an impact on historical events associated with the storied era of the 1960s. My endeavor really was to use their interest in Malcolm as a way of opening the door to their lifelong study of the longer movement that preceded his birth and persisted after this assassination.

As I designed the course, my hope was that the millennials who enrolled, armed with a greater appreciation for the particularities of that period, would resist the urge to fruitlessly ponder "What would Malcolm X do or think if he were alive today?" or, equally pointless, "Where is *our* Malcolm today?" I also had in mind those students and youth who had been involved in campus and community Black Lives Matter campaigns since their explosion in 2014. I wanted them to become more adept at recognizing and classifying the formal and diffuse ideologies that have given coherence, direction, and consistency to wide-ranging black agendas for social change.

As the recurrence of white supremacy continues to escalate a clamoring for reform that current structure of power relations can't, or won't, accommodate, it is imperative that scholars and activists alike develop the capacity to view themselves as being linked by more than just their collective trauma as people of color, or by a common desire for white-dominated institutions to make them feel "safe." My own assertion, which I shared throughout the course, is that a critically reconstructed black nationalism holds a key to envisioning alternatives to these political dead ends. As a social movement scholar and practitioner, I am cautiously optimistic that post-1960s initiatives like the Movement for Black Lives' policy demands—in calling for such things as reparations, black community control, and "independent Black political power and Black self-determination"—signal that present circumstances remain ripe for critically reconstructed black nationalist traditions and mobilizing frameworks bearing more liberatory possibilities than even in Malcolm's time.

NOTES

1. For fresh new interpretations of Malcolm's legacy, I suggest the *Journal of African American History*'s special issue on "The Legacy of Malcolm X: Black Nationalism, Internationalism, and Transnationalism" published in spring 2015, and Garrett Felber's edited online forum, "Remembering Malcolm," posted by the African American Intellectual History Society in 2017 (https://www.aaihs.org/online-forum-remembering-malcolm/). For any advanced undergraduate or graduate students in the course, I also recommend Graeme Abernathy's book *The Iconography of Malcolm X* (Lawrence: University Press of Kansas, 2013), which provides a visual arts approach to understanding his continuing cultural impact via photographs, paintings, film, and imagery in hip-hop music.

2. For further reading, students should see the *Journal of African American History*'s forum "Reflections on the Legacy of Malcolm X," published in the fall of 2013, and graduate students should be encouraged to read and critique Marable's biography for themselves.

The Long Hot Summers of the 1960s

Teaching the Racial Disturbances of the Civil Rights Era

SHAWN LEIGH ALEXANDER,

JOHN RURY, AND

CLARENCE LANG

The urban rebellions or uprisings of the 1960s (*riots* in popular parlance) were an important feature of the civil rights era, but one that many Americans still have difficulty understanding. Did they represent "the language of the unheard" or simply "self-defeating and socially destructive" behavior? Such questions have long been fodder for conversation and debate, although rarely in school classrooms.

The Langston Hughes Center (LHC) at the University of Kansas (KU) hosted a three-week summer institute in June 2017 for twenty-seven K–12 teachers to study race, the urban community, and civil disturbances, with the goal of bringing these important historical and contemporary issues into wider perspective. It employed a broad perspective informed by the humanities and social sciences to focus on the rebellions of 1967, involving interdisciplinary scholars from diverse viewpoints and differing racial and gender identities. Institute faculty members helped participating teachers make connections between prior incidents and today, encouraging them to think about issues affecting their own students in historical context. The goal was to enable educators to develop innovative, humanities-based classroom strategies for engaging critical subject matter about race and conflict in contemporary America. A vital reason for studying the civil rights era in American history, after all, is to better comprehend questions of racial inequity and social justice that continue to animate controversy and conflict today.

The Continuing Relevance of Civil.Disturbances

During the 1960s, black urban unrest rocked cities around the United States. These rebellions, frequently sparked by police violence, reached a fever pitch in July 1967 when massive disturbances occurred in Detroit and Newark. In the aftermath of that "long hot summer," President Lyndon B. Johnson's National Advisory Commission on Civil Disorders, also known as the Kerner Commission, concluded that the uprisings stemmed from patterns of racism that had splintered black and white America into two separate and unequal societies. As post-1960s black civil disturbances in such cities as Miami (1980), Los Angeles (1992), and Cincinnati (2001) have demonstrated, social inequalities and fragmentation along racial and class lines have remained persistent, making the watershed events of 1967 as pertinent today as ever.

The summer institute explored black urban disturbances during the fiftieth anniversary of the Detroit and Newark upheavals. Led by several resident faculty members from the University of Kansas and visiting scholars from institutions across the country, it also followed a series of more recent racial flashpoints that have echoed the 1960s-era rebellions. In August 2014, mass protests, community vigils, and sporadic looting erupted in Ferguson, Missouri, after a police officer killed an eighteen-year-old African American youth, Michael Brown. More serious civil disturbances occurred late in the fall when a grand jury failed to indict the officer who shot and killed him, Darren Wilson. In April 2015, a shorter but more disruptive episode of black civil unrest occurred in Baltimore after the death of African American Freddie Gray while in police custody. As in Ferguson, this drew a heavily armed police response, as well as comparisons to the 1960s.

As a point of origin for the growing popular demand that "Black Lives Matter," Ferguson became synonymous with a national conversation about black communities and local police, the methods and technologies of law enforcement, and the racial dynamics of criminal justice.

176

Renewed attention turned to geospatial patterns of race and inequality, the many dimensions of deprivation in black communities, and collective behaviors that count as "legitimate" forms of black protest. Reminiscent of the late 1960s, Ferguson also paved the way for new campus-based insurgencies in the fall of 2015 from the University of Kansas to Yale and, most appositely, the University of Missouri at Columbia. In this context, revisiting the urban disturbances of the civil rights era seemed especially pertinent.

Using Newark and Detroit as historical touchstones, institute faculty members sought to engage teachers in conversations that asked old questions anew: What events contributed to sparking these urban disturbances? What is the cultural and political significance of the nomenclature applied to them? What is the import of referring to these occurrences as *protests*, *riots*, *rebellions*, or *revolts*, or simply *civil disturbances* or *disorders*? The institute provided participants with primary documents, images, artistic representations, personal accounts, and other narrative resources that illuminate these issues for classroom use. They were also asked to consider the various groups in black urban communities that participated in these events and how gender may have influenced their participation. What were their motivations, perceptions, feelings, and goals, and the stories that have been told about them? Were these moments of social rupture organized or largely spontaneous? And ultimately, of course, what did the rebellions accomplish?

These and similar questions continue to puzzle many Americans and thus remain critically important to address in the schools and elsewhere. What relationship did these events have with what came to be known popularly as the *urban crisis*? Given the patterns of racial-spatial ordering that have emerged in US metropolitan areas *since* the 1960s, are the conditions giving rise to black urban disturbances today qualitatively different than in the past? Moreover, can placing these civil disturbances in a larger international context affect their meaning? And how do we situate them within the broader narrative of the civil rights movement in the United States and abroad? These issues were part of the planned curriculum for the institute as well.

Charting a Program of Study

It was one step to identify questions for an institute such as this, of course, and quite another to map a curriculum and instructional plan for three weeks of study and dialogue. The institute met Monday through Friday in morning and afternoon sessions and each week explored a particular theme. The first week examined the cultural and historical background of the civil disturbances that occurred in the 1960s and later, extending back to the latter nineteenth century. The second week focused on the urban rebellions of 1967 and 1968 and the community, state, and national responses that they evoked. Week three dealt with race relations and urban policy in the post-rebellion and post–civil rights era. These themes were explored in considerable depth, utilizing historical, literary, artistic, and oral sources made available on the institute's Canvas website. The goal was to inform participants and provide useful materials applicable to their own curriculum development projects. Although race was the central social category grounding this approach, faculty and participants also critically engaged questions related to class and gender, especially with regard to social constructions of black poverty, motherhood, and family that have influenced public responses to urban rebellions from the 1960s to the present.

In the mornings, resident and visiting faculty scholars provided academic talks grounded in current scholarship, addressing focal point questions and leading discussions of assigned readings. Afternoon sessions offered a continuation of scholar-led discussions and workshops by institute personnel to help teachers think about utilizing this material in the classroom. They also discussed instructional strategies to help students think historically about racial conflict. The late afternoons, evenings, and weekends, for the most part, were reserved for participants to read, maintain their portfolios, and work on curriculum projects with continued support from scholars, institute leaders, and summer institute colleagues.

Instructional methods included lectures by institute faculty, both resident faculty members and visitors. These presentations occurred in both large classroom settings and a more intimate seminar format. The use of PowerPoint slides with both text and images was routine, and these were made available on the institute website when possible, so that the teachers could readily access them afterward. The seminar format, with everyone sitting around a big table, encouraged questions and discussion from participants, who were generally not shy about sharing their perspectives. Conversation continued during lunch and dinner hours, which often were attended by both resident and visiting faculty.

Another frequently used instructional modality was small-group discussion of key questions or issues. This typically occurred following a lecture and entailed a question or prompt related to the topic at hand. Sometimes it called for each group, usual three to five participants, to take a position or develop an argument utilizing historical evidence from the lecture and/or readings. Occasionally it would lead to debate, as it did around the questions involving *looting* and *snipers* during the outbursts of the 1960s. A great deal of trust had to be established for individuals to freely express their opinions and for others to challenge them in a constructive manner. In most instances, resident faculty played the role of mediators, with discussion sometimes carrying into lunch or dinner to assuage feelings or ensure that misunderstandings did not persist. Altogether, however, all participants reported that they found these exercises to be among the most enlightening moments of the institute.

The institute assumed no prior background on the part of teacher participants. Upon arrival, participants received a copy of Malcolm McLaughlin's book, *The Long, Hot Summer of 1967: Urban Rebellion in America*; Ann V. Collins's *All Hell Broke Loose: American Race Riots from the Progressive Era through World War II*; and a number of articles on related issues.[1] These readings provided an overview of the key historical, political, and social underpinnings of the 1967 urban rebellions, and the progress and relapses since the Kerner Commission's report, to help them understand more contemporary developments.

The first week's program began with sessions on racial violence in history, key terms and ideas, and related issues, and discussions about how these fit into the larger context of American history as taught in schools. This portion of the institute aimed to provide a general introduction to racial violence in American history and establish a degree of mastery in foundational materials for use in their classrooms. Professor Shawn Alexander provided a conceptual overview of the key historical concepts that were utilized in the workshop, defining key terms such as *civil rights, black power, urban rebellions, riots,* and *neoliberalism.* He also provided an examination of lynching, terrorism, and racial pogroms, introducing material covering Ku Klux Klan activity and race riots of the late nineteenth and early twentieth centuries. Collin's opening chapter, "Race Riots: Structural Factors, Cultural Framing, and Precipitating Events," proved particularly useful in providing a framework for the participants to examine race riots and urban rebellions, as did Paul A. Gilje's introduction, "Why Study Riots?" in *Rioting in America* and Cathy

Lisa Schneider's *Washington Post* op-ed, "Five Myths about Riots."[2] There was also an extended discussion of pertinent primary documents and other materials, including, among other things, government documents on the Tulsa Race Riot, Chicago Race Riot, and the Harlem Riot of 1935, as well as poetry by Claude McKay, Sharon Olds, T. Thomas Fortune, and Langston Hughes.

. The first week also included an examination of the Red Summer of 1919, a particularly vicious year of white-on-black race riots. KU professor Bill Tuttle lectured on the infamous Chicago riot of that year, where he provided the participants with exclusive copies of his interviews with survivors of the riot. Subsequent discussions shifted to race riots in the mid-twentieth century, with an emphasis on outbreaks of violence in Harlem in 1935 and in Harlem and Detroit in 1943. Professor John Rury discussed racial violence over school integration during the 1940s and 1950s, culminating in riots at Little Rock in 1957. Finally, the film session was conducted on Saturday between the first and second weeks, led by Kevin Willmott, accomplished filmmaker, screenwriter, and member of the KU faculty. This session permitted institute participants to consider visual images and filmic depictions of black urban disturbances from the 1960s and 1970s. Willmott also screened and discussed the underappreciated film *Uptight* (1968).[3]

The second week of the institute shifted the focus to the urban uprisings of the 1960s and the events of 1967. It included presentations on a variety of topics, including the social and political context of the 1960s urban rebellions, conditions in Detroit and Newark, and protests by students that contributed to urban unrest during this period. We read poetry by Gwendolyn Brooks, Maya Angelou, Michael S. Harper, Larry Neal, A. B. Spellman, and David Henderson. Guest scholar Tony Bolden, a KU expert on poetry and blues, led a discussion of cultural responses to the urban disturbances.

The week also included field trips to the Black Archives in Kansas City and to the Dole Institute at KU, where students read newspaper accounts of this period and examined other historical artifacts, which proved essential to properly contextualizing the times. There was also an examination of developments in Kansas City, especially concerning civil rights activism, African American empowerment, and changes due to white flight to adjacent suburban communities.

In the final week of the institute, the focus shifted to an exploration of the aftermath of the upheavals of the 1960s and the uprisings of the post–civil rights era. Professor Clarence Lang led a session with a focus on national, state, and local organizational responses to the urban uprisings of the 1960s. This included an examination of the Kerner Commission's report and its effects on the transformation of urban communities following the 1967–1968 disturbances. Guest scholar Heather Ann Thompson guided participants through the rebellion in Detroit and its aftermath. In the afternoon session, Professor Thompson discussed the problem of black mass incarceration, a problem that emerged out of the upheavals of the 1960s. Visiting scholar Cathy Schneider addressed the question of why relatively few urban disturbances have occurred in the United States since the 1960s. Finally, Professors Alexander, Lang, and Rury led a discussion of events in Ferguson, Missouri, and Baltimore, Maryland, focusing on the economic, political, and social causes of the disturbances, along with responses from local communities.

On the institute's final Friday, teachers presented their projects, providing an opportunity for review and discussion of what they learned about the themes addressed in institute, with particular attention to how such knowledge and insight may prove helpful to others. This reflected work on portfolios utilizing resources available on Canvas and in their own research. Canvas and the institute website provided an easy-to-use and generally familiar interface, offering participants the opportunity to experiment with an online project in a supportive, secure environment. This was a crucial part of the institute's success.

How Did Participants Respond?

The teachers who participated in the institute represented a range of backgrounds and interests. About a third were African American, and all but a few were women. Perhaps a third were early career educators, and another third were within a decade of retirement. The largest group was social studies teachers, but many taught English as their primary subject. All but two worked in secondary schools, and one of those was a principal. They hailed from all parts of the country, with small groupings from Florida, New York, and Kansas. By and large it was a diverse group, but all shared an interest in learning more about the history of race and racial violence in the United States.

If there was an issue that came to define the experience for many of them, it was the question of nomenclature. There was consensus at the outset on the familiar use of the word *riot* to describe collective instances of racial violence in the past. But this was challenged in a number of ways. Institute faculty offered alternative terms to consider, and the readings addressed the question as well. The treatment of these historical episodes in Collins's conceptual framing of the question of racial violence was especially useful to many of the institute participants.

But on the very first day, one of the teachers described her own experiences in Detroit during the summer of 1967, when she became a participant in the events that unfolded at that time. Her recollection of the time was arresting and cast the somewhat abstract discussion of nomenclature into an altogether different light. Suddenly the group was confronted with the lived experience of someone who had once seen the moment as an opportunity to express longstanding frustrations. This made the question of *riot* versus *rebellion* far more palpable than anticipated and helped challenge the thinking of many of the participants in ways that were unexpected.

The first week's exploration of racial violence in the latter nineteenth and early twentieth centuries, when race *riots* entailed whites attacking blacks with intent to kill and destroy their property, led many to reconsider their familiar conception of the term. Discussion of the Chicago riot of 1919 proved especially illuminating. Other forms of white attacks on African Americans also were addressed, including lynching. Additionally, details of the "slow violence" in systematic degradation of African American schools, businesses, and other institutions in this period were discussed as well. All of this helped give meaning to the term *race riot* as a frenzied, forcefully violent assault by members of the dominant race on a minority group, with intent to restore or maintain conditions of inequality, oppression, and exploitation. The role of race was a focal point in this instance, as racial dominance was the very object of the various episodes in question.

As the focus of the institute shifted to the 1930s, 1940s, and beyond, however, the characteristics of *rioting* began to change as well. While whites continued to attack African Americans in Harlem and Detroit, African Americans also engaged in acts of violence to defend themselves and protest the inequality they endured. By the 1960s, of course, *race riots* were altogether different, as African Americans destroyed property and fought against police and other arms of state authority to protest the conditions of life in overcrowded, impoverished ghetto communities, especially the police violence they endured on a daily basis. Most institute participants recognized that this was quite different from the earlier episodes of racial violence. African Americans did not target white neighborhoods for attack, focusing instead on commercial properties in their own areas of cities. Most loss of life occurred within the black community, at the hands of the police. Most of the teachers could agree that terms such as *protest* or *rebellion* were better suited to these sorts of episodes than *riot*, which seemed better suited to the earlier events.

This did not mean that there was a lack of debate on these matters, as some participants questioned whether differences were really so great. Focusing on reports of snipers during the Detroit and Newark events and looting and destruction of property in nearly all such incidents, they wondered if the differences between earlier *riots* and later ones were significant. The case of white truck driver Reginald Denny, who was brutally attacked during the 1992 Rodney King protests in Los Angeles, brought these questions to the fore. One teacher wondered whether the treatment of Denny was any different from the lynch mobs of the earliest era, seemingly irrational violence against a member of a different race motivated by anger and hatred. In an ensuing discussion it was pointed out that the circumstances of this incident were quite different, in that the attack—while deplorable—was not intended to assert the dominance of a racial group or to exploit or oppress another group. Rather, the attack on Denny was an expression of anger, resentment, and frustration, the result of years of systematic discrimination and injustice. In the end, this was a perspective on the question of postwar racial violence in black communities with which all seemed ready to agree.

There had been a lively exchange of ideas throughout the institute's three-week duration, and the cross-fertilization of ideas and information was readily evident in the teachers' presentations, which drew on a wide range of resources, both from materials made available by the institute and from other sources.

Teaching the Civil Rights Era Today and Tomorrow

Given the history of racial violence in the United States, there can be little doubt that it is a vital theme in understanding the civil rights movement and most other periods of the country's history. The history of violent attacks on African Americans was a critically important issue during the long campaign for social and political equality during the postwar era and beyond, so examining it in considerable detail turned out to be quite fruitful for this group of teachers. The cataclysmic events of 1967 highlighted the limitations of the movement, at the same time that they deepened its demands for equity and social justice. This also certainly was true of the uprisings that shook the nation in the spring of 1968, following the tragic assassination of Martin Luther King Jr. And continued episodes of racial uprisings of this type are testimony to the unfulfilled goals of the movement, which is also a key element of teaching it. Events in Ferguson and Baltimore are only the most recent such episodes; it is hardly difficult to predict that there are more to come in the future.

In light of this, we offer the foregoing account of our experiences in conducting a summer institute for teachers on racial violence in American history, focused on the long hot summer of 1967, as an important dimension of understanding the civil rights movement. We hope that our effort in this regard proves helpful to colleagues at all levels of the educational system interested in teaching this critically significant aspect of our nation's history. It has much to teach us for today and for the future. We only hope that the vast majority of Americans will eventually learn to appreciate all of its varied dimensions and heed the cries of those whose lives were profoundly impacted by the decades of racial violence and protest, symbolized by the rebellions in Detroit, Newark, and innumerable other places throughout the land.

NOTES

1. Malcolm McLaughlin, *The Long, Hot Summer of 1967: Urban Rebellion in America* (New York: Palgrave Macmillan, 2014); Ann V. Collins, *All Hell Broke Loose: American Race Riots from the Progressive Era through World War II* (Santa Barbara, CA: Praeger, 2012).

2. Paul A. Giljie, "Introduction: Why Study Riots?," in *Rioting in America*, 1–11 (Bloomington: Indiana University Press, 1996); Cathy Lisa Schneider, "Five Myths about Riots," *Washington Post*, May 1, 2015.

3. Jules Dassin, *Uptight* (Paramount Pictures, 1968).

Power to the People!

*A Curriculum for Teaching
the Black Panther Party and the Transition
from Civil Rights to Black Power*

JAKOBI WILLIAMS

The Black Panther Party for Self-Defense (BPP) is the most iconic movement organization of the 1960s. Founded in 1966 by Bay Area activists Bobby Seale and Huey P. Newton, it evolved from a small group of black youth patrolling the police into a national organization with forty-nine chapters across the United States. The BPP's grassroots activism and revolutionary socialist ideology resonated with African Americans nationwide. At the same time, its pronouncements, posturing, and programs, which fascinated the media, frightened law enforcement. For better *and* worse, the Black Panther Party defined the Black Power era, making it the ideal organization through which to teach the transition from civil rights to Black Power.

The history of the BPP touches on crucial aspects of African American life, from lynching at the start of the twentieth century to mass incarceration at the beginning of the twenty-first. It also raises fundamental questions about the black freedom struggle, such as what does liberation mean to different generations of African American activists and how has heightened awareness of intraracial differences based on class, gender, sexuality, and region impacted the way people think about issues central to black freedom?

Over the last decade, I have developed a fifteen-week course on the history of the Black Panther Party. What follows is a description and explanation of that course, including a breakdown of the themes, suggested readings, films, and other sources that I assign. The material for the course can be adopted in its entirety or in discrete units to supplement instruction in a civil rights seminar or US history survey.

Week 1: Who Was Right, W. E. B. Du Bois or Booker T. Washington?

Readings: Ida B. Wells Barnett, "A Red Record," and W. E. B. Du Bois, *The Soul of Black Folks*, in *Norton Anthology of African American Literature*; Booker T. Washington, *Up from Slavery*. Documents: Martin Luther King Jr., "Letter from Birmingham Jail"; and Malcolm X, "The Ballot or the Bullet."

Since history does not happen in a vacuum, the first few weeks of the course are designed to provide historical context for 1960s black protest. The debate between Booker T. Washington and W. E. B. Du Bois at the turn of the twentieth century regarding the "Negro problem" serves as the springboard for diving into the black past. Forty years after the Civil War, America wrestled with what to do with African Americans in terms of full citizenship and equal protection under the law. Washington embraced an accommodationist approach, urging African Americans to acquire as much economic prosperity as possible under Jim Crow without upsetting racialized social norms. Du Bois argued against this position. He demanded that African Americans be recognized and protected under the law as full citizens. The debate and dilemma was shadowed by the real threat of death as whites used violence and terror to maintain the status quo. To make real the racial terror that African Americans faced, I show students a series of lynching postcards.

Sixty years later, Martin Luther King Jr. and Malcolm X engaged in a similar ideological debate regarding the "Negro problem," with King advocating for the use of nonviolent direct action and Malcolm arguing for self-defense. I have my students debate who was right, Washington or Du Bois, by examining the philosophical positions and organizing methods of Martin and Malcolm.

Week 2: Southern Segregation and the Roots of Black Power

Reading: Akinyele Umoja, *We Will Shoot Back: Armed Resistance in the Mississippi Freedom Movement*. Films: *Eyes on the Prize: Awakening* and *Two Societies*.

During the second week, the rural southern roots of Black Power as reflected in African Americans' embrace of armed self-defense are examined. Exploring the origins of Black Power challenges the Master Narrative view that locates the birthplace of Black Power in the urban North. Akinyele Umoja's *We Will Shoot Back* focuses on armed self-defense in Mississippi, highlighting the agency of black southerners. Umoja's work also demonstrates that African Americans were not just victims of southern racial violence but rather used guns to defend themselves and fight back. The two episodes of *Eyes on the Prize* explore both southern and northern engagement with armed self-defense.

Weeks 3 and 4: From Civil Rights to Black Power

Readings: Timothy Tyson, *Radio Free Dixie: Robert F. Williams and the Roots of Black Power*; Hasan Kwame Jeffries, *Bloody Lowndes: Civil Rights and Black Power in Alabama's Black Belt*. Film: *Negroes with Guns*.

The transition from civil rights protest to Black Power politics demonstrates the ways nonviolence and armed self-defense worked in tandem at the grassroots level. During these weeks, students are introduced to the southern roots of the Black Panther Party and the evolution of the practice and politics of armed self-defense. Two of the most significant works on this subject are Timothy Tyson's *Radio Free Dixie* and Hasan Kwame Jeffries's *Bloody Lowndes*, both of which examine iconic leaders and the movements they helped shepherd into existence. Tyson's book is a biography of Robert F. Williams. It also examines the liberation struggle in North Carolina, particularly the use of armed resistance by members of the NAACP. Jeffries's work looks at Stokely Carmichael and SNCC's political organizing project in Lowndes County, Alabama, which gave birth to the Black Power slogan and the original Black Panther Party.

Weeks 5 and 6: The Black Panther Party— The Beginning

Readings: Curtis Austin, *Up Against the Wall: Violence in the Making and Unmaking of the Black Panther Party*, chapters 1 and 2; Jakobi Williams, *From the Bullet to the Ballot: The Illinois Chapter of the Black Panther Party and Racial Coalition Politics in Chicago*, chapters 1–3;

Charles E. Jones and Judson L. Jeffries, "'Don't Believe the Hype': Debunking the Panther Mythology," in *The Black Panther Party Reconsidered*, chapter 1; Philip Foner, *Black Panthers Speak*, chapters 1, 3, and 7; Joshua Bloom and Waldo Martin, *Black against Empire: The History and Politics of the Black Panther Party*, chapters 1–6; Donna Murch, *Living for the City: Migration, Education, and the Rise of the Black Panther Party in Oakland, California*, chapters 1–5. Documents: The Black Panther Party for Self-Defense, "Ten-Point Platform."

The readings for this section cover the social, economic, and political conditions that gave rise to the BPP. They also explore the group's ideological development and examine its explosive growth from a local group to a national organization. The reading list is long, but several of the books are interchangeable. Austin, Bloom and Martin, and Murch all provide important historical context. Austin critiques racial violence, explaining how and why it influenced the party's founders, Huey P. Newton and Bobby Seale. Bloom and Martin survey the history of the BPP's early years. Murch's book brings to the fore the ways in which African American migration from the South and the struggle for quality education in the North merged in Oakland. Together, these works peel back the multiple, overlapping, contextual layers of the civil rights and Black Power eras.

My book, along with the anthology edited by Jones and Jeffries, further complicates the history of the BPP by debunking many of the popular myths and misconceptions that have sprung up around the organization. I also examine the BPP from a local perspective by looking closely at the BPP in Chicago. This approach reveals the sometimes stark differences between what was happening with the BPP at its national headquarters in Oakland and what was taking place in local chapters across the country. Indeed, to fully understand the BPP, which, at its height, had chapters in nearly every state, it is necessary to analyze the party from a local perspective.

Despite very real local variance, most BPP chapters shared some basic commonalities. Its members tended to belong to families that had migrated from the South in order to escape systemic racial violence and to secure life opportunities denied them because of Jim Crow. The North, of course, turned out to be much less than a land of milk and honey, which is why it is not surprising to find that BPP members also tended to be active in civil rights organizations prior to joining the BPP. Fred Hampton, the deputy chairman of the Illinois Chapter of the BPP, for example, held a leadership position in the NAACP before becoming a Panther.

Philip Foner's document collection offers a rich array of primary sources, including the BPP's Ten-Point Platform and Program, which serves as the basis for class discussion in this unit. Students are expected to utilize and rely on the reading material as they discuss and debate this document. As much time as possible should be allotted for this exercise, which always proves lively. I set aside two hours, and the students fill that time easily.

Week 7: BPP—Survival Programs

Readings: Dr. Huey P. Newton Foundation, *The Black Panther Party: Service to the People Programs*; JoNina M. Abron, "'Serving the People': The Survival Programs of the Black Panther Party," in *The Black Panther Party Reconsidered*, chapter 8; Jakobi Williams, *From the Bullet to the Ballot*, chapter 3; Joshua Bloom and Waldo Martin, *Black against Empire*, chapter 7; Donna Murch, *Living for the City*, chapters 6 and 7. Film: *Race: The Power of an Illusion*, episode "The House We Live In."

The Black Panther Party was founded as a direct response to structural racism, a concept that is sometimes hard for students to wrap their minds around. So I provide them with the following definition offered by law professor William Wiecek: "Structural racism is a complex, dynamic system of conferring social benefits on some groups and imposing burdens on others that results in segregation, poverty, and denial of opportunity for millions of people of color. It comprises cultural beliefs, historical legacies, and institutional policies within and among public and private organizations that interweave to create drastic racial disparities in life outcomes."[1]

The BPP's interest in structural racism manifested itself in the creation of "survival programs" to ensure equal access to food and land and nondiscrimination in employment, housing, education, health care, and justice. The documentary film *Race: The Power of an Illusion* looks at the history of the federal policies, laws, and judicial decisions that established and maintained structural racism in the twentieth century. As such, it serves as an excellent primer for examining structural racism.

The remaining reading for this unit documents the impact of the party's programs on poor people locally and nationally. J. Edgar Hoover, the long serving director of the FBI, labeled the BPP the "greatest threat to the internal security of the nation" primarily because of the grassroots appeal of the party's community service programs. The purpose of these programs was to eliminate the profit incentive from the daily human necessities that people needed to survive. The BPP offered its services free of charge and saw its work as a pragmatic, realistic, and tangible extension of Dr. King's Poor People's Campaign.

Week 8: BPP—Gender Dynamics

Readings: Robyn C. Spencer, *The Revolution Has Come: Black Power, Gender, and the Black Panther Party in Oakland*, chapters 1–3; Tracye Matthews, "'No One Ever Asks What a Man's Role in the Revolution Is': Gender and the Politics of the Black Panther Party, 1966–1971," in *The Black Panther Party Reconsidered*, chapter 12; Akua Njeri, *My Life with the Black Panther Party*; Jakobi Williams, *From the Bullet to the Ballot*, chapter 3. Films: *Comrade Sister: Women and the Black Panther Party; Free Angela Davis and All Political Prisoners*.

The majority of the BPP's members were women, which helps explain why the party was the only civil rights or Black Power organization to make the role of women in the movement and in society a focal point of discussion and action. In fact, many women defected from other movement organizations to join the Panthers because of the party's progressive views on gender equality. The Panthers also advocated for LGBTQ rights under their utopian banner of "Power to the People." Women in the party, however, still faced gender discrimination. Both Spencer and Matthews explore the history of the organization's internal gender dynamics through the experiences of Panther women.

There are several autobiographies written by women who held leadership positions in the BPP. Akua Njeri's autobiography, however, offers a firsthand account of a rank-and-file woman. Born Deborah Johnson, Njeri belonged to the party's Illinois Chapter. In 1968, she was eight months pregnant and lying next to the father of her unborn child, chapter leader Fred Hampton, when police stormed Hampton's apartment and assassinated him and Mark Clark. Her reflections pair nicely with my book on the Panthers, which provides insight into chapter-based differences when it came to the role and treatment of women in the organization.

Comrade Sister is a documentary made by Panther women. Through interviews with former BPP members Lynn French, Yvonne King, Ericka

Huggins, and others, it explores the multiple roles women played in the party. Unfortunately, *Comrade Sister* is hard to find. *Free Angela Davis and All Political Prisoners*, however, is more widely available. It explores the leadership and impact that women had on the black freedom movement, along with the kinds of repression they faced. It is a more than adequate substitute for *Comrade Sister*.

Week 9: BPP—Racial Coalitions

Readings: Jakobi Williams, *From the Bullet to the Ballot*, chapter 4; Amy Sonnie and James Tracy, *Hillbilly Nationalists, Urban Race Rebels, and Black Power*; Jeffrey O. G. Ogbar, "Brown Power to Brown People: Radical Ethnic Nationalism, the Black Panthers, and Latino Radicalism, 1967–1973," in *In Search of the Black Panther Party*; Laura Pulido, "Serving the People and Vanguard Politics: The Formation of the Third World Left in Los Angeles," in *Black, Brown, Yellow, and Left*, chapter 4. Films: *American Revolution II; Weather Underground*.

Interracial coalition politics was one of the greatest attributes and legacies of the BPP. No other group was able to draw on notions of class solidarity to unite African Americans with poor white southerners, Latinos, Asians, and Native Americans. The readings for this unit dispel the myth that the BPP was antiwhite, or worse, a black version of the Ku Klux Klan. The Panthers formed coalitions with poor people regardless of race and ethnicity. A common Panther slogan was "don't fight racism with racism; fight racism with solidarity." Williams, and Sonnie and Tracy, document the Panthers' alliance with Confederate flag–wearing southern whites to form the original Rainbow Coalition, which also included Latinos, among other racial and ethnic groups. Both Ogbar and I trace the Panthers' alliance with Latinos, while Pulido documents the history of the Panthers' Asian alliances. Essentially, the Panthers' coalition embodied the principles of Dr. King's Poor People's Campaign as it sought to empower and advocate on behalf of the nation's most marginalized people. By examining the relationship between the BPP and members of other racial and ethnic groups, students are introduced to the nuanced connections between resistance, racial coalitions, local movements, and the broader black freedom movement.

The films in this unit serve related purposes. *American Revolution II* traces the formation of the original Rainbow Coalition in Chicago. *Weather Underground* is a documentary about revolutionary white youth associated with the Students for a Democratic Society (SDS), who *unlike* the Panthers, actually waged war against the US government. The Panthers emphatically rejected the actions of the Weather Underground, dismissing them as acts of terrorism that failed to produce tangible results. Nevertheless, the BPP, which never engaged in an armed offensive against the state, but instead simply advocated for armed self-defense, a constitutional right, was subjected to extreme state repression in the form of assassinations and false imprisonment. The Weathermen were treated differently due to their racial and class privilege—their white skin and white wealth. Indeed, most escaped incarceration and assassination despite bombing numerous government buildings.

Weeks 10 and 11: Repression and Assassination— COINTELPRO

Readings: Ward Churchill and Jim Vanderwall, *The COINTELPRO Papers*, chapter 5; Ward Churchill, "'To Disrupt, Discredit and Destroy': The FBI's Secret War against the Black Panther Party," in *Liberation, Imagination and the Black Panther Party*, chapter 6; Jakobi Williams, *From the Bullet to the Ballot*, chapter 5; Joshua Bloom and Waldo Martin, *Black against Empire*, chapters 8–11; Robyn C. Spencer, *The Revolution Has Come*, chapters 4 and 5. Documents: COINTELPRO Images. Films: *The Murder of Fred Hampton*; *COINTELPRO 101*.

Arguably the most documented aspect of BPP history is the repression it faced at the hands of the state. The Panthers faced a barrage of illegal actions emanating from government agencies at all levels, including false imprisonment, beatings, torture, harassment, exile, and assassination. Churchill, Vanderwall, Bloom and Martin, and Spencer explore the illegal and unconstitutional actions of the FBI's domestic Counter Intelligence Program (COINTELPRO). I examine local state organizations such as Chicago's Red Squad, which was responsible for the death of Chicago Panther Fred Hampton. *The Murder of Fred Hampton* provides a history of Hampton's assassination, one of the clearest examples of state repression. Meanwhile, *COINTELPRO 101* offers an accessible overview and critical assessment of the FBI program.

Weeks 12 and 13: Aftermath of the Panthers

Readings: Akinyele Umoja, "Set Our Warriors Free: The Legacy of the Black Panther Party and Political Prisoners," in *The Black*

Panther Party Reconsidered, chapter 17; Jakobi Williams, *From the Bullet to the Ballot*, chapter 6; Robyn C. Spencer, *The Revolution Has Come*, chapters 6 and 7; Joshua Bloom and Waldo Martin, *Black against Empire*, chapters 12–16 and conclusion. Film: *Bastards of the Party*.

The BPP officially ceased to exist as an organization in 1982. The readings for these weeks explore the party's demise, the ongoing activism of its members, and the kinds of repression that former members faced. Bloom and Martin, Williams, and Spencer trace the group's organizational decline as well as its legacy, a legacy exemplified in electoral and interracial coalition politics, community service programs, education, and prison reform. Umoja highlights the struggle of political prisoners, while the film *Bastards of the Party* examines the ways that California street gangs, specifically the Crips and the Bloods, filled the social justice and leadership void created by the Panthers' absence.

Week 14: War on Drugs and Mass Incarceration

Reading: Michelle Alexander, *The New Jim Crow: Mass Incarceration in the Age of Colorblindness*. Film: *The 13th*; *Up the Ridge*.

The most important book about the black freedom struggle written in the last few years is Michelle Alexander's *The New Jim Crow*. It is a masterful work of exploration and advocacy that interrogates mass incarceration and colorblindness. Alexander's book demonstrates how many of the issues that the Panthers attempted to resolve continue to exist in new forms and under veiled methods. The documentaries *The 13th* and *Up the Ridge* further explicate the intricacies of law and punishment, including the exploitative system of mass incarceration.

Week 15: Black Lives Matter

Reading: Keeanga-Yamahtta Taylor, *From #BlackLives Matter to Black Liberation*. Films: *I Am Not Your Negro*; *#BlackLivesMatter*.

A course on the Black Panther Party specifically or on civil rights and Black Power more generally should also examine the most current political mass movement, the Movement for Black Lives. Taylor's work is a nuanced treatment of the movement, whose list of demands echoes the platform of the Panthers. Both the BPP and today's activists fighting for equality and inclusion organized around issues of land, bread, housing, education, employment, justice, and peace for all people regardless of race, class, religion, or sexual orientation. The two documentaries in this unit complement each other by analyzing the issues faced by the most marginalized African Americans in the 1960s, 1970s, and today, narrated by some of the most perceptive voices of the movement, including activist-writer James Baldwin.

Conclusion

State educational standards often identify the Black Panther Party as a 1960s organization worth studying, but far too often this is done simply to have a foil for expressly nonviolent groups. The Panthers, though, did not represent a dramatic break from early 1960s protest, but rather a logical extension of it. They continued the struggle for basic civil and human rights that was several generations old. In fact, quite a few BPP members belonged to traditional civil rights organizations before becoming Panthers. What's more, many of the party's goals mirrored those of older groups. In addition, Panther leaders, such as Fred Hampton, eclipsed some of the accomplishments of civil rights icons, including those of Dr. King, by forging coalitions with segments of society that had rebuffed them, including working-class whites.

Examining the BPP can greatly benefit students who are studying civil rights history. Most notably, it can help them understand the transition from civil rights to Black Power. It can also help them make sense of the party's many accomplishments, which are still visible today. These include free breakfast programs in schools, free health clinics, charter schools, legal aid clinics, and the many organic intellectuals who comprise the Black Lives Matter network, Dream Defenders, and advocates of LGBTQ rights.

NOTE

1. William M. Wiecek, "Structural Racism and the Law in America Today: An Introduction," *Kentucky Law Journal* 100, no. 1 (2011–12): 1–21.

PART FOUR

"The essence
of scholarship is truth"

*Sources for Teaching
the Civil Rights Movement*

Everybody Say Freedom

Using Oral History to Construct and Teach New Civil Rights Narratives

J. TODD MOYE

O ral history at its best recognizes people who are often ignored as experts on their own lived experiences [and] history."[1] So tweeted Jasmin Howard, a graduate research assistant for the Civil Rights in Black and Brown Oral History Project (CRBB, a project of which I am one of four codirectors) roughly three weeks into her experience as a CRBB interviewer in Deep East Texas in June 2016. She had just completed an interview with Betell Benham, an African American resident of Lufkin, Texas, about life under Jim Crow. It was an experience that drove home nearly all of the lessons I want my students to take away from oral history interviewing and that dramatized what makes oral history special, a difficult task worth doing. Prior to the interview Howard knew *intellectually* that she wanted to be the kind of historian who shows her respect for "local people" by taking their history seriously and by putting in the work to document social movements that the rest of society might dismiss as unimportant. Reflecting on the experience, she knew this *viscerally*: "Working on this oral history project has been life changing [and] it has also affirmed that this is exactly what I should be doing in life!"[2]

Howard, now a PhD student in history at Michigan State University, was not the first student to react this way upon diving into civil rights oral history, and she will not be the last. An oral history interview with a civil rights movement participant has obvious archival value, but the process of recording an oral history can have profound effects on the interviewer too. As Howard's experience suggests, it can be deeply affirming, even life changing. As educators, what more can we ask of a pedagogical tool?

An oral history is an interview between someone who participated in or witnessed something historic (in this case, a civil rights movement) and a prepared interviewer. To meet the commonly accepted academic definition, an oral history must be recorded and archived for posterity, but you may or may not decide that these steps are necessary for your own students' projects. The interviewer might be a graduate student like Jasmin Howard hoping to document an understudied or misunderstood aspect of civil rights history, in which case she has done extensive background reading to help her prepare questions before ever hitting the record button. The interviewer might be an elementary school student who knows little to nothing about the interviewee's background or the history he or she has witnessed, and can be expected to ask naive, even ignorant questions. Their interview might not even be recorded, much less archived. No matter. In all of these cases the student will learn actively, gain valuable insight, and develop important skills from the experience.

The act of sitting down with a participant in a civil rights movement, signaling that you think what the person did was important and that you are interested in hearing what they have to say about it, is a powerful action. (Indeed, simply having a deep, focused conversation with cellphones turned off becomes more radical and more important every day.) The story of American civil rights movements is the story of ordinary people doing exceptional things, people without access to power claiming a measure of it for themselves and sharing it with others. So whether or not they produce brilliant interviews worth archiving for posterity, students who have the chance to connect with the people who have participated in these movements cannot help but be empowered by the interview experience themselves.

Oral historians representing a diverse array of public, private, educational, community and governmental institutions have been at the forefront of efforts to document and interpret the history of the civil rights movement from its very beginnings, and they continue to explore the ways that the movement is recalled in individual, family, and national memories. I hope that this essay will convince you to create oral history assignments for your students, but even if you are not inspired to do that, you can expose your students to the mountains of oral history evidence that are widely available and accessible in print and online. I highlight a few—but by no means all—of the many collections oral historians have created. I also point out the ways that oral historians have been responsible for the corresponding revolution in the historiography of the civil rights movement, which, in contrast to a previous generation of scholarship, now covers a much broader chronological and geographical scope and focuses on the actions and mindsets of local people rather than the rhetoric of national leaders. Finally, I recommend the principles and best practices to follow if you decide to help your students create their own oral histories.

What I believe to be the first large-scale, systematic effort to record the memories of participants in the civil rights movement is Howard University's Civil Rights Documentation Project. Later renamed the Ralph J. Bunche Oral History Collection, the project recorded its first interviews in 1960, the year four college students from North Carolina sat down at a Woolworth's lunch counter designated for whites only and refused to leave until they were served. This nonviolent protest launched the nationwide, student-led sit-in movement. (Incidentally, Eliot Wigginton, a Georgia high school teacher, created oral history and folklife assignments for his students at around the same time; they resulted in the ground-breaking Foxfire project. K–12 educators have been doing oral history for educational purposes for roughly as long as university-based researchers have been doing it for archival purposes.) The collection, which is housed at Howard's Moorland-Spingarn Research Center in Washington, DC, includes nearly seven hundred interviews with narrators ranging from working-class direct action activists to elected officials and other leaders at the highest strata of government and society. The interviews were recorded in the 1960s and 1970s when movement memories were still fresh.

Howard University has not digitized the Bunche Collection transcripts or recordings to make them available over the web, but it is a tremendous resource for movement historians, and it set the bar high for the collecting efforts that followed in its footsteps. Over the last thirty years or so historians of the movement have taken a cue from oral history projects such as the Bunche Collection and turned their attention away from charismatic leaders and national organizations. They are now less likely to focus on what happened in the nation's capital, instead looking for ways that local struggles generated energy for the national movement. The interviews from the Bunche Collection have proven incredibly valuable to the historians responsible for this scholarly turn, and it is still an archive that every scholar of the movement must utilize.

A few university-based programs have been able to digitize their oral history collections and share them freely online, which makes them useful for anyone trying to create lesson plans that introduce students to primary sources. Their collections tend to focus on local or regional civil rights movements and figures who have escaped national notice. The University of Southern Mississippi in Hattiesburg has been at the forefront of efforts to document and interpret the movement in Mississippi, the Deep South state that produced arguably the most courageous civil rights activism, the most important organizing strategies, and the most venomous white resistance, through oral history, both in terms of collecting interviews and in making them available in creative ways to scholars and the public.[3]

The University of North Carolina's Southern Oral History Program (SOHP) is another university-based program that has been at the forefront of efforts to document the history of the movement by recording oral histories both with acknowledged leaders and with people from the grassroots whom the more recent generation of scholars have rediscovered.[4] The most important turn in the historiography of the movement over the past generation came in 2004, when Dr. Jacquelyn Hall, the longtime director of the SOHP, gave the presidential address to the Organization of American Historians on the theme of what she called the "Long Civil Rights Movement." The idea reflected a school of civil rights historiography that considers a much longer timeline than the traditional "Montgomery to Memphis" storyline did, and it really captured the imagination of American historians. It cannot possibly be a coincidence that someone so steeped in the act of listening deeply to what people had to say in oral history interviews would be the one to reconceptualize what the civil rights movement had been about in the first place. Hall, of course, is not the only historian to have done this, but I am genuinely struck by the fact—and it is a fact—that the historians who have been most responsible for this historiographical turn are also oral historians.

The CRBB Oral History Project, the one for which Jasmin Howard interviewed Betell Benham, is one of a new generation of projects that is born digital, and that uploads interviews—in this case, clips of interviews that have been indexed and tagged—to the web as quickly as they can be processed. Visitors to the project's website can search the interview database by subject, location, keyword, or interviewee name.[5] It differs from many other projects in that it aims to document and interpret both the Mexican American and African American civil rights movements as they developed in Texas communities and the ways that the movements sometimes worked together in coalition. High school teachers and college instructors are already using content from the interviews as teaching aids and assigning research projects around them, and the project's directors are working to integrate CRBB materials with state curriculum standards.

Community groups have also sponsored oral history research projects as a way of both documenting their own communities' histories and turning the research endeavor into a learning opportunity for school children, even a means toward social change on its own. The best example of this kind of oral history project is the one created by the Youth Program of the Rural Organizing and Cultural Center (ROCC) of Holmes County, Mississippi, which resulted in the book *Minds Stayed on Freedom*. The ROCC very self-consciously defined itself as an heir to the grassroots activist tradition of the Mississippi civil rights movement. In addition to educating and providing leadership training for young people, ROCC was "dedicated to combatting poverty and racism in Holmes County."[6]

According to their literature, "ROCC developed this oral history project as part of its effort to foster pride in local history and to develop youth leadership. The authors of *Minds Stayed on Freedom* are eighth and ninth grade students, most from low-income households, who spent thousands of hours researching the local movement, honing their questioning techniques, conducting interviews, transcribing tapes, editing their texts, and mastering the other tasks that went into the production of this book. Their success shows that ordinary people not only can make history, they also can best record it." This is actually a case where community-based oral history got out in front of the academic historians, who have been playing catch-up since ROCC published this book in 1991, but that wasn't the goal of the oral history project. ROCC conceived it as a project to empower students who were ill-served by their public schools; the contribution they made to the larger history of the civil rights movement was a happy coincidence.[7]

Various federal agencies and institutions have devoted considerable resources to collecting civil rights oral history. Presidential libraries from the Truman Library on have made special efforts to interview administration officials and others who either pushed for or reacted to the civil rights revolution. The historians of the US Senate and House oversee oral history projects that document the arguments for and against civil rights legislation within those bodies and show in great detail how the legislative sausage is made. These collections are valuable, but students have to approach them cautiously for obvious reasons—professional politicians know how to shape the record in ways that will benefit them most. The Library of Congress Civil Rights History Project, which was initiated in 2009, now features more than one hundred high-quality video interviews, all of which are available for viewing in their entirety online. This is obviously an important resource for researchers, but I anticipate that it will be used much more frequently by classroom teachers. According to the project's creators, "The recollections of interviewees cover a wide variety of topics about the freedom struggle, such as the influence of organized labor, nonviolence and self-defense, and the importance of faith, music, family, and friendships." The library's indexing system makes it easy to search across the interviews for discussion of particular events, figures, and places.[8]

The SNCC Legacy Project, detailed elsewhere in this volume, is one of the best projects I know of in which civil rights activists have reclaimed their own legacies and documented their own histories. It was founded by veterans of the Student Nonviolent Coordinating Committee, the organization that formed out of the sit-in movement of the early 1960s, who were dissatisfied with the ways that historians had portrayed them and who wanted to document their history on their own terms. Of course, as encouraging as this development is, it also comes with potential pitfalls. If government-sponsored projects have to be approached critically, so too do activist-sponsored projects. Good students of history approach any source skeptically, wondering what agenda lies behind the creation, archiving, and interpretation of a source. This is as much (but no more) the case for oral history sources as for other historical sources.[9]

Oral history projects have already documented tremendous regional variation in civil rights organizing, from state to state, from city to city, even from neighborhood to neighborhood.

In some communities religious leaders also became civil rights activists, but in others they hindered progress. In some places organized labor worked in very effective partnership with the civil rights movement, but in others labor institutions worked actively to obstruct the movement. Some communities did adhere to the nonviolent philosophy that Dr. King preached; others let it be known that they reserved the right to shoot back in self-defense, and did. In nearly all of the communities whose movements have been documented, women played a much more prominent role than the earliest generation of civil rights scholars gave them credit for. I encourage you to introduce your students to these complex variations within the African American movement and to help them find out what the movement looked like in their own community.

Of course, there are multiple oral history projects that address civil rights movements apart from the modern African American movement. They include Tejano Voices, a project sponsored by the University of Texas at Arlington, which interviewed the first generation of Mexican American elected officials in the state of Texas, and the ACT UP Oral History Project, which was sponsored by the San Francisco and New York City public libraries and documented an early generation of LGBTQ activism, among many others.[10]

These oral history projects and hundreds of others like them offer much more content than you and your students can possibly use in a short unit on the civil rights movement. Obviously, you will have to tailor assignments to fit the needs of your own class, but the reward of introducing students to these primary sources can be resounding. If you choose to devise your own oral history assignments, they can also serve as models for the project you and your students create.

Actually starting an oral history project may seem daunting. Before setting up the project you will want to read up on oral history methodology, and there is always another resource to consult. (See "Additional Resources and Further Reading" below.) You will want to read as many books and primary sources as you can about the civil rights movement as it existed on the national level and in your community, but there is always another book to read and another source to uncover. You won't want to look like a dummy in front of your narrator once you begin interviewing, so you will spend hours going over the questions you want to ask. It is easy to convince yourself that you need to do just a little more homework before launching your project and to keep repeating that cycle. But this is an endeavor for which experience is by far the best teacher, so just do it. As valuable as the resources listed below are, you and your students will learn much more from doing the project than you will from books and websites, so do it and commit to evaluating yourselves and learning from any mistakes you make.

You should first decide what your pedagogical objectives are and how an oral history project can help you meet them. How closely do you want your project to track curricular directives? Here you almost surely need to think beyond state standards. Nearly all states have curricular standards that call for at least basic coverage of civil rights history, but teachers who do little more than mention *Brown v. Board of Education* and Martin Luther King Jr. do not serve their students well. The major part of the problem here—and it is a significant problem— lies in the inadequacy of the standards themselves, but we have very little control over the state standards that are handed to us. We do have control over our classrooms and lesson plans.[11]

Who will you interview? Whether you know it now or not, your community had a civil rights movement. If you teach in the Deep South, someone in your town or city organized protests against Jim Crow. If you live in the Border South, Midwest, or Northeast, someone organized sympathy pickets or boycotts to show solidarity with the students who launched the sit-ins in 1960. Parents have organized for equal educational opportunities for children of color and poor children in every state in the union. Minority groups are fighting back against voting restrictions inside and outside of the South, and LGBTQ activists are demanding equal civil rights throughout the United States today. Civil rights history is everywhere.

Your state curriculum may define the civil rights movement narrowly and direct you to teach only about the "classical period" of the African American civil rights movement that lasted from the Montgomery bus boycott in 1955 until Dr. King's assassination in 1968. You can bring that history alive and connect your students much more effectively with the lessons it still has to teach us by sharing participants' archived first-person recollections and interpretations of what they did. Even better, you can have your students find and interview men and women who identify with the civil rights movements' ideals and organizing strategies. Whether or not these people participated in the narrowly defined 1954 to 1968 African American civil rights movement, the act of sitting down and absorbing information from them can be transformational for your students. Again, the story of civil rights movements is the story of ordinary people sacrificing and supporting one another to make their communities more just and more democratic. There is no better way to get this lesson across than to put students in a room with the people who have made these choices and to encourage them to find out what makes civil rights activists tick.

You may know a "gatekeeper" who can help you find a number of people who fit your criteria for interviews. If you do not, a local historical society may help, or research in your local newspaper may lead you to a few prominent names. Ask around—all oral history projects at every level depend at some point on word of mouth. Inviting someone, especially a stranger, to record an oral history can seem strange the first few times you do it, but you may be surprised how likely many if not most people are to share their time and memories with students. If you treat would-be interviewees respectfully and communicate that you are genuinely interested in hearing what they have to say, they are likely to respond generously.

Once you have identified gatekeepers, I encourage you to invite them to help you devise the project, and certainly to help you find additional interviewees. But the more work your students can do themselves to find interviewees for their project, the more they will buy into it. Explaining the project and inviting others to participate in it will help them develop communication skills. You may want them to create a flyer or a web site to solicit interviewees, which invites collaboration with your school's art teacher and/or IT specialist.

How long can you afford to spend on the project? Several middle and high school social studies teachers with whom I have worked in Texas find that the month left in the school year after the final round of standardized testing ends is perfect for a focused oral history project, but at this point in the school year they have to battle rapidly declining attention spans. You may have more time available and may want your oral history project to deliver historical content in time for your students to take advantage of it for end-of-year tests. Or you may teach in a school where standardized tests are less emphasized, in which case you can tailor a project to meet other goals. You may decide that oral history is better suited for a History Day project, or that only the students in an honors section have the discipline necessary to take on such a project, or that it is better suited for an extra-credit assignment or extracurricular activity. My point here is that oral history is flexible and versatile enough as a pedagogical tool to help you meet any number of objectives.

Will you archive your students' interviews? In other words, do you expect that your students will record interviews worth saving for posterity? Not all are, and you may devise a project in which the process is infinitely more important to you than the result, but several classroom projects have resulted in significant interviews that have been archived. Students have used these interviews not only to document historical events but also to interpret them and present their findings in creative ways. The *Minds Stayed on Freedom* project would be the classic example from civil rights–focused projects, but you can easily find other models on other historical subjects—for instance, the web-based projects developed by the "Telling Their Stories" Oral History Archives Project.[12]

If you do think you will want to archive the interviews, you will want to make prior arrangements with a local university or historical society, determine whether your school system has enough server space and expertise to house the interviews online, or look into the resources of the StoryCorps project. StoryCorps provides recording equipment, including a mobile recording studio, that allows ordinary Americans to interview loved ones and archives their interviews at the Library of Congress. You may have heard clips from StoryCorps interviews on National Public Radio's *Morning Edition*. The group released a smartphone app, which allows anyone to record an interview on a smartphone or tablet and upload it to a Library of Congress server, to great fanfare in 2015 and within weeks had archived thousands of short interviews. The app is simple to use even for adults (to say nothing of born-digital tweens and teenagers), produces decent enough sound quality, takes care of archiving in a snap, and makes its interviews available to anyone with an internet connection.[13] You may well find that it, or another app such as PixStori or one of the many others available, meets your classroom's needs perfectly.

At the elementary level, the goal of an oral history project should be to build empathy in students, to encourage them to connect with their elders, and to help them appreciate how much fun historical inquiry can be. I would consider any historical content they learn icing on the cake. Older students can learn lessons about the nature of historical inquiry and the ways that scholars produce new knowledge. High school and college students are certainly capable of recording interviews that are worth archiving and sharing with fellow scholars. The form of your class's oral history project should follow the functions you want it to perform. The Oral History Association's online Educator's Resource will help you think through all of these issues. It provides more than enough practical advice to help you launch your own project.[14]

Jasmin Howard, the graduate student whose observations opened this chapter, was profoundly moved by the raw emotion that seemed to erupt from deep within Betell Benham's soul when asked about Jim Crow–era violence in East Texas. In the moment of the 2016 interview Howard became conscious of connections that she and the narrator were making on multiple levels in real time: the narrator was recounting events that she had long sought to forget, and those memories understandably elicited emotions she had long tried to suppress. Benham, the interviewee, was surprised at her own reactions as she answered Howard's questions, and she commented on her present state almost parenthetically while she recounted past events. Oral history is the only kind of research that allows historical sources to interpret themselves in real time, in part because no other form of research so effectively "recognizes people who are often ignored as experts on their own lived experiences [and] history," as Howard put it. Participating in this kind of research can be electric, and it can lead students to the same reaction Jasmin Howard had. ("This is exactly what I should be doing in life!") Democratic in every sense, oral history is the best way for students to explore and internalize the lessons of the most democratic social movement in American history. I encourage you to share its possibilities with your students.

RESOURCES

Raines, Howell. *My Soul Is Rested: The Story of the Civil Rights Movement in the Deep South.* New York: Penguin, 1983.

Ritchie, Donald A. *Doing Oral History: A Practical Guide.* 3rd ed. New York: Oxford University Press, 2014.

Wood, Linda P. *Oral History Projects in Your Classroom.* Carlisle, PA: Oral History Association, 2001.

NOTES

This essay is adapted from a paper I delivered at the 2014 Congress of the International Oral History Association.

1. Jasmin Howard (@BlackHerstorian), Twitter, June 28, 2016, 4:17 p.m., https://twitter.com/BlackHerstorian/status/747901649952202752. I am grateful to Jasmin for allowing me to quote and analyze her tweets.

2. Jasmin Howard (@BlackHerstorian), Twitter, June 28, 2016, 4:12 p.m., https://twitter.com/BlackHerstorian/status/747900572351627264.

3. See University of Southern Mississippi's Center for Oral History and Cultural Heritage, https://www.usm.edu/oral-history.

4. See Southern Oral History Program, http://sohp.org.

5. See Civil Rights in Black and Brown Oral History Project, http://crbb .tcu.edu.

6. Youth of the Rural Organizing and Cultural Center, *Minds Stayed on Freedom: The Civil Rights Struggle in the Rural South—An Oral History* (Boulder, CO: Westview Press, 1991), xii.

7. Youth of the Rural Organizing and Cultural Center, *Minds Stayed on Freedom*, xii.

8. See Civil Rights History Project National Survey of Collections, American Folklife Center, Library of Congress, http://www.loc.gov/folklife/civilrights/.

9. See Student Nonviolent Coordinating Committee Legacy Project, http:// www.sncclegacyproject.org/.

10. See Tejano Voices, University of Texas at Arlington Center for Mexican American Studies, http://library.uta.edu/tejanovoices/; ACT UP Oral History Project, MIX—New York Queer Experimental Film Festival, http://www.actup oralhistory.org/.

11. On the inadequacy of state standards, see Southern Poverty Law Center, "Teaching the Movement: The State Standards We Deserve," 2011, https:// www.splcenter.org/20110920/teaching-movement-state-standards-we -deserve, and "Teaching the Movement 2014: The State of Civil Rights Education in the United States," 2014, https://www.tolerance.org/magazine/publica tions/teaching-the-movement-2014.

12. See "Telling Their Stories," Oral History Archives Project, Urban School of San Francisco, http://www.tellingstories.org/. For other examples, see "What Did You Do in the War Grandma? An Oral History of Rhode Island Women during World War II Written by Students in the Honors English Program at South Kingstown High School," 1989, http://cds.library.brown.edu /projects/WWII_Women/tocCS.html; "The Whole World Was Watching: An Oral History of 1968," South Kingstown High School and Scholarly Technology Group, Brown University, 1998, http://cds.library.brown.edu/projects/1968/.

13. See StoryCorps Archive, https://storycorps.org/ and https://archive .storycorps.org/.

14. See Oral History Association, "Oral History Association's Educator's Resource," http://www.oralhistory.org/educators-resource/, and "Principles and Best Practices for Oral History Education (4-12)," http://www.history .com/images/media/pdf/OralHistoryGuidelines.pdf.

Freedom Songs

Building a Civil Rights Playlist

CHARLES L. HUGHES

Music permeated the civil rights era. Mass meetings and marches rocked with freedom songs and gospel hymns. Folk, jazz, and pop artists became mainstays at rallies and fundraisers for movement causes. And the radio buzzed with soul and rock 'n' roll hits that captured the movement's energies and referenced its pivotal campaigns either directly or indirectly. To this day, our collective memory of the civil rights era is scored by anthems like Sam Cooke's "A Change Is Gonna Come," Aretha Franklin's "Respect," and the many versions of "We Shall Overcome" that echoed across the movement years. It is one of our deepest and most recognizable cultural soundtracks.

But music was more than just an accompaniment to this pivotal moment. Throughout the civil rights era, music was a site of struggle itself where musicians and audiences pressed for the same changes that motivated the larger campaign. Listeners sought access to African American–identified sounds and musicians, insisting that their ability to hear the uncontained energies of 1950s rock 'n' roll or the unmasked lyrical assertions of 1970s funk was connected to the larger push for racial justice. Artists such as Harry Belafonte and Nina Simone became prominent figures in the fight for freedom, using their prominence to make both artistic and economic contributions to the continuing struggle. And the music industry became a civil rights battleground, as African American musicians sought creative and commercial control over black-identified genres such as soul and jazz. In all respects, music offers a rich and complex glimpse into the movement era.

Given its ubiquity, significance, and continuing resonance, music remains a very powerful tool when attempting to understand the civil rights movement and communicating its many aspects to students. Music not only narrates the history of the movement but communicates its underlying dynamics in a manner that is both accessible and multi-faceted. It helps students and teachers unlock and interrogate some of the central concepts and debates in the movement era. As a classroom resource, music can be used not only as a helpful adjunct but also as an organizing structure around which to shape larger discussions of the civil rights and Black Power movements.

What follows is not an attempt to harness the vast diversity of movement music, nor does it offer a comprehensive guide to its many sonic pathways. Instead, I offer a brief discussion of some suggestions for incorporating music into larger discussions of movement ideology and strategy. Within that, I offer examples of songs and stories that I have found particularly useful and gesture toward how they may be incorporated into lectures or lesson plans. While I use these specific examples, I also encourage readers to look for others that I may not specifically address. The kind of presentation and analysis that I offer below can be applied to literally hundreds of other songs from this era, so I encourage both teachers and students to explore the possibilities of these methods in other songs or recordings.

One way to think about this as both a pedagogical and practical strategy is the "playlist" model that I have used as both an assignment and in-class activity. Inspired by the work of scholar and educator Craig Werner, whose broader influence permeates these pages, I have employed the creation of playlists as both an assignment for students and an ongoing in-class activity. I routinely assign a "historical playlist" essay as a final project, where students have to select eight to ten songs that capture the larger stories and themes of the course and then discuss why they chose these songs in accompanying "liner notes." I have also asked students to listen to particular playlists before class, ensuring that they will have familiarity with the music before we engage with it in class. Increasingly, I have abandoned the self-curated playlists in favor of those that students create themselves based on readings and classroom discussions. Given the widespread availability of recordings in the digital age, such playlists are easy to create and distribute.

More broadly, this playlist model—built around a diverse and flexible collection of songs—indicates the diversity and complexity of movement sounds and the movement itself. It encourages students and teachers to consider the music as a central component of the era, rather than using music as a stand-alone topic—such as the still-common use of a single class day to talk about "movement music" without much discussion the rest of the semester. It encourages collaboration, allowing each student to determine and debate the songs that matter most. Most importantly, perhaps, it promotes the practice of "call and response" that was so central to movement music and campaigns. As a form of what Werner calls "gospel politics," call and response "moves the emphasis from the individual to the community," requiring contributions from every member of that community and preventing anyone (including a leader) from having too much control over its direction.[1]

The process of call and response is central to the most obvious point of connection between the music and the movement: the "freedom songs" that became crucial to organizing and protest. Anthems such as "Oh Freedom" and "We Shall Overcome"—many descended from slave spirituals and the post–Civil War gospel church—are powerful documents of movement events and the energies that accompanied them. These songs enact the "beloved community" of the movement's grassroots organizing, both in terms of their interlocking voices and through lyrics that were adapted to fit particular situations. In different versions of "Ain't Gonna Let Nobody Turn Me 'Round," for example, performers call out specific challenges ("segregation") or even names ("Chief Pritchett," the sheriff in Albany, Georgia, who became that campaign's primary antagonist), circling back to the song's central message of perseverance and struggle.[2] Beyond their lyrics, freedom songs gained their power through their sound; the propulsive energy of "Woke Up This Morning with My Mind on Freedom" and the somber declaration of "We Shall Overcome" were as important to their meaning as their compelling lyrics. By presenting these songs to students (or, if you feel bold enough, having them perform them in class), teachers not only can re-create the energies of movement protest but also demonstrate its strategic approach.

Many of the most powerful statements on movement events emerged from artists who brought the freedom song into conversation with R&B, folk, and other genres.[3] By extending the reach of the freedom songs, they paralleled the insistence of movement activists on reshaping American political and social discourse by directly introducing the language of black struggle into the cultural conversation.[4] In soul music, artists such as Curtis Mayfield (whose group The Impressions recorded Mayfield-penned songs such as "Keep On Pushing" and "People Get Ready") or the Staple Singers (who performed alongside Martin Luther King Jr. and recorded songs such as "Freedom Highway" and "I'll Take You There") drew on black musical and political tradition in direct references to the "freedom songs" and the civil rights movement.[5]

A similar conversation took place in the folk revival of the early 1960s. Artists such as Joan Baez, Phil Ochs, and Odetta recorded some of the most explicit commentaries on movement events (including Baez's piercing "Birmingham Morning," recorded after the bombing of the 16th Street Baptist Church) and became regular performers at movement rallies, while ensembles such as the SNCC Freedom Singers shared their stages and repertoires. Most strongly symbolized by the image of African American and white performers singing "We Shall Overcome" at the 1963 Newport Folk Festival, this has become one of the most recognizable cultural images of the movement's early phase of nonviolent direct action and interracial alliance.[6] The political alliances were musical as well, with many folk artists in conversations that included both the freedom songs and their ambassadors on the pop charts.

One of the best examples is Bob Dylan's "Blowin' in the Wind." It was based on the Emancipation anthem "No More Auction Block," which had been recorded by everyone from the Fisk Jubilee Singers to Paul Robeson. It was inspired by the freedom songs of the SNCC Freedom Singers, who performed freedom songs for international audiences. It hit number one in a cover version by folk artists Peter, Paul and Mary, reflecting the growing prominence of civil rights–related material in the American musical mainstream. It was covered by The Staple Singers and Stevie Wonder, two of the era's most influential (and most political) R&B artists. And it inspired Sam Cooke's powerful soul anthem "A Change Is Gonna Come." Released after his death, and with clear lyrical referents to "We Shall Overcome" and other movement songs, this gospel-drenched recording reflected Cooke's growing political militancy—inspired by his friend Malcolm X—and was his first record to comment directly on the struggle in his lyrics. One could construct an entire class period or assignment around "Blowin' in the Wind," using it as a lens into a wider historical appraisal. This story reminds us that—far from being separate or oppositional—the worlds of folk, gospel, and pop were interlocked, with specific differences but a shared purpose that reflected similar diversity within the movement.

Additionally, this story reminds us that educators should be careful not to assume that movement music existed somehow separate from the pop mainstream. Although Sam Cooke began his secular career with songs that mostly avoided direct political commentaries, even such indirect material offers fruitful opportunities for analysis.[7] Particularly in the early days, politically charged lyrics by African American artists were largely absent from radio, so many artists masked political commentaries through misdirection and nuance. Such 1950s rock 'n' roll artists as Bo Diddley and Chuck Berry drew on humor, coding, and euphemism to create songs that commented on contemporary and historical conditions: Berry's brilliantly sly 1957 hit "Brown-Eyed Handsome Man," for example, addresses topics such as the rise of Jackie Robinson and the mistreatment of African Americans by the criminal justice system.[8] In the early R&B era, this obfuscation often took a distinctly gendered form. In songs such as The Platters' 1956 hit "The Great Pretender" or Smokey Robinson & The Miracles' "The Tracks of My Tears" from 1965, male singers express their inability to express or show their true feelings in the face of a world that does not know who they really are, a mixture of strength and vulnerability that paralleled the larger negotiations over what acceptable African American manhood looked like within an unfriendly American political context.[9] This was further demonstrated by early 1960s "girl group" songs such as The Chiffons' "Nobody Knows What's Going On in My Mind but Me" or The Shirelles' "Mama Said." In "Mama Said," the lead singer observes that "Mama said there'd be days like this," relating a generational lesson about pain and perseverance. "Mama Said" thus speaks to generational legacies of black women's activism, as well as the erasure of women's labor within a male-dominated movement narrative. By the late 1960s, when movement victories had pushed American popular culture to accept a greater level of directness and even militancy among African American musicians, such masking became less common. By asking students to grapple with masked meanings present in songs that do not announce themselves as "political" through protest content, we insist on a deeper level of analysis and more expansive vision of political music and politics.

This process also mirrors the reinterpretations through which movement activists and audiences sometimes recognized more militant messages in songs than were originally intended. Take, for example, Martha and the Vandellas' Motown hit "Dancing in the Street." After its 1964 release, the exuberant song symbolized the accomplishments of Motown Records as a profitable black-owned company that successfully marketed its recordings to both white and black audiences, as well as an anthemic party call ("an invitation across the nation") to cities such as Philadelphia and Washington, DC, that were centers of African American life. The song's meaning shifted when adopted by participants in the Detroit riot of 1967, who recognized a call to action that exceeded Martha Reeves's literal invocation to dance.[10] Asking students to follow their example and to consider how dance hits, love songs, and the like might be political helps expand our notion of what constitutes "political" music, destabilize our notion of movement struggle beyond its most common touchstones, and force us to grapple with the meaning of "politics" itself.[11]

The question "what is political?" relates directly to another key point—teachers must resist the temptation to limit discussions to lyrics. It is understandable to focus on words, but many of the most significant musical manifestations of movement changes from the 1950s through the 1970s came through melodies, rhythms, vocal style, instrumentation, and other sonic characteristics. Thus, students and instructors must be unafraid to tackle music-based questions. How does something sound? How do the instruments work together? How is the song structured and arranged? It is not necessary to be a musician or possess a knowledge of music theory; there are numerous ways to think and talk about sound that do not require fluency in musical terminology. In fact, given that most listeners (and many musicians!) do not possess this knowledge, it is more instructive to encourage students and oneself to think about music without utilizing specialized language. This can in part be accomplished by thinking about how something *sounds*— even descriptors such as *excited*, *sad*, or *troubled* can be appropriate.

To return to 1950s rock 'n' roll, the genre's uncontained musical energy and stylistic blending illustrates its challenge to segregation more directly than most of its lyrics. The primary objections to the music of Elvis Presley, Chuck Berry, and others—criticisms that were ubiquitous throughout the era from politicians, religious leaders, and other critics—centered on the "jungle rhythms" and chaotic arrangements

that supposedly signaled the music's dangerous racial and sexual politics. Fans of rock 'n' roll, too, heralded the music's wild and excitable
sounds—from the intense vocals of Little Richard to Bo Diddley's
unique guitar style—as a symbol of positive cultural change and a contrast to mainstream American culture.

This is particularly observable when discussing the phenomenon of
white "cover versions" of songs by popular African American artists in
the rock 'n' roll era. This has become a standard story in the longer history of disparities faced by African American artists, attempts by white
authorities to diminish black influence (musical or otherwise) on white
teenagers, and debates over cultural appropriation. Specifically, rock
'n' roll provides a perfect opportunity to talk about its broader musical challenge. The work of white pop singer Pat Boone—who recorded
several songs by black rock pioneers—is particularly instructive, and
Boone's covering of Little Richard's "Long Tall Sally" has led to one of
my most consistently successful course activities. Here, I ask students
to compare the Little Richard's original version with Boone's subsequent cover. The lyrical differences are minimal—although Boone does
erase the song's apparent connection to a cross-dressing prostitute in
New Orleans—but the significant sonic differences between Richard's
furious boogie and Boone's restrained smoothness produces an unmistakable contrast. (To make this point even more directly, I use the
filmed Little Richard performance of the song in the 1957 film *Don't
Knock the Rock*, during which Richard's androgynous appearance and
suggestive movements toward his largely white audience amplify his
challenge to cultural norms.) Rock 'n' roll's transgressions against the
musical boundaries erected by white cultural gatekeepers in the 1950s
symbolized the rising strength of the movement and presaged the political and cultural innovations to come.

No genre understood the politics of musical liberation in the civil
rights era more than jazz. Jazz has never been a solely instrumental
medium, of course, and some of the music's greatest vocalists—Billie
Holiday, Nina Simone—have created vivid and significant movement
anthems like Holiday's "Strange Fruit" and Simone's "(To Be) Young,
Gifted and Black."[12] Not only do jazz vocalists deserve to have their
lyrics considered in the framework detailed previously, but—like their
counterparts in folk, R&B, rock 'n' roll, and the rest—we must also consider their vocals as fluid and instructive instruments. Still, despite
these important caveats, I have found the greatest contribution of jazz

215

to a civil rights curriculum to be forcing students to think sonically. The jazz of the 1960s and 1970s is filled with artists and composers whose work tread this terrain. Compositions such as Max Roach's "Freedom Now Suite," Charles Mingus's "Haitian Fight Song," and John Coltrane's "Alabama" (a wordless saxophone re-creation of Martin Luther King's elegy for the victims of the 16th Street Baptist Church bombing) directly addressed movement events and their historical precedents. And new genres embraced liberatory possibilities that linked them to similar futurism and Afro-diasporic strains in Black Power in the 1970s. Particularly crucial was the genre of free jazz, inaugurated by saxophonist Ornette Coleman in his titular 1961 album. The idea of "free jazz"—also called by Coleman a "collective improvisation"—offers a chance to think through conceptions of *freedom* in both music and society at the height of Black Power. Playing Coleman's music, students can be asked to discuss what exactly is "free" about this music, what it represents, and from what it represents a departure. This groundbreaking work meant that—more than any other genre, with the possible exception of soul—jazz became a topic of discussion among the Black Arts Movement, Afrocentric scholars and others who linked their recentering of human experiences to the music and ideology of jazz. The expansion of jazz throughout the 1960s and early 1970s both fueled and paralleled the accomplishments of the movement during the same period.[13]

Although jazz was often positioned as the musical linchpin of Black Power liberation, such transformations occurred in pop music as well. During the late 1960s and early 1970s, the demands of activists and artists led to an increased willingness of record companies (including a growing number of black-controlled labels) to release material that was consciously linked to Black Power. One way to trace this is through the rise of funk, which rose to prominence in the early 1970s as a Black Power link between the musical roots of soul music and the new possibilities pioneered in jazz. Funk was primarily defined by rhythm, and the music amplified the strength and depth of the beat. But the opportunity offered by funk extended to a variety of new possibilities, including extended song length, less reliance on standard song forms, and the incorporation of Afro-diasporic musical influences that created a musical palette that matched the expansive thematic visions offered by funk artists. Although it could be brooding or even cynical, funk was primarily about the sonic celebration of blackness. The musical assertions amplified the political messages in anthems such as James Brown's 1968 "Say It Loud (I'm Black and I'm Proud)," where the piercing, pulsing rhythms of the band and Brown's vocals complement lyrics that call for political and economic liberation and introduce listeners to nearly every plank of the Black Power platform. Funk's celebrations also allowed for new visions of black life, such as Parliament-Funkadelic's discussions of black-controlled worlds in outer space or in the "Chocolate City" (title of a 1975 song) triggered by "white flight" abandonment but built by Black Power. And funk created space for a new level of openness and frankness, about everything from black female sexuality to what the Isley Brothers called "the bullshit going down" in their anthem "Fight the Power" (whose title and tone were later remixed by hip-hop artist Public Enemy in 1989).

Despite the Isleys' directness in "Fight the Power," their songs—and others from the funk era—reveal that (as with other genres) the changes play out in music as in lyrics. One of the best ways to think about this is to trace songs by artists whose careers began in 1960s soul but who turned to funk in the early 1970s. The aforementioned Isley Brothers began in the early 1960s as a Motown group whose joyous, gospel-inflected party music (including the original versions of "Shout!" and "Twist and Shout") reflected the early promise of the 1960s movement.[14] By the 1970s, the Isleys had updated their sound (recording longer, funkier, and more intricate material) and their look (with the tailored suits of the early days replaced by hats, capes, and African-inspired designs) for the Black Power age. Such work serves a particularly important goal in illuminating the continuities between the early civil rights years and the later Black Power era; although these are sometimes presented in stark divide, the music of the Isleys and others reveal their similarities.

Another key artist in this regard is Aretha Franklin. Franklin's career extends from gospel and "freedom songs" in the late 1950s to pop and jazz crossovers in the early 1960s to becoming the "Queen of Soul" in the Black Power years. Franklin's music and iconography offer very helpful avenues to trace the new possibilities for black artists in the civil rights and Black Power years. (Even a nonmusical demonstration of the transformation of Franklin's look from straightened hair and makeup in the early 1960s to Afros and dashikis in the early 1970s provides a vivid illustration.) Comparing the sound of Franklin's earliest recordings (many of which are rooted in the pop and jazz of the previous decade) with the celebratory funk and soul of her biggest hits suggests a larger transformation. This is not to suggest that the earlier music is worse or somehow less "real"; such misstatements must be resisted to avoid presenting false narratives of authenticity or declension in the music and the movement.[15] But tracking the differences can be very fruitful to think through with students in the context of other discussions of the continuities and changes that defined the 1960s and 1970s.

Such musical comparisons also reveal differences between versions of the same lyrical material. For example, Otis Redding's original version of "Respect" offers a pleading (and male) take on a song that—when performed later by Aretha Franklin—is reborn as an assertive anthem for black women. These changes are *not* lyrical, since (with a few minor changes) Franklin and Redding sing the same words. But the musical differences offer a means of understanding how Franklin's recording sounded a clarion call not only for a new era of Black Power, but specifically for the assertion of a black feminist consciousness. The two versions of "Respect" thus become a simple and effective lesson in charting both the continuity of women's participation in the movement and a growing demand that such participation be acknowledged and respected.

As crucial as it is to engage with songs and recordings as historical texts, it is also important to remember that no music exists outside of the contexts of its creation and consumption. Getting away from the particularities of musical texts actually offers some of the most important demonstrations of its political power. A discussion of recording studios reveals crucial questions about the possibilities and limitations of integration, particularly in famous stories such as Stax in Memphis or Motown in Detroit. Additionally, radio stations, record stores, and concert venues became the sites of literal and figurative battles over segregation and representation, from the attack on Nat King Cole in Birmingham in 1956 to James Brown's famous performance in Boston after Dr. King's assassination. And music's presence or absence animated its own set of protests, whether from soldiers in Vietnam (who clashed over the presence or absence of soul and jazz records on their military bases) or musicians themselves, who organized in the late 1960s to demand that Black Power's economic and social assertions be extended to the leadership and activities of record companies. In order to get to these questions, it is crucial to incorporate musical spaces into the analysis of civil rights sites, to consider musicians and listeners as

political actors, and to think about how these stories confirm or complicate our understandings of the larger battles for access and representation. What makes musical spaces similar or different to lunch counters,
schools, or other obvious sites of civil rights struggle? What does musical activism look like? What were the possibilities and limitations of
music as a liberatory enterprise?

Music was a crucial space of movement activity, whether through
the assertions of artists and fans, or the broader discourse created by
the sounds, lyrics, and spaces through which it traveled. At times, it
was a hopeful vision of a "land of 1000 dances" (to borrow the title of a
Wilson Pickett soul hit) that married the movement's highest aims with
its persistence and energy. Other times it noted the ambivalence of
movement activities and ideologies, particularly as the 1960s pro-
gressed, and a new set of internal and external challenges exposed deep
wounds within its political coalition and social fabric. These trends and
debates existed throughout the music of the period, even in songs that
have nothing obviously to do with the civil rights movement or American politics.

They also extend forward to music created after the civil rights era,
particularly in hip-hop and other genres that (sometimes literally) sample and remix the music of the past for a new set of political and social
conditions. By the late 1970s, the sounds and energies of the music—
like the movement—had developed into a new musical genre and cultural movement, hip-hop, that built many of its recordings on the music
of the 1960s and 1970s and remixed the desires and strategies of the
movement era into a new set of political and social contexts. Even into
the present, when #BlackLivesMatter marchers sing Kendrick Lamar's
"Alright" and new-era feminists rally around Beyonce's call to "Formation," the musical groundwork of the civil rights period—like the organizing traditions and social assertions that defined the movement's
politics—continue to hold great resonance and offer important opportunities to connect to students whose lives and times have their own
playlists that offer rich additions to the historical call and response. So
keep listening.

Assignment Ideas

- Compare several musical responses—from multiple genres—on
  the same movement event or theme. For example, responses to the

16th Street Baptist Church bombing in Birmingham, Alabama, by Joan Baez, John Coltrane, and Phil Ochs.

- Write an essay discussing an important topic in civil rights history using *only* musical sources as texts.
- Trace a particular artist's responses to the movement over the course of their career and contextualize within the larger story. Potential artists could include Miles Davis, Bob Dylan, Aretha Franklin, The Isley Brothers, Nina Simone, and Sly and the Family Stone.
- Look for discussions of music in movement memoirs. How do the authors present their relationship to music? What kinds of music do they discuss? Potential memoirs could include Melba Pattillo Beals's *Warriors Don't Cry*; Elaine Brown's *A Taste of Power*; John Lewis's *Walking with the Wind*; Anne Moody's *Coming of Age in Mississippi*; or Assata Shakur's *Assata*.
- Create a "visual history" of movement music that does *not* include sound. While this seems counterintuitive, a focus on how iconography and imagery changed or varied during the civil rights era provides an important glimpse into many of the same issues. This can be framed chronologically (tracing the story of movement music over a period of years) or as a "snapshot" of a particular year or campaign.
- Conduct oral histories with musicians, movement activists, and listeners about the music of the era, how it affected them, and—if relevant—their experiences in creating it.
- Trace contemporary music that harkens back (directly or indirectly) to the civil rights and Black Power era. There are many artists and songs that refer to movement activities (particularly in today's #BlackLivesMatter context) and also to the music of the civil rights era. Explore how this worked, using historical analysis as a basis.

SUGGESTED READINGS

Beals, Melba Pattillo. *Warriors Don't Cry*. New York: Pocket Books, 1994.

Berry, Chuck. *Chuck Berry: The Autobiography*. New York: Harmony Books, 1987.

Brown, Elaine. *A Taste of Power: A Black Woman's Story*. New York: Doubleday, 1992.

Chang, Jeff. *Can't Stop Won't Stop: A History of the Hip-Hop Generation*. New York: St. Martin's Press, 2005.

220

Estes, Steve. *I Am a Man! Race, Manhood, and the Civil Rights Movement*. Chapel Hill: University of North Carolina Press, 2006.

Feldstein, Ruth. *How It Feels to Be Free: Black Women Entertainers and the Civil Rights Movement*. New York: Oxford University Press, 2013.

Hughes, Charles L. *Country Soul: Making Music and Making Race in the American South*. Chapel Hill: University of North Carolina Press, 2015.

Kelley, Robin D. G. *Africa Speaks, America Answers: Modern Jazz in Revolutionary Times*. Cambridge, MA: Harvard University Press, 2012.

Kelley, Robin D.G. "'We Are Not What We Seem': Rethinking Black Working-Class Opposition in the Jim Crow South." *Journal of American History* 80, no. 1 (1993): 75–112.

Kot, Greg. *I'll Take You There: Mavis Staples, the Staple Singers, and the March up Freedom's Highway*. New York: Scribner, 2014.

Lewis, John. *Walking with the Wind: A Memoir of the Movement*. New York: Simon & Schuster, 1998.

Lordi, Emily J. *Black Resonance: Iconic Women Singers and African American Literature*. New Brunswick, NJ: Rutgers University Press, 2013.

Monson, Ingrid. *Freedom Sounds: Civil Rights Call Out to Jazz and Africa*. New York: Oxford University Press, 2012.

Moody, Anne. *Coming of Age in Mississippi*. New York: Random House, 1968.

Ramsay, Guthrie. *Race Music: Black Cultures from Bebop to Hip-Hop*. Berkeley: University of California Press, 2005.

Redmond, Shana L. *Anthem: Social Movements and the Sound of Solidarity in the African Diaspora*. New York: New York University Press, 2014.

Shakur, Assata. *Assata: An Autobiography*. London, Zed Books, 1988.

Smith, Suzanne E. *Dancing in the Street: Motown and the Cultural Politics of Detroit*. Cambridge, MA: Harvard University Press, 2003.

Thomas, Pat. *Listen Whitey! The Sounds of Black Power, 1965–1975*. Seattle, WA: Fantagraphics Books, 2012.

Vincent, Rickey. *Party Music: The Inside Story of the Black Panthers' Band and How Black Power Transformed Soul Music*. Chicago: Chicago Review Press, 2013.

Ward, Brian. *Just My Soul Responding: Rhythm and Blues, Black Consciousness, and Race Relations*. Berkeley: University of California Press, 1998.

Weisbard, Eric. *Top 40 Democracy: The Rival Mainstreams of American Music*. Chicago: University of Chicago Press, 2014.

Werner, Craig. *A Change Is Gonna Come: Music, Race and the Soul of America*. 2nd ed. Ann Arbor: University of Michigan Press, 2006.

Werner, Craig. *Higher Ground: Aretha Franklin, Stevie Wonder, Curtis Mayfield, and the Rise and Fall of American Soul*. New York: Crown Books, 2004.

Wolff, Daniel. *You Send Me: The Life and Times of Sam Cooke*. New York: William Morrow, 1995.

NOTES

1. Werner, *A Change Is Gonna Come*, 12, 14. Werner's book is the single most influential text on my understandings of music in the movement—it offers crucial concepts and numerous specific examples.

2. Two of the best collections were released by Smithsonian/Folkways and are readily available: the compilation *Voices of the Civil Rights Movement: Black American Freedom Songs, 1960–1966*, which features numerous recordings made live at mass meetings and other rallies, and the album *Songs My Mother Taught Me* by activist Fannie Lou Hamer, which includes numerous gospel and work songs that inspired Hamer's activism.

3. A particularly fascinating subset of the civil rights movement music is that recorded by activists themselves, including members of the Black Panther Party and other groups. For more information on this, see Thomas, *Listen Whitey!* and Vincent, *Party Music.*

4. It is perhaps no surprise that when introducing the Voting Rights Act of 1965, President Lyndon Johnson invoked "We Shall Overcome" in his address to Congress.

5. For discussions of this process, see Werner, *Higher Ground*, and Kot, *I'll Take You There.*

6. A particularly important and somewhat unsettling story concerns the origins of "We Shall Overcome" in the activism of black female workers in Charleston, South Carolina. Told by Shana Redmond in *Anthem*, the story of the song's journey from the shop floor to an international audience reveals a story that offers important complication to the aspirations of the folk revival and the utopianism of many chroniclers of the early civil rights movement.

7. With Cooke, the aspirational "Wonderful World" or the work song "Chain Gang" are but two examples. For more on Cooke's life and career, see Wolff, *You Send Me*. Werner mentions "Wonderful World," Cooke, and the larger practice of R&B masking in *A Change Is Gonna Come*, 36–37.

8. Berry describes this creative process in his autobiography, a helpful resource when talking about the artist and his contexts. See Berry, *Chuck Berry: The Autobiography.*

9. For a nonmusical discussion of this, see Estes, *I Am a Man!*

10. See Smith, *Dancing in the Street.*

11. One helpful theoretical formulation that could be utilized here is Robin D. G. Kelley's suggestion of movement "infrapolitics," developed from James C. Scott, political activism that exists outside (or beneath) that which is understood as politics but which nonetheless possesses important effects within the fight for equality. Kelley articulates these ideas in his 1997 article "'We Are Not What We Seem.'"

12. See Feldstein, *How It Feels to Be Free.*

13. See Kelley, *Africa Speaks, America Answers*.

14. For a particularly good discussion of the Isleys, see Weisbard, *Top 40 Democracy*.

15. For deft deconstructions of this simplification, see Feldstein, *How It Feels to Be Free*, and Lordi, *Black Resonance*.

Two Thumbs Up

Movies and Documentaries to Use
(and Avoid) When Teaching Civil Rights

Hasan Kwame Jeffries

ocumentaries and movies are highly effective tools for teaching civil rights history. They make the movement come alive, breathing life into the nameless and faceless masses who mobilized and organized for change. People are generally aware of Rosa Parks's role in the Montgomery bus boycott but are wholly unaware of the thousands of black domestic workers who made victory possible by refusing to ride the buses for an entire year. Films add depth and dimension to the famous leaders who spearheaded the struggle, such as Martin Luther King Jr. Everyone knows who Dr. King is, but too few know him beyond sound bites from his "I Have a Dream" speech. And films generate empathy by capturing and conveying deep emotion, such as the paralyzing fear brought about by night riders. It is one thing to read about racial terror; it is another thing entirely to see it in high definition.

The pedagogical power of film is strengthened when documentaries and movies are paired with one another. The lessons learned in the former are reinforced in the latter. Pairing films also sharpens critical analysis of popular narratives of the movement. People are conditioned to believe what they see on screen. Pairing films challenges this basic assumption when what appears in a documentary, such as the presence of black women in leadership positions, fails to show up in a movie.

An explosion of films on civil rights history over the last twenty-five years has created abundant options for using film in the classroom. Scores of documentaries have been produced, touching on subjects ranging from the origins of the movement to its aftermath. Although fewer movies have been produced, and their subject matter has been less varied, the selection is still strong.

Of course, not all films are equal. There are good ones that get the basic history correct and great ones that totally disrupt the Master Narrative. There are also terrible ones that reinforce the Master Narrative, and God-awful ones that simply fabricate history. Yet nearly all of them are useful, with the best ones revealing the truth about the past, and the worst ones exposing entrenched falsehoods. Thus, films about the movement, from the exceptional to the dreadful, that examine a broad cross section of subjects, from the origins of racism to contemporary civil rights struggles, can significantly deepen understanding of civil rights history.

Racism has shaped the contours of America from the earliest days of the Republic, fueling the need for a civil rights movement. *Race: The Power of an Illusion* (2003) is a great primer for discussing the role of racism in American society. The three-hour documentary begins by explaining race as a pseudoscientific invention designed to justify European capitalist exploitation of African labor. It then pivots toward racism, moving quickly beyond personal prejudice to look at the racialization of political structures and economic systems. Finally, it looks specifically at the racialization of the housing market to illustrate the harmful effect racial discrimination has had on contemporary African Americans.

I Am Not Your Negro (2017) explores racism in a completely different way, from the perspective of civil rights–era essayist James Baldwin. But it is equally effective as a springboard for an opening discussion on the need for a civil rights revolution. Using Baldwin's searing words, the documentary draws viewers in, making the pain of the black past feel present. For some, Baldwin's indictment of white Americans for their commitment to white supremacy will confirm long-held suspicions. For others, it will be a revelation. But for all, it will prompt deep introspection, a necessary ingredient for frank and honest conversation.

Civil rights protest challenged contemporaneous patterns and practices of racial discrimination. For much of the twentieth century, this meant taking on Jim Crow. *The Rise and Fall of Jim Crow* (2002) provides a thorough overview of Jim Crow and the black response to it. The four-hour documentary explores the history of segregation from emancipation through World War II, chronicling both its formal and informal manifestations in the South and beyond. The second and third episodes, which examine the black experience from *Plessy v. Ferguson* in 1896 through the start of the NAACP's school desegregation campaign in the 1930s, is particularly useful for establishing the movement's precursors and preconditions.

Dramatizations of black life during the era of legal segregation help make clear that Jim Crow was much more than just a bundle of unfair laws. *Mudbound* (2017) explores personal interactions across and on either side of the color line in the Mississippi Delta during World War II. The film's gaze is intimate, providing a close look at the racialized customs that simultaneously separated and tied together black tenant farmers and white landowners, showing how Jim Crow linked black fates to white fortunes. *The Great Debaters* (2007) chronicles the trials and triumphs of the debate team at Wiley College, a historically black college in Marshall, Texas, during the Depression. One scene in particular, "The Pig Farmer," effectively re-creates the kind of life-threatening, random encounters that African Americans often had with whites and is worthy of showing on its own. *Something the Lord Made* (2004), the story of pioneer heart surgeon Vivien Thomas, explores the less dramatic, daily indignities of segregation, rendering unmistakable the ways that Jim Crow customs, as practiced by both individuals and institutions, stifled human potential at great cost to society. The movie parallels the documentary *Partners of the Heart* (2002) but is far more emotionally engaging.

Two films set in the Jim Crow era that are inspiring tales of persistence and perseverance but are far less useful as overviews of the period are *Hidden Figures* (2016) and *Loving* (2016). Although both films treat their subjects thoughtfully and compassionately, and each has the added benefit of revolving around black women, which too few films do, neither provides a clear enough sense of the scale and scope of segregation to effectively convey the intractable nature of Jim Crow. Another film set in the Jim Crow era that is of no use at all is *The Help* (2011). The movie fixates on normalizing white privilege and black subservience and completely marginalizes the Mississippi freedom movement.

Violence was the cornerstone of Jim Crow. Whites resorted to it to regulate black behavior, control black labor, and steal black wealth. The documentary *Banished: How Whites Drove Blacks out of Town in America* (2006) examines three incidents of early twentieth-century racial violence that resulted in black landowners losing their lives and property. It also shows how the land grab impeded black economic upward mobility for generations. *An Outrage* (2017) takes a personal look at lynching through the eyes of its victims and their descendants. It is a hauntingly moving portrayal of Jim Crow's strange fruit.

The kind of mob violence that led to lynching can be hard to fathom, but *Rosewood* (1997), which depicts the 1923 racial pogrom in the all-black town of Rosewood, Florida, reveals the mechanics of lynch mobs, including the rapidity with which they formed, and captures the unspeakable horror of their murderous rampages.

White sheriffs rarely protected the targets of racial violence, and white judges and juries almost never provided justice to victims. Instead, they worked to uphold Jim Crow laws and enforce Jim Crow customs. Few cases illustrate this better than that of the Scottsboro Boys. *Scottsboro: An American Tragedy* (2000) recounts the conviction of nine innocent black teenagers accused of raping two white women in Alabama in 1931. *Slavery by Another Name* (2012) takes a broader look at the justice system under Jim Crow by detailing the ways white southerners used convict leasing to reestablish and maintain white supremacy after Reconstruction. It is a harrowing account of brutal capitalist excess.

A southern prison labor camp, not unlike Mississippi's infamous Parchman Prison Farm, is the backdrop for *Life* (1999), a comedy featuring Eddie Murphy and Martin Lawrence as two would-be bootleggers sentenced to life in prison for a murder they did not commit. The film touches on many of the themes discussed in *Slavery by Another Name*, including judicial malfeasance, creating the opportunity for critical analysis of popular representations and misrepresentations of segregation.

Depicting black suffering during the Jim Crow era makes clear why African Americans were so desperate for change. Highlighting black organizing during the same period is just as important because it demonstrates African Americans' refusal to accept the status quo. *Birth of a Movement: The Battle against America's First Blockbuster* (2017) describes the effort led by William Monroe Trotter, a Boston-based activist and

The Birth of a Movement: The Battle against America's First Blockbuster (courtesy of Northern Light Productions)

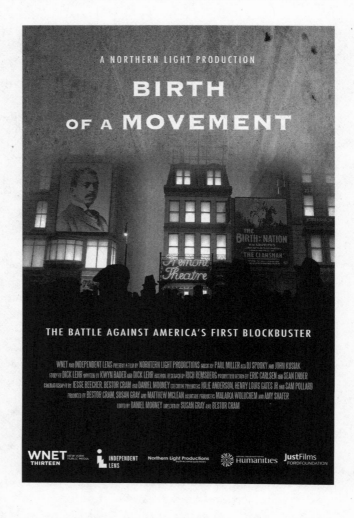

newspaper editor, to ban D. W. Griffith's white supremacist propaganda film *Birth of a Nation*. *Marcus Garvey: Look for Me in the Whirlwind* (2000) examines the life of the Jamaican-born activist, who through the Universal Negro Improvement Association (UNIA) and its newspaper, the *Negro World*, spread the gospel of black nationalism and Pan-Africanism. Much like these documentaries, *10,000 Black Men Named George* (2002), a fictionalized account of civil rights activist A. Philip Randolph's effort to organize the Brotherhood of Sleeping Car Porters in the 1920s, introduces viewers to a grassroots campaign that not only challenged Jim Crow but also helped create the organizing infrastructure that enabled the civil rights movement to flourish years later.

World War II looms large in civil rights history. "Deadly Calling," the third episode of *The War* (2007), provides a useful overview of the black wartime experience at home and abroad, albeit interspersed between stories of military developments overseas. *The Black Press: Soldiers without Swords* (1999) probes much deeper by tracking the unheralded effort of black journalists to advance democracy for black soldiers on the frontlines and for black citizens on the home front. *In Their Own Words: The Tuskegee Airmen* (2012) uses oral history to zero in on the civil rights hardships and military heroism of black flyers. By contrast, the major motion picture *Red Tails* (2012) omits the airmen's fight against racial discrimination on US soil before, during, and after their time in the army. An egregious oversight, it nonetheless creates an opportunity to use the film to interrogate the idea that black military service and sacrifice were enough to rid whites of racial prejudice.

When northern black servicemen and servicewomen who had been stationed in the South returned home, they were unable to escape racial discrimination. Like the waves of black southerners who had left the region during the war years, they could not outrun white supremacy. To be sure, a different kind of Jim Crow reigned up north, but it was still Jim Crow. Neither New York nor Cleveland nor Oakland turned out to be the fabled Promised Land.

Goin' to Chicago (1994) demystifies northern Jim Crow by examining the lives of a group of older black Chicagoans who migrated from the Mississippi Delta. A common experience in nearly all of their personal stories is housing discrimination. *The Pruitt-Igoe Myth* (2011), which explores the creation and collapse of a massive public housing complex in St. Louis, masterfully unpacks housing discrimination, including the central role played by the state and federal governments. The movie *Fences* (2016) is the perfect complement to these documentaries. Set in Pittsburgh, it shows how working-class African Americans tried to get the most out of life despite the constant pressure of racial discrimination. Sports animated the protagonist in *Fences*, Troy Maxson, like nothing else in life. Baseball in particular was his salvation and refuge, and to hear him tell it, he was spectacular. But sports did not unburden him of the weight of racism, just as it did not relieve those in the real world who either toiled in segregated black leagues or broke into white professional leagues. Their struggle provides a window through which to view not only the intersection of race and sports but also Jim Crow America, especially in the North.

Unforgivable Blackness: The Rise and Fall of Jack Johnson (2004) chronicles the first black heavyweight boxing champion's brazen exploits in and out of the ring during the first part of the twentieth century. *Jesse Owens* (2012) follows the journey of the 1936 Olympic gold medalist in track and field from Cleveland to Berlin, highlighting the many obstacles Jim Crow placed before him. *Olympic Pride—American Prejudice* (2016) pushes beyond the Owens narrative to share the experiences of the seventeen black athletes, including two black women, who joined Owens on the 1936 US Olympic team. *Only the Ball Was White* (1980) provides an excellent overview of the Negro Leagues, a key example of a black parallel institution. "Shadow Ball," the fifth "Inning" of *Baseball* (1994), also explores the Negro Leagues and its star players but in greater depth. *Jackie Robinson* (2016) offers a detailed glimpse of the on-the-field achievements and off-the-field civil rights advocacy of the Brooklyn Dodgers' legend. *Black Magic* (2008) looks at the history of basketball at historically black colleges and universities and the impact desegregation had on the sport, black athletes, and black coaches, while *Breaking the Huddle: The Integration of College Football* (2008) does the same for football. And *Muhammad Ali: Through the Eyes of the World* (2001) tells of the far-reaching impact that the boxing great's stand against white supremacy and opposition to the Vietnam War had on people.

Sports movies abound, making it possible to pair nearly all of these documentaries with direct cinematic counterparts. *Race* (2016), *42* (2013), and *Ali* (2001) are biopics about Jesse Owens, Jackie Robinson, and Muhammad Ali, while *Glory Road* (2006) and *Remember the Titans* (2000) revolve around the integration of college basketball and high school football. But every one of these films treat civil rights more or less the same—racism is reduced to personal prejudice practiced by a handful of rednecks; it is overcome by black athletes through nonviolent perseverance; and it is rejected by whites once they witness African American athletes performing at a high level. The usefulness of these films, then, is mainly as prompts for analyzing the shortcomings of normative narratives of the persistence and eventual demise of Jim Crow.

Much like movies on race and sports during the Jim Crow era, movies specifically about the civil rights movement tend to follow the Master Narrative, with storylines revolving around preachers and presidents and a heavy emphasis on nonviolence. Documentaries about the movement, however, are generally much better, shifting the focus away from great men and broadening the range of strategies and tactics beyond nonviolence.

Eyes on the Prize remains the gold standard for documentaries on the civil rights movement. Its fourteen hour-long episodes draw on a rich array of primary source material, including original broadcast news footage and interviews with movement leaders and foot soldiers, to weave together an accessible overview of the movement. It is not, however, without shortcomings. At times it is overly event and leader driven, especially its early episodes, causing the complexity of the movement, including its geographic diversity, to be lost. The pacing is also a bit slow for today's younger viewers, who have grown up watching films with more visual activity. It is best used, then, selectively, in segments, as an introduction to key events and people.

By contrast, *Soundtrack for a Revolution* (2009), which tells the story of the movement through freedom songs, pulsates with energy. Civil rights music inspired, encouraged, and energized movement participants, who are called on here to explain their purpose and importance. Although contemporary artists, such as John Legend, perform the songs, the arrangements are traditional. Unfortunately, so too is the narrative arc. The film adheres too closely to the Montgomery to Memphis framework, privileging the experiences of Dr. King above all else.

Lee Daniels's *The Butler* (2013), whose lead character, Cecil Gaines, serves as a valet to eight US presidents, is one of a small handful of movies that attempt to engage the entire history of the civil rights movement. Not surprisingly, its take on the movement is conventional, emphasizing decisions made in the Oval Office over those made at mass meetings. Indeed, the movement does not even seem to exist until Gaines arrives at the White House, and it loses steam completely when Black Power emerges. In this sense, it is a classic depiction of the Master Narrative and should only be shown as such. At the same time, the film re-creates a few pivotal movement moments that are almost always ignored on screen, most notably the nonviolent direct action workshops led by Rev. James Lawson in Nashville, Tennessee, in 1959.

Most treatments of the civil rights movement are far less ambitious than *Eyes*, *Soundtrack*, or *The Butler*. Rather than tackling the subject as a whole, they focus instead on a specific event, historical figure, or both. Beginning with school desegregation, *The Road to Brown* (1990) traces the history of the NAACP's southern school desegregation campaign, which culminated in the US Supreme Court's landmark ruling in *Brown v. Board of Education*. The film introduces Charles Hamilton Houston, the architect of the NAACP's strategy, and shines a light on the segregated communities involved in the cases. *Mr. Civil Rights: Thurgood Marshall and the NAACP* (2014) recounts the NAACP's long legal battle to desegregate southern schools that Marshall, a protégé of Houston, helped lead. The biopic *Marshall* (2017) dances around the edges of this history, choosing instead to focus on Marshall's early courtroom activism outside the South. Laurence Fishburne's one-person play, *Thurgood* (2011), however, fits perfectly with these documentaries. It is unusually comprehensive in its coverage of the courtroom challenge, and Fishburne's performance is masterful. In fact, *Thurgood* is strong enough historically and theatrically to be shown on its own.

It is well established that the civil rights movement did not begin with *Brown*, but the Supreme Court ruling, along with the murder of Emmett Till and the start of the Montgomery bus boycott one year later, are critically important to the movement's evolution. Together, they mobilized new constituencies and created new possibilities for pursuing change.

The Murder of Emmett Till (2003) details the events surrounding the lynching of the fourteen-year-old Chicago boy at the hands of two white men in Money, Mississippi, making direct connections to the Great Migration and rabid white resistance to *Brown*. The filmmaker's interview with Mamie Till, young Emmett's mother, in which she describes the impact of her son's murder, is particularly powerful. "Awakenings, 1954–1956," the first episode of *Eyes on the Prize*, discusses the death of Till and the emergence of the Montgomery bus boycott, showing how their combined force pushed the movement in a new direction. The movie *Boycott* (2001), which is based on historian Stewart Burns's edited collection of oral histories with movement participants, stands out as the best film or documentary on the Montgomery protest. It makes clear the mechanics of the movement, depicts the central role of women, and portrays King as he was—a reluctant leader struggling to catch up to his people.

Returning to school desegregation, the crisis in Little Rock, Arkansas, in 1957 is explained succinctly in "Fighting Back, 1957–1962," the second episode of *Eyes on the Prize*. This segment nicely sets up *Nine from Little Rock: Pioneers of Desegregation* (1964). This documentary short, filmed seven years after the highpoint of the conflict, profiles the lives of the nine black students who desegregated Central High School. *Little Rock Central: 50 Years Later* (2007) shares the perspectives of students and community members five decades removed from the crisis, creating an opportunity to discuss school segregation and desegregation in a contemporary context.

The Little Rock Nine were the vanguard of southern student protest, which exploded into full public view with unimaginable energy in February 1960 with the lunch counter sit-ins. *A Force More Powerful* (1999), which examines a half-dozen, nonviolent, direct action campaigns across the globe during the twentieth century, draws on rare archival footage to take viewers inside the Nashville sit-in movement, revealing the practicalities of a nonviolent campaign. Meanwhile, *Fundi: The Story of Ella Baker* (1981) introduces viewers to veteran activist Ella Baker, the guiding force behind the Student Nonviolent Coordinating Committee (SNCC). Baker infused SNCC with a commitment to grassroots democratic organizing, enabling the organization to catapult the movement forward in the early 1960s.

Some of the tough decisions that SNCC activists had to make are beautifully dramatized in *Freedom Song* (2000), a fictionalized account of a SNCC direct action and voter registration campaign. Rather than focusing on a single, large-scale, mobilizing event, *Freedom Song* hones in on the slow, hard work of organizing, making grassroots activism visible, a rarity in movies. *Freedom Song* also touches directly on the Freedom Rides, making it a terrific companion for *Freedom Riders* (2011), which tells the story of the more than four hundred African American and white activists who traveled to the South in 1961 to challenge segregation in interstate travel.

Young people remained at the forefront of the struggle in 1963. In Birmingham, Alabama, they forced white elected officials and business leaders to desegregate downtown by taking to the streets and filling the city's jails. *Mighty Times: The Children's March* (2004) documents their courage and heroism. There was, however, a steep price to be paid, and four young people paid it with their lives when Klansmen bombed Birmingham's 16th Street Baptist Church. *4 Little Girls* (1997) revisits that horrible moment, recalling the lives lost and explaining the far-reaching and long-lasting impact of their deaths.

The next year, in St. Augustine, Florida, young people conducted wade-ins at beaches and a swim-in at a hotel pool to desegregate

Mighty Times: The Children's March (courtesy of the Southern Poverty Law Center)

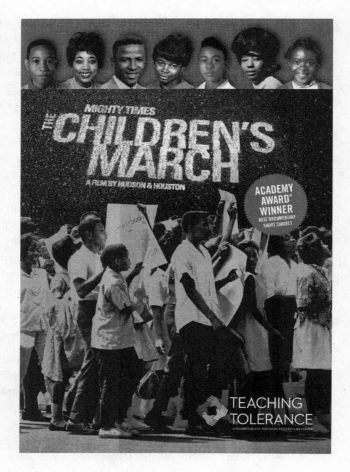

America's oldest city. Often overlooked, the struggle in "Florida's Birmingham" drew national attention to the brutality that undergirded Jim Crow, helping to bring about the Civil Rights Act of 1964. *Dare Not Walk Alone* (2008) places St. Augustine back in the national narrative, connecting the actions of local people with those of Martin Luther King Jr. and President Lyndon B. Johnson. But only the first half of the eighty-minute documentary examines the movement in 1964. The second half looks at local black life nearly fifty years later, pointing out the underlying reasons for the persistence of poverty, rising incarceration rates, and failing schools. A sobering reminder of the movement's limits, this part of the film creates an opportunity to reflect on the long-term impact of the fight for civil rights.

Whereas St. Augustine has been underemphasized, Freedom Summer has been overemphasized, owing to the participation of large numbers of northern white students who joined the effort to break segregationists' stranglehold on Mississippi. *Freedom Summer* (2014) chronicles the events of those intense months, from the formation of freedom schools to the Mississippi Freedom Democratic Party's Atlantic City challenge. *Freedom on My Mind* (1994) covers the same subject but looks more closely at the years leading up to 1964, providing a much better sense of the Mississippi movement's evolution. The experiences of one white activist are the subject of *An Ordinary Hero: The True Story of Joan Trumpauer Mulholland* (2013), creating space for dialogue about the role of whites in the movement.

The flipside of white participation in the freedom struggle—white opposition to it—is covered in *Spies of Mississippi* (2014), which examines the state of Mississippi's use of intelligence gathering, economic coercion, political intimidation, and murder to thwart the freedom struggle. *Neshoba: The Price of Freedom* (2011) turns a spotlight on organized racial terror groups by looking at the infamous murder of three civil rights workers by Klansmen at the start of Freedom Summer.

More movies have been made about civil rights in Mississippi than have been made about any other civil rights topic, but with the notable exception of *Freedom Song*, none are especially good, and a few are just plain bad. Of the latter, *Mississippi Burning* (1988), possibly the most watched civil rights film of all time, tops the list, having managed to make the movement's success hinge totally on the wit and wisdom of white FBI agents. It is worth showing only to interrogate a fabrication of movement history.

Selma (2015) is everything that *Mississippi Burning* is not. It centers African Americans—they are the primary shapers of their own destiny, and it portrays the FBI with much greater accuracy, as more adversary than ally. These reasons alone make it worth watching. But as a depiction of the 1965 Selma voting rights campaign, it is not without flaws. Local Alabama activists take a backseat to national leaders, and advocates of self-defense, especially within SNCC, are depicted as overly emotional and irrational. This is not totally unexpected because the movie is actually a biopic, a portrayal of Dr. King revolving around his civil rights leadership and nonviolent approach to change. As such, it works well with the documentaries *Citizen King* (2005) and *King in the Wilderness* (2018), which examine the final years of King's life; *The March* (2013), which goes behind the scenes of the 1963 March on Washington for Jobs and Freedom; and *At the River I Stand* (1993), a chronicle of King's time with striking Memphis sanitation workers shortly before his death. It also pairs nicely with *King: A Filmed Record . . . Montgomery to Memphis* (1970), which pulls together rare footage of King delivering some of his most important speeches, including "I Have A Dream."

As seen in *Selma*, King's outsized presence in civil rights narratives obscures key elements of the freedom struggle, chief among these being self-defense. *Negroes with Guns: Rob Williams and Black Power* (2004) addresses this oversight by sharing the story of Williams's armed defense of the black community in Monroe, North Carolina, and full-throated advocacy of self-defense via the radio waves. *Deacons for Defense* (2003), a fictionalized account of the Deacons for Defense and Justice, the armed self-defense group founded in Jonesboro, Louisiana, in 1964 to protect local movement participants, including nonviolent activists, complements *Negroes with Guns* perfectly. The story of the Deacons, which is ably captured here, demonstrates the ways armed self-defense could make nonviolent direct action possible and compel reluctant federal officials to act on behalf of African Americans.

But it is neither the Deacons nor Rob Williams who come most immediately to mind when thinking about African Americans and armed self-defense, but rather Malcolm X. Even in *Selma*, the former spokesperson for the Nation of Islam (NOI) makes a cameo appearance as the foil to King's nonviolence. Malcolm, of course, was much more than a voice of black rage; he was an astute political thinker with a constantly evolving worldview, which comes across clearly in *Malcolm X: Make It Plain* (1994), the most comprehensive documentary on his life. Spike Lee's artful *Malcolm X* (1992) is also a viable option for introducing Malcolm as it cleaves closely to *The Autobiography of Malcolm X*.

Malcolm lived his entire life in the Midwest and the Northeast. Treatments of his life, therefore, can be used to offer insights into the northern freedom struggle. So too can *The Hate That Hate Produced* (1959), a news exposé on the NOI. Although the program frames the group as a black supremacist cult, the interviews with Malcolm, NOI spiritual leader Elijah Muhammad, and NOI members are revelatory in terms of perspectives on racism from black northerners who rejected integration.

236

The view of moderate, mainstream black northerners comes across in two biographies. The first is *Adam Clayton Powell* (1989), which explores the life and politics of the outspoken civil rights activist who represented Harlem in Congress in the 1940s, 1950s, and 1960s. And the second is *The Power Broker: Whitney Young's Fight for Civil Rights* (2012), which delves into the political machinations of the head of the National Urban League.

The sentiments of everyday black northerners trapped in declining, deindustrializing, urban centers are discernible through documentaries on the uprisings of the mid- to late 1960s. *July '64* (2006) offers insights into the thoughts of ordinary African Americans in Rochester, New York, through its exploration of the causes and consequences of the three-day rebellion that took place there in the summer of 1964. *Revolution '67* (2007) does the same for African Americans living in Newark, New Jersey, during that uprising three years later. Both documentaries work with *Detroit* (2017), a severely flawed dramatization of the murder of three African Americans by police at the Algiers Motel during the 1967 Motor City rebellion. The documentaries make visible what is rendered invisible in *Detroit*, most notably the local movement and the institutionalized nature of police terror.

Urban uprisings offer a convenient entry point for discussing the transition from civil rights to Black Power, but jumping immediately from one to the other misses Black Power's southern roots. "Out of the Shadows," the first episode of *Black America since MLK: And Still I Rise* (2016), and "The Time Has Come, 1964–1966," the seventh installment of *Eyes on the Prize*, explain the genesis of Black Power in SNCC's Lowndes County, Alabama, organizing project. The *Black America* episode also introduces the Oakland, California, Black Panther Party for Self Defense (BPP), the most iconic organization of the Black Power era.

The BPP straddles the civil rights and Black Power periods, making it the ideal organization for studying the transition between the eras. *The Black Panthers: Vanguard of the Revolution* (2015) offers a rich and engaging overview of the BPP, although it privileges what was happening at the party's headquarters in Oakland over everything else. The documentary short *Emory Douglas: The Art of the Black Panthers* (2015) provides a succinct, yet revealing, look at the political thinking of party leaders, rank-and-file members, and supporters. And *The Murder of Fred Hampton* (1971) exposes the government's criminal conspiracy to

Black America since MLK: And Still I Rise (courtesy of PBS)

crush the BPP that led to the assassination of Hampton, the Chicago Panthers' bold, brash, and brilliant leader.

The Black Panthers are generally treated harshly in movies. In *Forrest Gump* (1994), and more recently in *The Butler*, they are mocked as gun-toting, wannabe revolutionaries who contributed nothing to the movement other than violence. Scenes from both films are worth showing as examples of gross mischaracterizations in popular portrayals of civil rights and post–civil rights black radicalism. The scene in *Forrest Gump* is especially worth deconstructing because it is the only exposure most students have to the BPP and Black Power.

A notable exception to these kinds of distorted depictions emanating from Hollywood is *Blood Done Sign My Name* (2010), an account of white racial violence and black protest in the small town of Oxford,

North Carolina, in 1970. The film casts Black Power protest as an extension of civil rights activism and treats Black Power advocates as serious
political thinkers. Both of these points are also well made in *Scarred
Justice: The Orangeburg Massacre, 1968* (2008), which examines black
activism at South Carolina State University and investigates the murder
of three students by state troopers. The emphasis on student activism in
both films makes pairing them together work for the purpose of discussing the emergence of Black Power.

"Move On Up," the second episode of *Black America since MLK*,
covers the 1970s, providing a good sense of those areas of black life
where civil rights victories had made a substantial difference and those
areas where radical change was still needed. The final three episodes of
Eyes on the Prize do similar work, but in a bit more detail. Meanwhile,
The Black Power Mixtape, 1967–1975 (2011), a compilation of interviews
with activists and movement footage shot by Swedish journalists during
the period, offers a narrower kind of overview of the era by analyzing
Black Power ideology as a response to conditions left unaddressed by
the civil rights movement.

Finally, there are several noteworthy documentaries on contemporary topics through which to explore the legacy of the movement. The
development of hip-hop, from the streets of the Bronx to the concert
stages of Europe, is chronicled in *Hip Hop Evolution* (2016). *Letter to the
President* (2005) and *Let It Fall: Los Angeles 1982—1992* (2017) examine
the devastating impact that Reaganomics had on the African American
community, the former through rap music and the latter through the
1992 Los Angeles uprising. The cultural influence and economic exploitation of black athletes at predominantly white universities is the subject
of *The Fab Five* (2011). *OJ Made in America* (2016) ties all of these themes
together into a coherent and compelling narrative of black life from the
1960s through the 1990s by chronicling football legend O.J. Simpson's
phenomenal rise and spectacular fall. The destruction wrought in New
Orleans by decades of discriminatory housing policy and the federal
government's grossly negligent response to Hurricane Katrina is explored in *When the Levees Broke: A Requiem in Four Acts* (2006). *The House
I Live In* (2012) and *The 13th* (2016) offer micro- and macro-level views
of mass incarceration. *The Central Park Five* (2012) and *Every Mother's Son*
(2004) take intimate, deeply personal looks at unconstitutional police
practices and their collateral consequences. And *Whose Streets?* (2017)
tells the story of the Ferguson, Missouri, uprising in 2014, from the

killing of eighteen-year-old Michael Brown by local police to the birth of the Movement for Black Lives, from the point of view of the activists who led it.

There are very few major motion pictures on contemporary civil rights topics as powerful as *Fruitvale Station* (2013), a heart-wrenching dramatization of Oscar Grant III's last day alive. The twenty-two-year-old African American was shot and killed by Bay Area transit police on New Year's Day in 2008. The film is the perfect complement to any of the documentaries on contemporary topics, especially the ones on mass incarceration and policing, including *Whose Streets?*

Documentaries and movies are incredible resources for teaching civil rights history, and never before have so many been available for classroom instruction. The best ones can truly deepen understanding of the movement, but even the worst ones can be used to make clear what the struggle was about. The right documentary, paired with the right movie, can help students wrap their minds around even those aspects of the movement that are the hardest to comprehend.

A Rich Record

*Using Primary Sources to Explore
the Civil Rights Movement*

JOHN B. GARTRELL

The word *archives* has a different connotation for nearly everyone. In many cases, it conjures up a familiar image at the end of the Steven Spielberg blockbuster *Raiders of the Lost Ark*, where the iconic Indiana Jones character is inquiring of a government agent where the recovered biblical relic, the Ark of the Covenant, is being held. The government agent dramatically replies that the ark is in the hands of "top men," and the next scene shows an unlabeled crate being nailed shut and stored in what appears to be an endless warehouse among countless other unlabeled crates.

In a more modern and digital representation, the word *archive* is quite often applied to someone's meticulously curated iTunes music library, complete with burned vinyl, CD, and downloaded albums. This musical archive is no doubt a prized collection of all a person's musical favorites that is constantly at risk with any given software update and launch of a newer, sleeker device.

To some degree, both of the aforementioned examples are a part of what an archive truly is. Archives can often be very large, full of boxes on seemingly endless shelves, but it would be near criminal in the archives profession if none of those boxes had labels! And archives can be full of digital files (music or document files) and personally curated to reflect a creator's taste or collecting preference. The difference, however, is that a traditional archive as an institution is governed by a set of principles to not only save history but to preserve and objectively describe the materials therein, for use by the general public. It is the job of an archives to be able to assist researchers, teachers, and students by providing documentation so history can be told, retold, revised, and reconsidered in perpetuity. With that charge in mind, the archivist assigned to any given collection can be a valuable ally in the exercise of historical exploration. The inherent value in doing primary source/archival research, particularly when it comes to mining the history of the civil rights era, cannot be understated.

For even the most seasoned researcher, archives can frequently be a challenge to navigate. But a few insider tips can be helpful in undertaking the initial foray into archival research. The first thing one should be aware of is whether a particular archive collects civil rights history. Although the civil rights era is often recognized as a relatively old topic in American history from our modern viewpoint, it is still a frontier in the world of archival collecting. This is largely because most archival collections are donated posthumously, and many of the veterans of the movement are still alive today. An archive in a particular region simply may not have civil rights materials because of this, so it is always a good idea to reach out to an archivist before starting research to see whether there are materials related to civil rights in a given collection.

The second thing one should be aware of is that archives have varied collecting missions and purposes. A key example of this is the difference between an archive at a local/regional library or historical society, a municipal or state archive, and an archive at a research college or university. In the case of a local/regional library or historical society, the collections are typically reflective of the community surrounding the institution. Occasionally, there were forward-thinking archivists or librarians who began collecting these materials in the late 1970s and early 1980s because they felt the movement had a great impact locally and needed to be documented, so some archives may have more extensive holdings than others. There is a good chance local newspapers and magazines would be housed in these types of institutions, alongside personal papers and files of community activists and organizers. Municipal and state archives are generally charged with documenting the history of a city or state and are tremendous resources for exploring the legal side of the movement. It is important to remember that each time someone went to jail, or sued to have a school desegregated, or debated changing a law in a city council or state legislature, documents would have been created by the city or state in each of these instances. These repositories are critical to understanding how the government reacted to and through the movement and speak to our collective civic understanding of how our society functions. Finally, a college or university archive is charged with documenting the history of an institution of higher education. The civil rights movement was unquestionably buoyed by the activism of a younger generation of college and university students. Institutions of higher education in the late 1950s, 1960s, and 1970s found themselves in the crosshairs of intergenerational conflict reflective of the change in society at large. Coinciding with the rise of student activism, leaders of the movement frequented college campuses to deliver lectures and speeches to both share and recruit for a given cause. Colleges collecting documents about the activities on campus during this key period of their institution's history are wonderful repositories of information on the movement.

These are just three different categories of archives, and hopefully one can see the importance of what each can contribute to the study of the movement. To be sure, there is overlap in the kinds of collecting interests in these types of repositories. For instance, a state archive may have records from a state university, or a university may have taken interest in collecting the history of the community surrounding the school, but again, there are plenty of options in the kinds of archives one will encounter, and understanding the kind of material they collect is a key step.

After choosing the type of archive in which to perform research (though it is certainly worth it to explore them all), it is important to understand what kind of materials might be at your disposal. The categories of records from this time period (mid-twentieth century) are wide-ranging and dynamic; keep in mind that as technology evolves so too does the historical record. There are, of course, paper records, which include but are not limited to personal letters, staff and organization files, memorandums, court/legal documents, and journals. There are audio and visual materials such as photographs, media and personal videos, phonograph records, audiotapes, drawings and cartoons, and oral histories. There are also ephemeral materials such as posters, bumper stickers, banners, buttons and pins, flyers, and material culture. The archivist is charged with describing all of this in a way that is objective and user-friendly to researchers. It is admittedly a difficult task and one that is constantly being refined. But herein lies another benefit to

Duke University undergraduates exploring primary resources from Duke University's David M. Rubenstein Rare Book and Manuscript Library. (courtesy of John B. Gartrell)

students working with archival materials, the process of performing research to find an archival source that applies to their topic.

Armed with the understanding of the range of archives and categories of materials that they can hold, teachers can settle on the materials that might best be used in the classroom. Visual materials, such as documentary photographs, can be a critical point of entry for students, particularly younger ones. The photographs and even television newsreels of the era provide a literal snapshot moment involving key actors and events from the era. They allow students to put a face to the names of the movement but also provide the opportunity to flesh out how images can impact perception of the movement. Some of the most iconic images of the period still have a visceral effect for the generation that lived through that time. How did *Jet Magazine's* publication of Emmett Till's ravaged body raise the awareness of the dangers of southern violence for northern residents? What impact did the video of the first Selma-to-Montgomery march have in the passing of the 1965 Voting Rights Act? How did television in general bring the realities of the freedom struggle into the American conscience? This foray into visual materials provides for critical conversations in the classroom and can easily be connected to the way we use audio and visual technology to chronicle present-day movements.

Printed media would be another crucial source for critical analysis by students. Before the advent of social media, which has opened new horizons in our present society with the ability to track social movements in real time, newspapers, magazines, and newsletters were the crucial organs, even more so than television, for consuming the ongoing events that took place in the twentieth century. A wonderful exercise for classroom exploration would be comparing and contrasting different kinds of print media. All too often scholars study the movement as if it existed only in the periodic reports of major national publications such as the *New York Times* or *Washington Post*. But archival sources range well beyond these popular titles and provide far more depth to our understanding. Consider having students mine titles of black newspapers such as the *Chicago Defender*, *Afro-American Newspaper*, or *Pittsburgh Courier*. These papers, with large circulation numbers in the North and South, had reporters on the ground long before mainstream media began reporting on the injustices taking place in the Deep South. These media outlets were also critical in connecting migrant African Americans in the North with news from back home about relatives left behind. Publications such as the NAACP's *Crisis* magazine, or SNCC's *Student Voice*, were key in communicating organizational strategies, tactics, and firsthand accounts from the frontlines. The exercise of comparing and contrasting these kinds of sources is eased by the fact that print media generally covered the same story over the duration of the movement. The difference, of course, is the audience who would receive the message. Just as with the visual media, print media and its prominence greatly shaped the public's perception of the events that took place during this period.

Organizational records are another source for students to use in the classroom. Instead of simply learning the alphabet soup of civil rights organizations (CORE, SCLC, NAACP, SNCC), studying the papers of these and other organizations will give students an inside perspective on the workings of these groups. The papers of these respective organizations are generally organized by layers of administration, correspondence, inter-office communication, press releases and news, research files, and general files. There is also a distinction between the work of the national headquarters and the local branch or office. The NAACP is a great example of this. While the head office in New York City was delivering direction and aiding the local and state branches, the latter frequently applied the marching orders from the headquarters to fit the

245

constituents they served. In addition, using more local records will no doubt reveal conflict between the objectives of that local branch and the national branch. This approach to archival research, looking at the history of organizations, is an important connection for students regarding how activists and organizers got work done in a group context. It will also highlight the reality that these organizers often both collaborated and disagreed with one another.

In order to make the movement even more personal for students, I highly recommend a deep dive into personal papers. Although an individual may have been involved with an organization, and there may be papers of that person in the records of that organization, if the personal records of the individual are extant, they could prove the richest of any archival record. Personal papers of an individual involved in the movement could be easier to wade through than voluminous organizational papers, or even audio and visual materials. In personal papers, one may find drafts of speeches or other writings and receive insight into how these were crafted and delivered, or correspondence with family and friends that reveals anxiety and fear, strength and courage, or a touch of humor, or perhaps even a journal or diary. These materials from an individual do the key work of humanizing some of the giants of the movement. Analysis of personal papers can indeed be eye-opening for students to indicate that they too could be the propellers of social movements in the near future.

Research conducted in the archive allows students to read, hear, and even see the materials from the period as events were happening. There is no third voice interpreting what students are engaging with as they might typically find in a textbook or monograph—only the primary source and the student's voice matter. This is key to developing critical thinking skills and becoming an expert in the subject matter. By going straight to the source, students can also learn more about the environment in which a person in history was living, empathize with the decisions made by historical actors in moments of crisis, and peer into the personal lives of the "great men and women" of the period to understand them as humans and not simply as icons or martyrs. And at its best, archival research will render new perspectives to historical interpretation and debunk previously written narratives bound by bias and prejudice.

The Revolution Was
Not Televised but
It Is Available Online

Using the SNCC Digital Gateway to Tell
Civil Rights History from the Bottom Up

KARLYN FORNER

In the age of Google, access to information is not a problem. Students no longer have to rely on encyclopedia
entries or bound books on library shelves to get the information they
need. But internet searches present another problem: too much information. When students google the civil rights movement, the results
number in the millions. Often, the number one hit is not the best source
of information, and rarely do students—or anyone else for that matter—
go beyond the first page of results. Resources putting forward a grassroots, bottom-up history of the movement get buried in searching for
civil rights. Instead, familiar but partial stories of heroes such as Dr.
Martin Luther King Jr., Rosa Parks, and President John F. Kennedy get
new play, and themes such as nonviolence and lunch counter integration overwhelm those of empowerment and economic justice. The challenge of today is helping students figure out which sources are reliable
and how to understand and use them.

More and more digital collections that document the movement are
becoming available, creating unprecedented access to materials that
used to be shut away in physical archives. Many of these collections

reveal a nuanced, complex, and people-centered version of the movement. For example, the Oral History Digital Collection at the University of Southern Mississippi makes available interviews with stalwarts of the Mississippi Movement such as Amzie Moore, Fannie Lou Hamer, and Aaron Henry.[1] The Civil Rights History Project of the Library of Congress lets students listen to and watch oral history interviews with movement veterans in which they describe how they came into the movement and why their actions mattered.[2] The inner workings of the Mississippi Freedom Democratic Party (MFDP) and the Congress of Racial Equality (CORE) are revealed in their organizational papers made available in the Wisconsin Historical Society's Freedom Summer Collection.[3] These digitized documents and audiovisual materials give students a window into how the movement worked on the ground, what local people and organizers cared about, and how the nation responded to this grassroots effort for change.

But digital collections come with some of the same problems as the wider internet, namely the sheer volume of information available. It does not take much for a student or the general public to get overwhelmed by the thousands of pages and hours of interviews. The prospect of clicking through hundreds of search results turns away all but the most intrepid historian. For students and teachers, the issue is not only how to find documents but how to make sense of them. Sources are overwhelming without a framework in which to understand them. And without a framework that puts the grassroots, bottom-up narrative of the civil rights movement front and center, it is easy to fall back on the Master Narrative and focus only on the most well-known people and events, Dr. King and the March on Washington instead of the Mississippi Freedom Democratic Party's challenge at the 1964 Democratic National Convention or the organizing of the first Black Panther Party in Lowndes County, Alabama. Too much primary source material is a good problem to have, but even rich digital collections need context.

This is where websites such as the SNCC Digital Gateway website and the Civil Rights Movement Veterans website come in.[4] Their purpose is to connect students to the raw materials of the movement—letters, oral histories, photographs, and publications—while also contextualizing that material through the framework of grassroots organizing, empowerment, and small *d* democracy.

Both the Civil Rights Movement Veterans and SNCC Digital Gateway websites were created by the activists themselves, committed to

Screenshot of the homepage of the SNCC Digital Gateway. (SNCC Digital Gateway, SNCC Legacy Project)

reframing the movement as the people-centered, empowering struggle for change that it was. For these veterans of the southern freedom struggle, civil rights history is not a completed chapter in the American story of democracy and progress. While the Civil Rights Act of 1964 and the Voting Rights Act of 1965 are the oft-celebrated fruits of their labor, legislation did not mark the end of the movement. Young organizers and local people came together in an attempt to make real the potential of American democracy. The movement was about people taking control of their own lives and making change, from their daily interactions to city halls and county courthouses and all the way up to the halls of Congress. In this framework, themes of grassroots organizing and empowerment take precedent over big events and great heroes. This is the story of the movement that organizers and local communities know and remember.

The Civil Rights Movement Veterans (CRMVet) website documents the history of the southern freedom movement from the perspective of those who were there on the ground. Here, the movement starts before the Supreme Court's *Brown v. Board of Education* decision in 1954 and continues after the call for Black Power in 1966, and its focus stretches beyond a narrowly defined vision of civil rights. "At heart, the Freedom Movement was a demand for social and political equality, an end to economic injustice, and a fair share of political power for Blacks and other non-whites," CRMVet explains. Above all, CRMVet tells the story of local people transforming their own lives through extraordinary acts of courage.[5]

The CRMVet website offers an enormous and wide-ranging collection of primary source documents. WATS line logs from the Student Nonviolent Coordinating Committee (SNCC) document the day-to-day harassment civil rights workers faced while organizing in the rural South. Reports reveal the challenges organizers faced in everything from gaining the trust of the people with whom they worked to dealing with logistics in transportation and housing. Publications from the NAACP, SCLC, SNCC, and CORE, as well as local organizations, bring to light how organizations conveyed the work and goals of the movement to a national audience.

CRMVet also includes reflections and ongoing analysis of the movement by veterans. Tributes when a fellow organizer passes capture stories from the deep relationships that sustained workers. An Our Thoughts page contains commentary by movement veterans on issues today as well as on the movement. An extensive timeline describes and contextualizes events from across the spectrum of the movement, focusing on how each experience shaped later decisions by those involved. Collections of primary source documents related to particular events link back to this timeline. Every section of the CRMVet website undercuts the Master Narrative.[6]

The magnitude of material available on CRMVet provides a wealth of teaching possibilities. Documents, reports, and letters are grouped by type, year, organization, and event, which easily tailor to different lesson plans. For example, a lesson about the Voting Rights Act of 1965 could direct students to the document collection for the Lowndes County Freedom Organization (LCFO). There a SNCC research report details the conditions in Lowndes County, Alabama, prior to 1965, when no black person in the 80 percent black county was registered to vote. In another report, a SNCC staffer describes the conditions in tent city, a makeshift settlement whose inhabitants had been evicted from their homes for registering to vote. Other documents detail how Lowndes residents decided to form an independent political party for the purpose of winning control of local government and improving the daily conditions of their lives. Two comic books designed for political education illustrate how organizers connected with residents and formed the first Black Panther Party. Instead of a story about marchers being beaten on a bridge and President Lyndon Johnson responding, a lesson on the Voting Rights Act becomes one of community organizing and political power. The majority of the material on CRMVet lends itself to these kinds of lessons.

Similarly, the SNCC Digital Gateway (SDG) website connects students and teachers to grassroots stories of the movement and the primary sources that document it. SNCC was born from the student sit-in movement in the spring of 1960. Under the guidance of Ella Baker, the organization of young people moved from direct action, focused on lunch counters and greyhound buses, to grassroots organizing, partnering with local communities in the Deep South in a fight for voting rights. Its experiences in voter registration pushed SNCC and local people toward forming independent parties to win political power. But SNCC soon learned that, in the words of SNCC staffer Courtland Cox, "the vote was necessary but not sufficient."[7] This understanding led SNCC into economic development work and building coalitions internationally and with other movements in the United States.

The SNCC Digital Gateway website grew out of a partnership between SNCC veterans and documentarians, scholars, librarians, and administrators at Duke University dedicated to telling the history of the southern freedom struggle in a new way. SDG puts SNCC's overarching commitment to empowerment—whether personal, political, or economic—at the center of the story. It focuses on how young SNCC activists united with local communities in the Deep South during the 1960s to take control of their political and economic lives. Together, they built a grassroots movement for change that not only transformed the lives of ordinary people but also transformed the nation. The SNCC Digital Gateway uses Black Power as an interpretive lens that puts political power, economic justice, agency, and empowerment front and center. It creates a way for looking at local communities before SNCC arrived, the grassroots organizing work SNCC did in partnership with local people, and how the movement continued in a multitude of different forms after SNCC ended.

SDG weaves together grassroots stories of the movement with primary source materials and new interpretations by movement veterans. These stories about people, events, organizing, and ideas feature letters, interviews, photographs, reports, and other documents, selected from larger digital collections, to give a deeper context and provide a starting point for further research. SDG brings this history to a new generation. The subtitle of the site is "learn from the past, organize for the future, make democracy work." Understanding what SNCC did, how they did it, and who was involved is central to contemporary attempts to secure full citizenship and equality of opportunity for all.

The SNCC Digital Gateway is divided into six major sections: People, Timeline, Our Voices, Inside SNCC, Map, and Today. Each section is designed to give students and teachers a different entry point into SNCC's history. Whether by people and places or events and ideas, having multiple ways to engage SNCC's history lets teachers choose the approach that fits their students best. Maybe that is digging into the profiles of the young Mississippians who joined the movement, reading through the primary source documents, listening to oral histories, and comparing their experiences and what they hoped the movement would accomplish. Or perhaps it is by investigating how and why local movements played out differently in places such as Greenwood, Mississippi, and Lowndes County, Alabama.

The SNCC Digital Gateway goes beyond names, dates, and places to focus on how SNCC's experiences shaped its subsequent organizing, how the organizers themselves were organized, and how ideas evolved over time. Students using SDG will encounter rich primary source material explained in a way that emphasizes the actions of people and themes of growth and empowerment. A breakdown of the sections of the website follows to assist teachers in assessing how SDG could be most useful in their classroom.

People

SNCC worked to empower people, to help them take action to determine and define their lives. The story of the movement is a story of thousands of people. The People section of the SNCC Digital Gateway tells the stories of dozens of these individuals. It divides them into categories—SNCC staff, local people, mentors, supporters, and more—to help users understand what role these groups played in the movement. The profiles on the SNCC Digital Gateway are not mini-biographies; they tell stories illustrating how individuals came to the movement and why they were important. Each profile connects students with photographs, oral histories, and documents about that person and the places they worked. Often, the selected documents are only a sampling of available material. By following the links to the primary sources in the profiles, students can dig deeper into the digital collections where the materials came from.

Timeline

The Timeline offers a chronological history of SNCC's organizing. Using event pages that have a similar structure to the profiles, SDG details what happened, why, and what came after. Each event page features a short narrative telling the story of that event and situating it in the historical context. The SNCC Digital Gateway tells history through stories, and the narrative of each event puts front and center the people making decisions and taking action. Like the profiles, events feature selected digitized primary sources, which allow students to delve deeper into the history and locate additional materials.

The Timeline section is divided into five periods that define different stages of SNCC and the broader freedom struggle. The periods mark phases of SNCC, from direct action in the early 1960s to organizing independent political parties in the later 1960s and SNCC's legacies. Dividing events into periods helps students see how SNCC evolved over time. SNCC's understanding of the task at hand and the tools for accomplishing it continuously shifted based on the experiences organizers were having on the ground. These periods help define that development:

1. SNCC: Origins and Founding (1943–1960) explores the post–World War II activism—the return of black veterans, growth of NAACP branches in the South, the murder of Emmett Till—that laid the foundation for SNCC's organizing and shaped the thinking of the young people who would start the sit-in movement.
2. Direct Action to Voter Registration (1960–1962) traces SNCC's birth out of the sit-in movement and its early involvement in direct action campaigns such as the Freedom Rides, to its shift to voter registration work and grassroots organizing in the Deep South.
3. Voter Registration to Freedom Parties (1962–1965) explores how voter registration efforts helped SNCC grow into an organization of organizers and pushed SNCC and local people toward political organizing and building parallel parties such as the Mississippi Freedom Democratic Party.

253

4. Freedom Parties to Black Power (1965–1969) explores how SNCC—with a growing understanding that the vote was necessary but not sufficient—turned to organizing independent parties and economic cooperatives and pursuing international connections.

5. SNCC Legacies (1968–Present) traces SNCC's legacy, both the work of its members and its organizational legacy, in the decades after SNCC workers moved on and became involved in other movements, campaigns, and undertakings.

Inside SNCC

The Inside SNCC section of the SNCC Digital Gateway breaks down how the organizers organized, delving into the inner workings of SNCC. Popular history of the movement celebrates marches and dramatic showdowns at the courthouse, but SNCC had an entire behind-the-scenes structure that supported its organizers out in the field. SNCC's national office in Atlanta was its administrative headquarters, operating a communications department, a research department, staff photographers, the Sojourner Motor Fleet, the Freedom Singers, and more. Meanwhile, northern Friends of SNCC organizations and an office in New York raised both funds and national support. SNCC's administration made sure that the field organizers had what they needed to organize effectively and that the nation got word of what was going on in the Deep South. But while SNCC's national office made sure its field staff received their $9.64-after-tax-paycheck, it was SNCC's culture that sustained its young organizers. The SNCC Culture section highlights SNCC veterans explaining what it was like to be a part of SNCC and what kept them going. The Inside SNCC section breaks down SNCC's history like a how-to guide—or an activist's playbook—for young organizers today.

Our Voices

The Our Voices section brings to the forefront themes that are woven throughout SNCC's organizing work and traces how ideas in SNCC evolved over time. Each Our Voices section is authored by an individual SNCC veteran or by multiple activists in conversation with each other. History has acquired a reputation of being only about names and dates, but ideas were central to people's participation and the aspirations of the movement. Some of these include freedom education, grassroots organizing, women's involvement, land ownership, economic development, internationalism, and more. In each section, SNCC activists reflect on a theme that they saw as central to the movement and lay out its importance using narrative, audiovisual materials, and documents.

Map

SNCC organized in diverse places. Each community had its own sheriff, mayor, business leaders, and plantation owners, all committed to maintaining white supremacy by any means necessary. These particularities of place mattered to the young organizers in SNCC. Before starting a project in a new community, SNCC's research department compiled data about each location, so field secretaries could understand the lay of the land. The map on the SNCC Digital Gateway lets students explore how different places shaped SNCC's organizing work. It's a portal that brings students to the people who worked in, and the events that happened in, a specific place, and lets them examine how the movement developed over time in local communities.

Today

The Today section features contemporary activists reflecting on how SNCC's work continues to be relevant to their organizing today. It is divided into nine questions that speak to enduring themes at the heart of SNCC's organizing, such as building coalitions, controlling the narrative, organizing a meeting, and employing different strategies and tactics. Here, young organizers from Dream Defenders, Black Youth Project 100 (BYP100), United We Dream, Moral Mondays, the NAACP, and more break down their thinking, their approach, and the challenges they face. Teachers can use the Today section to explore how SNCC's organizing continues to inform today's struggles for self-determination, justice, and democracy.

The SNCC Digital Gateway and the Civil Rights Movement Veterans websites are two of the best digital resources for telling a grassroots story of the movement and connecting students to the letters and reports, and the voices and thoughts of those who made history.

For lesson plans and ideas about how to actually teach this history in the classroom, educators should turn to two organizations, Teaching for Change and the Zinn Education Project.[8] The Civil Rights Teaching website, a project of Teaching for Change, provides lessons and resources that highlight the role of individuals in creating change and walks teachers through strategies for using document-based learning to teach the civil rights movement.[9] Lessons range from using SNCC's work in Lowndes County to help students understand the Voting Rights Act to teaching the Montgomery Bus Boycott and examining the radical vision of Dr. King. These lessons take well-known heroes and events and use them to teach a more nuanced, complex history of the movement. Likewise, the Zinn Education Project takes this same approach to the entirety of United States history and provides lesson plans that stress "the long struggle for human rights and full democracy in the United States."[10]

Taken together, these digital resources address two of the major challenges educators face when teaching the civil rights movement from the bottom up: helping students find reliable sources and establishing a framework in which to understand them. Both the Civil Rights Movement Veterans and SNCC Digital Gateway websites provide the framework and resources needed to teach a more expansive history of the movement beyond the Master Narrative.

ADDITIONAL RESOURCES

1988 SNCC Conference, "We Shall Not Be Moved," Trinity College (http://digital repository.trincoll.edu/sncc/). A ten-part series of video recordings of "We Shall Not Be Moved: The Life and Times of the Student Nonviolent Coordinating Committee, 1960–1966," a conference held at Trinity College, Hartford, Connecticut, April 14–16, 1988.

Freedom Summer Digital Collection, Wisconsin Historical Society (http://content .wisconsinhistory.org/cdm/landingpage/collection/p15932coll2). Includes over 30,000 pages of official records of organizations, personal papers of movement leaders, letters, diaries, images, and newsletters documenting the Mississippi Freedom Summer Project of 1964. Featured collections include the Amzie Moore papers, Ella Baker papers, and Mississippi Freedom Democratic Party papers.

Courtland Cox Papers; Faith Holsaert Papers; Judy Richardson Papers; Joseph Sinsheimer Papers; SNCC 40th Anniversary Tapes, Duke University (http://library .duke.edu/rubenstein/findingaids/). The Courtland Cox Papers feature material related to the Drum and Spear Bookstore and the Sixth Pan-African

Congress. The Faith Holsaert papers contain correspondence related to SNCC's organizing in southwest Georgia. The Judy Richardson papers include materials from her years on SNCC's staff in Atlanta and Mississippi; her involvement at Drum and Spear Bookstore; and her work on the *Eyes on the Prize* documentary series and *Hands on the Freedom Plow* book. The Joseph Sinsheimer papers include oral history interviews with activists from the Mississippi Movement. The SNCC 40th Anniversary tapes document the SNCC fortieth anniversary conference held at Shaw University in Raleigh, North Carolina, in 2000.

Digital Collections, University of Southern Mississippi (http://digitalcollections.usm.edu/). Includes photographs, oral history transcripts and audio, letters, and other documents about local struggles for civil rights in Mississippi. Featured collections include Herbert Randall Freedom Summer photograph collection and a large number of oral histories with veterans of the Mississippi Movement.

Civil Rights History Project, Library of Congress (http://www.loc.gov/collections/civil-rights-history-project). Features video-recorded oral history interviews and transcripts with a wide range of activists involved in the 1960s freedom struggle. Many interviewees participated in national organizations, such as the NAACP, SNCC, and CORE, and the interviews cover a broad geographical area and topical range.

Take Stock (http://takestockphotos.com/). Features images made by activist photographers personally dedicated to the cause of social justice. The Civil Rights Collection contains some 27,000 images taken by photographers such as Matt Herron, George Ballis, and Maria Varela, in Mississippi, Louisiana, Alabama, and Georgia in the mid-1960s.

Eyes on the Prize Interviews, Washington University (http://digital.wustl.edu/eyesontheprize/resources.html). Includes interviews from the fourteen-part series *Eyes on the Prize*, which debuted on PBS stations in 1985 and 1988 and is considered the definitive documentary on the civil rights movement.

Jim Peppler Southern Courier Photograph Collection, Alabama Department of Archives and History (http://digital.archives.alabama.gov/cdm/landingpage/collection/peppler). Features 11,000 photographs documenting the civil rights movement and social conditions in central Alabama taken by Jim Peppler, a staff photographer for the *Southern Courier.*

Mississippi State Sovereignty Commission Records, Mississippi Department of Archives and History (http://www.mdah.ms.gov/arrec/digital_archives/sovcom/). Includes approximately 133,000 pages of material from Mississippi's state-sponsored, counter–civil rights agency from 1956 to 1973. Material includes investigative reports, correspondence, speeches, and a large amount of published material.

KZSU Project South Interviews, Stanford University (http://www.oac.cdlib.org/findaid/ark:/13030/tf7489n969/). Includes interview and meetings with civil rights workers and local activists in the South, recorded during summer

1965 by Stanford students affiliated with the campus radio station KZSU. Features interviews with members of CORE, the MFDP, the NAACP, SCLC, and SNCC and transcribed action tapes of civil rights workers canvassing voters, conducting freedom schools, and participating in demonstrations.

Civil Rights Digital Library, University of Georgia (http://crdl.usg.edu/). Assists users in discovering primary sources and other educational material from libraries, archives, museums, and public broadcasters on a national scale. Includes a digital video archive of historical news film and serves as a civil rights portal by connecting users to related digital collections.

Notes

1. Oral History Digital Collection, University of Southern Mississippi, http://digitalcollections.usm.edu/.

2. Civil Rights History Project, Library of Congress, http://www.loc.gov /collections/civil-rights-history-project.

3. Freedom Summer Collection, Wisconsin Historical Society, content.wis consinhistory.org/cdm/landingpage/collection/p15932coll2.

4. SNCC Digital Gateway, http://snccdigital.org; Civil Rights Movement Veterans, http://www.crmvet.org.

5. "About the CRMVet Website," Civil Rights Movement Veterans website, http://www.crmvet.org/about1.htm, accessed July 26, 2016.

6. Julian Bond quoted in Charles E. Cobb Jr., *This Nonviolent Stuff'll Get You Killed: How Guns Made the Civil Rights Movement Possible* (New York: Basic Books, 2013), 247.

7. Courtland Cox quoted by Judy Richardson, opening remarks, "In the Mississippi River: Heroes and Sheroes: A Tribute to Those Murdered and Martyred in Mississippi," Freedom Summer 50th, Jackson, Mississippi, June 27, 2014, Civil Rights Movement Veterans website, http://www.crmvet.org /comm/judyr14.htm, accessed July 26, 2016.

8. Teaching for Change, http://www.teachingforchange.org; Zinn Education Project, http://zinnedproject.org, accessed July 29, 2016.

9. Civil Rights Teaching, http://civilrightsteaching.org.

10. Zinn Education Project website.

PART FIVE

"Strong people don't need strong leaders"

Methods for Teaching the Civil Rights Movement

Stay Woke

Teaching the Civil Rights Movement through Literature

JULIE BUCKNER ARMSTRONG

The wake-up call opens a long history of civil rights cultural productions. The initial scene of Richard Wright's 1940 novel *Native Son* jolts Bigger Thomas out of bed with an alarm clock and, soon after, a rat, which Bigger chases around his family's cramped quarters armed with an iron skillet. Bigger wins the battle, but his ultimate war—against an oppressive racial caste system—is for his own humanity. Lorraine Hansberry's 1959 play *Raisin in the Sun* similarly begins with a demand for its main character Walter Lee Younger to "do some waking up in there." His wife Ruth's words foreshadow the play's main idea and link back to Wright's novel. Walter Lee not only must get up to start his day. He must stand up, become fully human—a man, not a rat, his sister Beneatha says—to help his family claim their share of the American Dream. Spike Lee's 1989 film *Do the Right Thing* echoes these earlier works. The first shot after the opening credits focuses on the face of disc jockey Mister Señor Love Daddy, who holds and sounds an abrasive alarm clock. "Waaaake up! Wake up, wake up, wake up!" Mister Señor Love Daddy cries. His audience is the Bedford Stuyvesant neighborhood surrounding the radio station, and especially the film's protagonist Mookie, who must learn how to "do the right thing" after white police officers strangle his friend Radio Raheem. After the real-life deaths of Michael Brown (2014), Sandra Bland (2015), and others in police custody, the Black Lives Matter movement adopted the wake-up call as social media hashtag: #staywoke. Erykah Badu popularized the phrase in a 2008 song, "Master Teacher," challenging listeners to become politically conscious, educated about history and—as the works of Wright, Hansberry, and Lee suggest—to stand up for a humanity continually under siege, whether one's own or one's fellow citizens.

The wake-up call's persistence highlights the possibilities and complications of teaching the civil rights movement through literature—possibilities and complications that emerge from a similar place. Consider the textual examples discussed so far, which range across genres and decades. The options overwhelm. For many educators, Harper Lee's 1960 novel *To Kill a Mockingbird*, which examines segregation-era Alabama through the eyes of a precocious white narrator named Scout, remains the default option. However, writers from Ida B. Wells to Charles W. Chesnutt, Langston Hughes, and Lillian Smith began tackling the fight against Jim Crow decades earlier, leaving behind a rich legacy of poetry, drama, fiction, and memoir. That legacy continues with works about the people, places, and events of the movement's classic phase. Authors such as Gwendolyn Brooks, James Baldwin, Amiri Baraka, and Alice Walker bring readers into the turmoil of a transformational social moment. More contemporary writers—Claudia Rankine, August Wilson, Ta-Nehisi Coates, and others—help audiences connect past to present in thoughtful and thought-provoking ways. Clearly, literary works from and about the movement will open students' eyes. Instructors should prepare for the difficult conversations that arise from that moment of awakening, especially from students who have no desire to "stay woke." As Margaret Early Whitt states in the introduction to *Short Stories of the Civil Rights Movement*, "literature helps us *feel* history" (x). Those feelings can include anger, guilt, sadness, and frustration, and they can spoil the best-intentioned lesson plan. Instructors should also prepare for class to go well. Richard H. King explains that literature "inform[s] us in the deepest sense about certain ethical and political dimensions of the way we 'are' in the world" (163). This essay offers resources, themes, and strategies for facilitating such a positive outcome, for turning complications into possibilities.

Resources

The amount of literature available for teaching the civil rights movement is formidable but manageable, in part because of the

Claudia Rankine, *Citizen: An American Lyric* (cover design by John Lucas, used with permission of Graywolf Press)

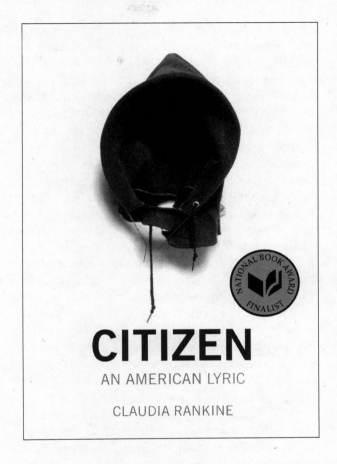

many excellent resources that have become available during the past two decades. This body of work parallels the explosion of historical scholarship and reflects its efforts to create more nuanced movement narratives. Twenty years ago, an article such as this one would have been rare. More common were those such as King's, calling for academics to draw upon literature more frequently and effectively. The intervening years have seen a substantial rise in criticism and teaching resources. Scholars such as Minrose Gwin, Christopher Metress, Sharon Monteith, and Brian Norman demonstrate how literary responses operate as historical artifacts and as ways of constructing memory. Multiple anthologies—some new, some old—provide a range of works from and about the movement and show how literature has always marched arm in arm with civil rights protest, as authors tap into the power of words as weapons, bridges, and tools for speaking out, making sense, and remembering.

Anthologies that focus on specific genres—Whitt's *Short Stories of the Civil Rights Movement* (2006) and Jeffrey Lamar Coleman's *Words of Protest, Words of Freedom: Poetry of the American Civil Rights Movement and Era* (2012)—depict a complex movement of everyday people fighting for their rights and their lives. Whitt organizes her volume thematically, focusing on school desegregation, sit-ins, marches and demonstrations, acts of violence, and works that take a retrospective view. The movement that emerges is sometimes brutal, as in James Baldwin's "Going to Meet the Man" (1965), a graphic depiction of how racism and violence are passed down through generations; sometimes humorous, as in Michael Thelwell's "Direct Action" (1963), which uses a toilet to change the notion of "sit-in"; and sometimes conflicted, in stories such as Anthony Grooms's "Negro Progress" (1994), where the protagonist cannot commit to joining the forces of social change. The movement as seen from Coleman's poetry anthology is equally layered. Sections cover events such as the Selma Voting Rights March and late 1960s urban uprisings; places such as Mississippi and Birmingham; and people such as Medgar Evers, Dr. Martin Luther King Jr., Malcolm X, and the Black Panthers. What becomes clear from reading this volume is the movement's literary and cultural significance. Going well beyond conventional beliefs that the movement was a southern phenomenon or an African American concern, Coleman assembles a roll call of major international poets from the second half of the twentieth century, including Aimé Césaire, Nicolás Guillén, W. H. Auden, Derek Walcott, Denise Levertov, Allen Ginsberg, Robert Lowell, Adrienne Rich, Léopold Sédar Senghor, Carolyn Kizer, Yevgeny Yevtushenko, and Galway Kinnell. *Words of Protest, Words of Freedom* clearly demonstrates that an anthology specifically devoted to one genre can represent a movement's depth and breadth.

Several multigenre anthologies provide very different perspectives on the movement and social change. *Black Fire: An Anthology of Afro-American Writing*, edited by Amiri Baraka and Larry Neal, came out in 1968 and remains available in print and electronic formats. Including essays, poetry, fiction, and a much wider selection of drama than other collections, *Black Fire* helped define the Black Arts Movement. Few other works can better represent the spirit of the times and give students access to significant cultural voices, such as Sun Ra and Dingane Joe Goncalves, that do not appear in more recent texts. Similarly, Toni Cade Bambara's *The Black Woman: An Anthology* became in 1970 many readers' introduction to writers such as Nikki Giovanni, Audre Lorde, and Alice Walker; to women's leadership roles in the movement; and to black feminism. As in *Black Fire*, the wake-up call in *The Black Woman* to gender equity reflects its historical moment's energy and offers students insights into important questions and debates of the times: "The Pill: Genocide or Liberation?" Bambara (writing then as Toni Cade) provocatively asks. A more recent anthology that brings together poetry, fiction, drama, and essays is *The Civil Rights Reader: American Literature from Jim Crow to Reconciliation*, which I coedited with Amy Schmidt. This volume presents readings from a long civil rights movement that begins with segregation's institutionalization and continues into an era that some call "post–civil rights" and others the "New Jim Crow." The "problem of the Twentieth century is the problem of the color line," W. E. B. Du Bois claims in a passage from *The Souls of Black Folk*. Selections from Claude McKay, Ralph Ellison, Flannery O'Connor, Amiri Baraka, Walter Mosley, Toi Derricotte, and others bear out that prediction, raising the question of how far the twenty-first century must continue before that problem gets resolved.

Themes

The anthologies discussed above, separately or in combination, equip instructors to teach a full course on movement-related literature or to select texts for part of a course according to specific people, places, or events. Those who choose to look beyond anthologies will find even more texts from which to choose. Common themes include heroes and martyrs, consciousness raising, segregation and white supremacy, forms of resistance, and human relationships. Instructors should know that literature performs different cultural work from history. One expects students to come into a civil rights classroom with little factual knowledge, usually derived from television, Hollywood films, music, social media, and other forms of popular culture. Literature is yet one more form of representation. However, it can prepare students to think critically and creatively about the facts they encounter. Literary works take readers into imaginative spaces that documentary resources do not. They show us how history is experienced, felt, and remembered in individual human lives—shaping memory into beauty and truth.

Heroes and Martyrs

A significant amount of movement literature engages iconic figures in ways that create a more complex understanding of civil rights leadership, heroism, and martyrdom. For example, contemporary fiction and graphic narrative on Dr. King—such as Julius Lester's *All Our Wounds Forgiven* (1994), Charles Johnson's *Dreamer* (1999), and Ho Che Anderson's three-volume *King* (1993–2003)—portray the minister as a flawed, complicated man rather than an idealized, sanitized hero. Similarly, the civil rights poems in Rita Dove's *On the Bus with Rosa Parks* (2000) compose a more nuanced figure than the familiar image of the seamstress who was so tired one day that she just sat down on a bus and refused to get up. Students who do not know much beyond the Master Narrative may be surprised to find that some of the more compelling works in terms of literary representation involve Medgar Evers and Malcolm X. Some may be unfamiliar with Evers, the Mississippi organizer that Byron de la Beckwith assassinated in 1963. Evers's death generated a number of works, including Eudora Welty's short story "Where Is the Voice Coming From?" Written days after the event and told from the (then unknown) murderer's perspective, the story is one of the most chilling to come out of the movement. Although students are likely familiar with Malcolm X's name, they may know less about the way both his life and his death galvanized the Black Power and Black Arts movements. *The Autobiography of Malcolm X*, written with Alex Haley and published in 1965, is one of the most important memoirs to come out of this time period, for its models of self-determination and diasporic identity formation. Malcolm X's assassination, also in 1965, became a touchstone for writers from Gwendolyn Brooks and Robert Hayden to Sonia Sanchez and Amiri Baraka.

Raising Consciousness

Raising consciousness is a predominant theme of civil rights–related literature, especially that produced during the moment. Key wake-up calls came in response to acts of violence—against heroes such as Martin, Medgar, and Malcolm, and especially against child and young adult victims. Perhaps the most famous case was the 1955 murder of fourteen-year-old Emmett Till in Money, Mississippi. His brutal death, the photo of his disfigured body in *Jet* magazine, the acquittal of two white men charged with his murder, and their later confession in an infamous *Look* magazine article galvanized civil rights and Black Power movement activists alike, symbolizing the rupture between national ideals and realities that the movement strove to rectify. Christopher Metress's *The Lynching of Emmett Till: A Documentary Narrative* (2002) gathers selections from journalism, memoir, poetry, and fiction to show the extent to which the case registered far beyond its place and time. In *Emmett Till in Literary Memory and Imagination*, Metress has catalogued over 150 literary representations of Till's death, such as Anne Moody's memoir *Coming of Age in Mississippi* (1968), James Baldwin's play *Blues for Mr. Charlie* (1964), Bebe Moore Campbell's novel *Your Blues Ain't Like Mine* (1992), and Marilyn Nelson's cycle of poems, *A Wreath for Emmett Till* (2009). Other young victims addressed in literature include three civil rights workers murdered in Mississippi during Freedom Summer 1964 (Elizabeth Nunez's *Beyond the Limbo Silence*, 1992), and four girls killed in the 1963 16th Street Baptist Church bombing in Birmingham, Alabama (Anthony Grooms's *Bombingham*, 2001, and Sena Jeter Naslund's *Four Spirits*, 2003).

Sometimes literature raises consciousness through a different form of violence: not by calling attention to historical events but by describing horrific fictional scenarios or employing graphic language as shock value. Playing upon readers' emotions in hopes of fostering social change is a literary protest strategy that connects the civil rights movement to its abolitionist roots through works such as Frederick Douglass's *Narrative of the Life of Frederick Douglass* (1845) and Harriet Jacobs's *Incidents in the Life of a Slave Girl* (1861), both of which describe the brutal treatment the enslaved received from their enslavers. Writers who participated in the anti-lynching efforts of the late nineteenth to mid-twentieth centuries often drew upon exposé and grotesque social realism to make their case. Ida B. Wells, in *Southern Horrors* (1892) and *A Red Record* (1895), Elisabeth Freeman and W. E. B. Du Bois in "The Waco Horror" (1916), Walter White in "The Work of a Mob" (1918), and Richard Wright in "Big Boy Leaves Home" (1938) provide a template for later movement writers to draw upon. Seen within the context of these works, the brutal depiction of violence in works such as Baldwin's "Going to Meet the Man" and Junius Edwards's *If We Must Die* (1963) seems at least consistent if not less distressing. Some of the more controversial engagements of racial stereotypes in Eldridge Cleaver's memoir *Soul on Ice* (1968), Amiri Baraka's 1964 play *Dutchman*, and his 1966 poem "Black Art" make sense in this context as well. The times themselves were often shocking, and writers insisted that their audiences take note.

Segregation, White Supremacy, and Privilege

While some writers focus on the most visible and egregious forms of racism, others work to expose the underlying and interlocking structures of oppression. Sickness is a common metaphor used to describe that system, as authors outline symptoms and search for cures. In *Killers of the Dream* (1949), Lillian Smith casts segregation as a social "illness" that allows some people to have power over others because of their race, gender, class, and other forms of privilege. Likewise, Moody, in *Coming of Age in Mississippi*, wonders about her chances against the white "disease." In Moody's memoir, one learns quite a bit about specific movement-related events, people, and places, but her title indicates that she wants readers to focus on her "coming of age," her awakening into the racist, sexist southern way of life. Moody vividly describes the toll that fighting against that system exacts on her own health, and on the lives of people such as Till and Evers—demonstrating that the struggle to defeat that system will be long and difficult, because it has stood firmly in place for a very long time. In *Your Blues Ain't Like Mine*, Campbell uses the "Honorable Men of Hopewell" to show the interconnected, long-lasting relationship between money, race, and power. The Honorable Men, whose roots in the town extend back to the slave-holding South, continue to manipulate property taxes, the local education system, regional economic health, and even medical care so that they win and everyone else—including poor whites and all blacks—loses. Campbell is not alone in showing that when rich white men meet in dark smoky rooms, a black person's health—or life—will soon be at stake. The literature of segregation and civil rights has relied upon this trope for over a century, in novels such as Charles Chesnutt's *Marrow of Tradition* (1901), James Weldon Johnson's *Autobiography of an Ex-Colored Man* (1912), Carson McCullers's *Clock without Hands* (1961), and John Oliver Killens's *'Sippi* (1988).

An equally long and ongoing literary tradition informs that segregation and privilege are not limited to the US South. Angela Davis's

Autobiography (1974) focuses on her organizing efforts in Southern California. Malcolm X's *Autobiography* and poetry about the Black Panthers look north and west. Two of the most profound personal essays written during the movement, Baldwin's "Notes of a Native Son" (1955) and his 1963 letter to his nephew in *The Fire Next Time*, come out of his experiences growing up black and gay in Harlem. Both Richard Wright's and Lorraine Hansberry's wake-up calls focus readers' attention on Chicago. In *Raisin in the Sun*, the "system," which Walter Lee refers to as Mr. Charlie, rather than Jim Crow, comes in the not-so-subtle form of the neighborhood association that wants to keep the Younger family out. Like Moody and Campbell, Hansberry also makes clear the intersections of race, gender, and class prejudice. Tensions exist between Walter and Beneatha's boyfriend George, who is wealthy and college educated, as well as between Walter and Beneatha, who dreams of becoming a doctor, a career not seen as appropriate for a 1950s-era woman. *Clybourne Park*, a 2010 play by Bruce Norris, revisits Hansberry's intersectional themes for contemporary audiences and examines the Youngers' move against newer forms of racially inflected neighborhood change. Ta-Nehisi Coates's memoir, *Between the World and Me* (2015), also collapses the distance between space and time in its attempts to unpack structures of oppression and privilege that exist throughout the Unites States and persist into the present day. Coates takes his title from a 1935 Wright poem that depicts a lynching and his epistolary form from Baldwin: the book is an open letter to Coates's son about being a black man in the United States. Coates's passionate prose and cogent arguments remind readers that locating white supremacy and privilege in the past or in one particular region acts as a way of containing and minimizing. As Malcolm X famously said in 1964, "America is Mississippi."

Forms of Resistance

Complex problems demand complex solutions. The philosophies and strategies of nonviolent direct action are traditional reference points for student knowledge about the civil rights movement—most likely because Dr. King's 1963 "Letter from Birmingham Jail" is so often assigned in high school and college courses to teach subjects including writing, rhetoric, history, and political theory. Literary works reveal characters engaging in a variety of protest forms from individual acts of defiance to more revolutionary tactics. Moody's *Coming of Age in Mississippi* and Davis's *Autobiography* provide excellent points of comparison between the activism that specifically targeted segregation and that focused on structural racism. A strategy shared in both books: singing in jail keeps up one's spirits and dignity. One place that Moody learns to fight back is through her work as a teenage domestic, at first through strategic silence—listening to her white employers talk about segregation when they think she is not listening, and later through strategic action—quitting jobs when employers do not treat her well. Each time, she grows braver, paving the way for later courage as a movement activist. A range of texts similarly reveals characters engaging in small, but significant, acts of workplace resistance. August Wilson's 1983 play *Fences* sees protagonist Troy agitating for African Americans, him in particular, to be hired as sanitation truck drivers instead of collectors—that he lacks a license is beside the point. Walter Mosley's 1997 story "Equal Opportunity" has ex-con Socrates persistently applying for, and getting, a supermarket job that he knows he will lose once his jail time is discovered. In Natasha Trethewey's poem "Drapery Factory, Gulfport, Mississippi, 1956" (from her 2000 collection *Domestic Work*), a supervisor gets a distinctly female surprise when inspecting women's purses for possible theft as they leave the building.

While these texts provide a spectrum of ways that individuals and groups take action, others raise questions about whether the most effective tactics involve nonviolence or more aggressive tactics. Protestors participate in traditional forms of direct action in both Grooms's "Negro Progress" and Killens's *'Sippi*, but when white backlash threatens their communities, black men with guns keep watch. Retribution is a key theme of both Alice Walker's *Meridian* (1976) and Toni Morrison's *Song of Solomon* (1977). In the latter, the character Guitar belongs to a vigilante group called the Seven Days. Because he is the "Sunday Man," he is tasked with bombing a white church after the deadly bombing of a black one in Birmingham. Meridian, the title character of Walker's novel, struggles with the concept of retaliation that her friends embrace. For Anthony Grooms, in *Bombingham*, violence breeds only more violence. His protagonist Walter, traumatized by childhood events in Birmingham, grows up to be a military sharpshooter in Vietnam, perceiving the need for reconciliation and healing but also measuring their distance.

Human Relationships

Perhaps one of the most productive ways of bringing literature, especially fiction, into the civil rights movement classroom is to discuss the ways that political, economic, and other social transformations affect personal relationships. Baldwin's essays famously make clear the connections between self, family, and society. In Grooms's *Bombingham*, domestic life marches on while demonstrations take place down the road. Walker's *Meridian* and Killens's *'Sippi* look provocatively at dating relationships in the movement, especially interracial ones taboo at the time. Other books, such as Rosellen Brown's *Civil Wars* (1984) and *Half a Heart* (2001) and Danzy Senna's *Caucasia* (1998), examine

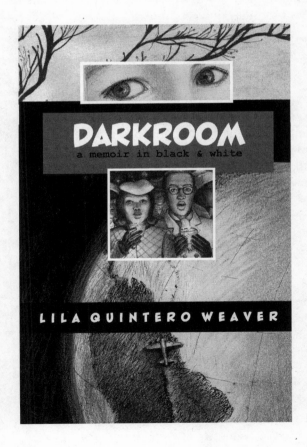

Lila Quintero Weaver, *Darkroom: A Memoir in Black and White* (used with permission of University of Alabama Press)

how the movement affected future generations, with the latter two books focusing in particular on participants' children. Several recent graphic narratives offer students an excellent introduction to the movement from the perspective of friendship, love, and family. Howard Cruse's *Stuck Rubber Baby* (1995), set in 1963, navigates the thicket of gay and straight sexuality, politics, friends, and family within a milieu complicated further by antiblack and antigay violence. *The Silence of Our Friends* (2012) by Jim Demonakos, Mark Long, and Nate Powell juxtaposes the stories of two families, one black and one white, navigating friendship and civic responsibility in 1967 Houston. Lila Quintero Weaver's *Darkroom: A Memoir in Black and White* (2012) narrates the movement story from an immigrant's perspective, offering a verbally and visually artful rendering of the ways individuals strive to make whole fractured identities, families, and communities.

Teaching Problems and Solutions

Because literature of the movement so often deals with fundamental issues of individual and civic identity, conversations about that literature can become fraught with difficulty. Civil rights educators battle students' lack of knowledge, firmly entrenched positions, and responses to writing that provocatively engages hearts and minds. For every text that attempts to wake up—or shake up—readers, one exists to help them work through troubling ideas and times. One might make the same remark about literary responses to the civil rights movement as author Finley Peter Dunne said of newspapers, whose job is to "comfort the afflicted and afflict the comfortable." Even the most common "afflictions," however, can be approached as teaching opportunities.

Readers often confuse historical fiction with historical fact. Works such as *Your Blues Ain't Like Mine* and *Bombingham* may be deeply rooted in specific events or places; the point of reading Campbell's and Grooms's novels, however, is not to measure how closely they mirror reality but to consider what they reveal about their topics' broader cultural significance, meaning, and value. Even memoir takes liberties with facts in search of narrative coherency and artistic truth. Anne Moody and Malcolm X, who rely on faulty memory like any human, also construct themselves as heroes of their own stories. With the literary representation of any movement-related person, place, or event, classroom discussions should cover, at minimum, basic issues about genre, artistic movement, rhetorical situation, and the publication marketplace. For example, a variety of documentary and creative resources exist about the 1963 bombing of Birmingham's 16th Street Baptist Church, including photographs, video clips, newspaper accounts, oral histories, memoir, poetry, fiction, and film. Instructors might ask students to compare Eugene Patterson's newspaper editorial "A Flower for the Graves," written for white southerners, to Dudley Randall's poem "Ballad of Birmingham," written for a northern black audience. These works use similar imagery, a child victim's shoe, to raise consciousness about the magnitude of violence occurring in the Jim Crow South. More recent texts that treat the same event—Christopher Paul Curtis's young adult novel, *The Watsons Go to Birmingham* (1963) and Grooms's *Bombingham*—have a different thematic focus: the difficultly of healing from a moment remembered as both an individual and cultural trauma. Contemporary works that look back often say as much about the present as they do about the past.

Although most movement-related literature tries to bring about greater awareness and deeper understanding of racial and social justice, some texts rely upon narrative conventions that, intentionally or not, reinforce stereotypes and systems of privilege. Instructors can help students pinpoint examples in assigned readings and other forms of popular culture. Alfred Uhry's 1987 play *Driving Miss Daisy* and the novels *Sugar Cage* (1992) by Connie May Fowler and *The Help* (2009) by Kathryn Stockett point to the popular "best friend" plot where white and black characters, often in an employer-employee relationship, either team up to solve a problem or wind up working well together after initial conflicts, giving the illusion that issues such as structural racism and white privilege will magically disappear if "people would just get along." A key component of this plot is white redemption, where characters change their attitudes about race after witnessing dramatic events. These moments of enlightenment differ from wake-up calls in not challenging characters, or readers, to channel their awareness toward social action. They suggest that whites need only to recognize a problem, not participate in solving it. Some earlier works—such as Lettie Hamlett Rogers's *Birthright* (1957) and Elliot Chaze's *Tiger in the Honeysuckle* (1965)—verge on complicating this narrative by asking characters to make tough choices. Others, such as *To Kill a Mockingbird*, assume that their narrators will "do the right thing" after their eyes are opened. Yet this novel relies on its own familiar trope, that of the sacrificial black, who must die so that others can see. The difference between Harper Lee's Tom Robinson and Spike Lee's Radio Raheem lies in the awakened character's privilege. Scout can choose whether or not to walk around in Tom's shoes. Mookie cannot change his race like he changes his sneakers.

One of the most difficult aspects of teaching this literature is navigating conversations where some students see what others cannot. Talking about topics such as privilege and racial violence can be hard enough when they are "safely" confined to the past and explosive when they appear in the present day. Whether students wake up to Richard Wright or #BlackLivesMatter, civil rights issues affect their personal and political lives in ways that some are just learning how to recognize. A wise teacher once said that no bad classes exist, only opportunities to reflect. These opportunities can begin with informal writing that students can share or not, anonymously or with their names, as appropriate to the situation. Most feel comfortable saying on paper what they will not out loud. Another good exercise asks students to defer to the literature— imagining how difficult conversations might play out between characters and writers. Doing so acts as a classroom pressure valve, deflecting strong emotions back into texts. Students can also consider how they would respond if they were channeling the words of authors such as James Baldwin or Audre Lorde. The short answer is that both would insist upon the importance of remaining awake to injustice and ready to stand up for what is right. The beautiful world that Erykah Badu seeks in "Master Teacher" may exist only in "dreams, dreams, dreams." Literature provides tools for imagining that more perfect reality.

RESOURCES

Armstrong, Julie Buckner, ed. *The Cambridge Companion to American Civil Rights Literature*. New York: Cambridge University Press, 2015.

Armstrong, Julie Buckner, and Amy Schmidt, eds. *The Civil Rights Reader: American Literature from Jim Crow to Reconciliation*. Athens: University of Georgia Press, 2009.

Bambara, Toni Cade, ed. *The Black Woman: An Anthology*. 1970. Reprint, New York: Washington Square Press, 2010.

Baraka, Amiri, and Larry Neal, eds. *Black Fire: An Anthology of Afro-American Writing*. 1968. Reprint, Baltimore: Black Classic Press, 2007.

Coleman, Jeffrey Lamar, ed. *Words of Protest, Words of Freedom: Poetry of the American Civil Rights Movement and Era*. Durham, NC: Duke University Press, 2012.

Dubek, Laura. *Living Legacies: Literary Responses to the Civil Rights Movement.* New York: Routledge, 2018.

Gwin, Minrose. *Remembering Medgar Evers: Writing the Long Civil Rights Movement.* Athens: University of Georgia Press, 2013.

Jones, Suzanne. *Race Mixing: Southern Fiction since the 1960s.* Baltimore: Johns Hopkins University Press, 2006.

King, Richard H. "Politics and Fictional Representation: The Case of the Civil Rights Movement." In *The Making of Martin Luther King and the Civil Rights Movement*, edited by Brian Ward and Tony Badger, 162–78. New York: Washington Square Press, 1996.

Metress, Christopher, ed. *The Lynching of Emmett Till: A Documentary Narrative.* Charlottesville: University of Virginia Press, 2002.

Metress, Christopher. "Making Civil Rights Harder: Literature, Memory, and the Black Freedom Struggle." *Southern Literary Journal* 40, no. 2 (Spring 2008): 138–50.

Monteith, Sharon. "Civil Rights Fiction." In *The Cambridge Companion to the Literature of the American South*, edited by Sharon Monteith, 159–73. New York: Cambridge University Press, 2013.

Norman, Brian. *Neo-Segregation Narratives: Jim Crow in Post-Civil Rights American Literature.* Athens: University of Georgia Press, 2010.

Norman, Brian, and Piper Kendrix Williams, eds. *Representing Segregation: Toward an Aesthetics of Living Jim Crow, and Other Forms of Racial Division.* Albany: State University of New York Press, 2010.

Pollack, Harriet, and Christopher Metress, eds. *Emmett Till in Literary Memory and Imagination.* Baton Rouge: Louisiana State University Press, 2008.

Varlack, Christopher A. *Critical Insights: Civil Rights Literature Past and Present.* Hackensack, NJ: Salem Press, 2017.

Whitt, Margaret Earley, ed. *Short Stories of the Civil Rights Movement: An Anthology.* Athens: University of Georgia Press, 2006.

"Nonviolence is impossible"

Role-Playing in the Classroom

WESLEY HOGAN

When people think of the civil rights movement, nonviolence is everywhere and nowhere. Everywhere mentioned, and nowhere understood. Some people think it blankets the whole civil rights movement, that it is the movement's single most distinctive feature. Scholars in the last two decades have shown how misleading that idea is. Nonviolence was more of a "one-off" tactic, used sporadically, yet to great effect. We now know that most tactics used in the movement were *not* specifically associated with nonviolence—they involved economic boycotts, lobbying, community organizing, nonretaliation, and self-defense.[1]

Regardless of whether one thinks nonviolence was the whole movement, part of the movement, or a bit player in a larger drama, nonviolence seems strange to almost everyone. "Violence is as American as cherry pie," as movement veteran H. Rap Brown noted.[2] The vast majority of people in the United States are culturally much more familiar with the idea of an eye-for-an-eye and defending ourselves. From George Washington through Nat Turner to John Wayne and Michael B. Jordan, our cultural and political heroes are often those who use violence to fight physically for their freedom. The value of this role play is how clearly it focuses students on how *difficult* it is to be a nonviolent actor. It isn't the weak who fall back on nonviolence; it's only for the strong. Too often students will miss this entirely and dismiss nonviolence as passivity—"I would never let someone spit on me." If students are going to understand the political lever nonviolence provides, we've got to do a better job of teaching it.

Nonviolence presents three tricky questions for almost everyone who tries to teach and learn about it: How did it work? Why was it so difficult to do? And why did it work in some places so effectively and not others?

The challenge in the classroom is simple, if profound. Nonviolence is so different than what most people have experienced in their lives. In my experience teaching about it in college, high school, and community settings, an individual can't understand how nonviolence worked by listening to a first-person account, reading a book, or watching a film. All of those modes take place in people's heads. Nonviolent tactics and strategies are somatic—they don't make sense if you just "think" or "talk" about them.

Role play, in my experience, is thus the best route to giving students a quick, immersive experience to then discuss, read more about, and explore. Still, before they do a role play where they *feel* what it is like, students who've heard about nonviolence or watched a film say things like, "I'm not the kind of person who lets someone step on my neck." Once you put them in a role-play situation, suddenly a whole range of practical possibilities emerge. They understand why even people who were not philosophically nonviolent used this tactic, and why it was so effective. They understand the deep humanity of protestors that the tactic conveys to neutral bystanders and opponents. They grasp how complex the police officers' roles could be in confronting protestors. They understand how confusing it was for shopkeepers who found their lunch counters occupied by sit-in protestors. They see why sometimes these tactics failed, or why people engaging in these tactics sometimes experienced a bond akin to that developed by comrades in war.

If one was teaching civil rights movement history in Burma, or Vietnam, or another context where theories and practices of nonviolence were culturally more widespread, perhaps one would not need to put people literally "in the shoes" of the sit-in students. As it is, to teach the remarkable history and profound bravery of the mostly black youth who revitalized the civil rights movement in the spring of 1960 in the United States, the immersive experience vastly speeds up students' understanding and their ability to see and feel nonviolence's power. It is a limited power. Yet when it works, they understand why.

Setting Up the Classroom

As with any immersive experience, the first rule is to do no harm. In order to prevent harm, the teacher has to know three things extremely well: the subject, the class, and oneself. On the first topic, read up on the sit-ins using the resource section at the end of this chapter. Second, know your class: Who are the bullies? Who talks more than others? Who feels marginalized already? It's vital that you know the students and that you are the person in control of that class. This is not an exercise to do before the students know and trust you. If you haven't built an environment of trust in the classroom, avoid the role play. And finally, you have to understand who you are as the person carrying this knowledge to the next generation. It is vital, for example, for me to be aware of myself as a white woman, an activist-scholar, and a person with a long history in antiracist organizing; and the students have to know that I know this about myself. I have to know that I am going to take an active role in structuring the role play, and that I have the back of every kid in the class who could feel marginalized. I have to be clear that I will jump in to interrupt any student acting out of ignorance or acting to foster stereotype.[3]

Think through where and when you plan to do the role play. I've been teaching this for fifteen years. In 2006, in the wake of Hurricane Katrina, it raised different issues for students than in 2009, right after President Obama's election, and yet again the role play felt extremely straightforward to teach in these two eras compared to how complicated it was to teach it in 2016, three years into the viral video sharing of police killings of black youth on social media and the emergence of the Movement for Black Lives. Another way to say this is that the volatile period of the 2010s requires situational awareness. If you tried to teach this role play in 2015, with a majority-white class, three weeks after Dylann Roof murdered nine devout black Christians in Charleston, no one would be able to effectively play the white thugs. It simply wouldn't work. On the other hand, teaching it immediately after the 2017 Charlottesville riots where twenty-year-old white Ohioan James Fields Jr. murdered white antiracist nonviolent activist Heather Heyer, it could work well, since students might be open to learning more about Heyer and the views for which she gave her life. Finally, it is important to let people in the building nearest your classroom know what is happening a few weeks ahead of time, and remind them a day or two before. The role play is loud, and depending on your building, can be disruptive to other classes. Explaining to colleagues what you are doing, and why, often can be extremely helpful.

The sit-in role play requires almost no prior preparation on the part of students. There are materials they can read or watch beforehand, but in my experience, there are real advantages to sharing this material afterward instead. Students enter the class, and before anything else I ask them to drop their usual classroom expectations. "Today, we're going to try something a little different. All I need from you is a sort of radical openness to something different from most of what we've experienced in this society in our daily lives. I'm going to ask you to sit in someone else's mindset for twenty to forty minutes. If you don't buy it at the end of the class, no problem. I just want you to experience it and respond in a way that feels true to you."

"Here's the back story. From 1865 until 1960, African Americans were not allowed to eat meals in public restaurants, pubs, or lunch counters across the South. A small group of primarily black college students changed this forever in the spring of 1960. On February 1, 1960, four students at North Carolina A & T—Franklin McCain, Ezell Blair Jr., David Richmond, and Joseph McNeil—sat-in at the Greensboro, North Carolina, Woolworth's. A wave of similar sit-ins followed. In the end, they signaled a new phase of the civil rights movement in which student activists moved to center stage. Twenty thousand students— most of them at historically black colleges and universities (HBCUs)— had desegregated over two thousand lunch counters across the South within a few months. Today we're going to figure out how they did it."

I ask for volunteers. "The role play will work—or not—based on one group, the 'white thugs.' I need people in the room who feel angry today. It doesn't matter if you're angry with parents, or a boyfriend or girlfriend, a teacher, an employer. I just need people who can channel their inner frustration and anger." Teaching this in a majority-black setting for a decade, I found that students who volunteered to be white thugs found this so different from their usual identity that they stepped into it relatively quickly—they were clear that they were acting a part. They understood white thugs were a historical and present-day reality, and that acting the part was critical to the success of the role play. They didn't feel that much conflict. Nonblack students often find this much more challenging. "Are people going to think I really feel antiblack sentiments if I act out this part?" To overcome this requires some additional support: I've often said, "Don't focus on the racism of the thugs for the purposes of acting this part. Instead, find that part of you that is angry, and frustrated, and act it out. If you don't fully embrace the inner thug, which all of us can find, it simply won't work." I ask for five to nine volunteers and give them each the following piece of paper:

THUG: Drop your concern for anyone but yourself and your fellow thugs. If you don't act your part full-out, the role play will not work. So it's up to you. Channel all your anger, all your frustration, into getting these trespassers out of the restaurant. Don't act like it's a role play. Act like they are invading your home, and you must get them out to protect your loved ones.

Channel this mindset: These people in this restaurant are a direct threat to your way of life. They are diseased, filthy, and dangerous. If they sit in your usual restaurant, soon they will be in your church, next to you in the pew. They will be married to your brother or sister. You will never find peace, because they are dangerous and out to corrupt your whole way of life. You must remove them: by ridicule if possible, by force if necessary. You may harass them, mock them, mess with them, and physically remove them. If you physically punish them, however, *you* can be arrested and they will win. To be clear, there can be no physical violence. I will cut the lights if I see anything getting out of control or if anyone from the sit-in group asks to stop. At that point you need to stop everything immediately.

Once they all have a paper, I ask the thugs to go in the hall, come up with a "Plan A" and a "Plan B" to get the sit-in students out of the restaurant. They leave, and I ask for sit-inners, also five to nine people, who are willing to experiment with a very different way of being for twenty minutes. "I need you to let go of the usual ways most of us have been taught to live. Many times, parents and other important people tell us to stand up for ourselves always, to fight if we have to, in order to maintain our personal dignity, 'Don't let anyone mess with you. Protect your little brother or sister.' Nonviolence is a different tactic, and for the next twenty minutes only, I'm asking you to dive in, explore it. It has amazing power." I then pass out pieces of paper to each sit-in volunteer:

NONVIOLENT ACTIVISTS: You must agree to obey the following rules of nonviolent resistance:

280

1. *Under no conditions* are you to strike back, either physically or verbally. Violence of spirit is even worse than striking back.
2. *Do not laugh out.* Do not leave your seat until your leader has given permission.
3. *Do show yourself friendly and courteous* at all times. Do refer information seekers to your leader in a polite manner.
4. Do sit straight, always face the counter.
5. Remember the teachings of Jesus, Gandhi, Martin Luther King Jr. Love and nonviolence is the way.

REMEMBER: Those who break the rules undermine the sacrifice of everyone else.

I ask them to come to the front, pull a chair and desk with them, and line them up next to each other like a lunch counter. "Strategize together while I get the rest of the class set up. You can link arms. You can sing. You can distract yourselves. You too need Plan A, Plan B, and maybe Plan C. When the thugs come at you, make sure you have some responses up your sleeves."

While the thugs and the sit-in people strategize separately, I pull the rest of the class closer together. "The next key person is the restaurant owner. A hard worker, someone who's put much of their work and money into this business. They aren't political. They just want to make a living. Who feels like they can do this role?" That person receives this piece of paper:

RESTAURANT OWNER: You have poured your life savings into this restaurant. If you don't serve at least twenty to thirty customers a day, you cannot pay your rent, your bills, or your waitresses, and you will quickly lose your business, all that you've worked so hard for. People are afraid of the sit-ins, the sit-ins drive away business, so you are very eager to convince the students to leave peacefully. If the police must be brought in, customers will be scared away. You're not anti-Negro, but you do not want trouble. Your goal is to keep serving as many customers as possible, and if you serve Negroes, you are convinced you will lose all your white customers.

Next, we need a few police officers—three or four. Two is fine if the class is small. "Your role is strange," I begin. "You are between a rock and a hard place. You're white. You can't arrest the white thugs, even if they're doing horrible, illegal things. You're trying to get the nonviolent people out of the restaurant. The mayor is on your case, so you have to be very careful. Read this and figure out some possible strategies together":

POLICE OFFICER: You have been told two opposite things by the mayor: you must keep blacks out of the downtown lunch counters, and you have to do this without arresting anyone. If blacks are allowed to eat at lunch counters, whites will stop going downtown to shop. If you arrest people for peacefully sitting-in, the city will look hateful on the national level, and people will stay away from shopping downtown. The city's most powerful merchants have told the mayor in clear terms: keep the sit-in people out, but do so peacefully. *Money must keep flowing downtown.* So that is your job. If you are rude, violent, or abusive toward anyone in this situation, you will reflect badly on your city, and people will stop shopping there.

The rest of the class remains. Usually these people are glad they escaped the role play. I make sure they know I expect them to volunteer later for round two as actors. For now, I split them up into four groups, to watch closely and report to the group as a whole after round one. I assign groups to watch the thugs, the sit-in people, the restaurant owner, and the police. I give them an "observer" sheet, and ask them to read it over. "During the role play, too much is happening too fast for any of us to catch it all. I need you to get up close to the role play. You *can't* sit at the back of the classroom. Come up close, and write down what you see your group doing." All students also receive this handout before the role play starts:

Circle your role below:

1. Your first role was: THUG   SIT-IN STUDENT   COP   OWNER   OBSERVER

2. Your second role was: THUG   SIT-IN STUDENT   COP   OWNER   OBSERVER

After the role play has run each time, please answer the following questions based on the roles you played. (Don't answer the questions if you didn't play the role.)

THUG

1. What is your response when the sit-in people ignore you?
2. How do you feel about verbally attacking people who you don't personally know?
3. How do you feel about committing public violence? Is it hard or easy?
4. How do you respond when the white police try to calm you down and ask you to leave?
5. What, if anything, was most successful in getting the sit-in students to physically fight back?

SIT-IN STUDENT

1. What is your emotional response when the thugs begin threatening, pushing, name-calling? Be sure to name all the emotions that run through your head.
2. How do you feel about remaining nonviolent? Is it easier, or harder, than getting violent?
 i. FOR MEN: Is it equally hard to remain nonviolent when one of your female peers is attacked, compared to when a male peer is attacked?
 ii. FOR WOMEN: How do you feel about the men in your group remaining nonviolent when you are harassed or attacked?
3. What worked best to keep everyone in your group nonviolent? Be sure to describe nonverbal actions as well as what you may have said.

POLICE OFFICER

1. How did you feel as a police officer watching the students getting beaten and not doing anything?
2. How did you feel as a white person watching the students demanding equal treatment?
3. How hard was it to end the situation peacefully? Explain what the barriers were to a peaceful resolution.

RESTAURANT OWNER

1. Why didn't you let the students be served?
2. How do you think ongoing sit-ins will affect your business?
3. What do you want the police to do?
4. How do you want this to be resolved?

OBSERVER

You have the most important job of all. Please write down *all observations*: who is rolling their eyes, who looks mad, who looks scared, who is tuning out, etc. Pick one group to observe (police officers, sit-in students, thugs, restaurant owner) and write down everything you observe.

1. How could this be resolved without violence?
2. What seems hardest for individual students about remaining nonviolent? For thugs? For the owner? For police?
3. Who takes the initiative in your group, and how do others in your group respond?

I then go into the hallway and check with the thugs. Do they have questions? Do they understand their role is the key? What are some of their plans? I tell them I will be standing by the light switch. If I see anything that requires us to stop, the lights will go off, and they need to cease. I tell them to barge into the classroom in exactly five minutes.

Back in the classroom, I tell the sit-in students that if they look directly at me and nod, or if they say "Stop," I will turn off the lights and the role play will cease immediately. I ask the observers to come closer, with their pens and paper. I say to the restaurant owner, "You're up! These people have just begun to sit-in at your restaurant. It's your job to get them out. When you exhaust your options, call the police. Police, be ready to come, but do not intervene until the owner calls. Begin."

I stand by the light switch and watch. Almost always, the thugs aren't thugish enough. The sit-in people hold their ground, the owner is eloquent or not, the police are ineffective. I hit the lights, end it, and ask the thugs to go back out in the hallway and come up with a better plan. While they're out, I check with the sit-in people. "What's your plan when they escalate?" We brainstorm. Sometimes they are uncomfortable singing or linking arms. I encourage them, "People had to come up with off-beat and innovative tactics to keep their seats in these situations. Try new things. See what gets the thugs off their rhythm. Try ignoring them and not looking at them. Try looking directly at them, and calmly engaging them. Sing louder than they're yelling." Often this isn't necessary, because the students come up with innovative and interesting things with encouragement—often things I've never seen. "OK, I'm going to tell the thugs we're ready." Then we rerun the role play.

If the thugs do their job, sit-in students inevitably get a strong taste of the tactic. They "know" it's a role play, and yet people violate their personal space, yell at them, throw bits of paper at them, take off their glasses, muss their hair. They experience how that feels, and what it is like to remain calm, to stay together with their group. The "police" are often beside themselves with frustration—they realize they have almost none of the tools of power besides brutality or arrest or both. The "owner" often tries repeatedly to plead with the students, either with grace and persuasiveness, anger and frustration, or simple un-enforceable threats. If the role play works, it always escalates, as that is the nature of the tactic. When nonviolent people hold their ground, thugs have to escalate in order to get them out of their seats. It is a simple, yet profound realization. Once the role play gets to that point, I turn off the lights, and ask everyone to stay where they are.

"Now is the most important part of today's class. People need to listen more closely than they might normally do to one another. You only saw part, and felt part, of the role play. So I'm going to start with the sit-in people. I'll go down the line. Tell me what this experience was like for you."

Students respond with an incredibly wide range of reports. I validate each experience verbally and encourage them to share their thinking, feeling, and analysis. Students report things like, "I didn't realize how difficult it was to have people in my space"; "I wish I didn't know how bad it felt to have people yell at me"; "No one deserves the things people said today; I felt both lesser to hear it and greater to be standing against it." Sometimes people say, "It didn't affect me much, I knew it was a role play." But more often than not, they explore the experience and begin to ask new questions about the sit-ins themselves. "How did people learn to do this? Where did this idea come from?" We investigate the difference between those who used it only as a tactic, because it effectively dramatized the undemocratic nature of Jim Crow for the world, and those who began to see nonviolence as a way of life. "Once they participated," I say, "some 1960s students felt transformed. They felt they could always put their bodies on the line against injustice. They began to see nonviolence as a way of life. It turned them in a whole new direction." I sometimes circle back in subsequent classes to highlight the lives of those who used nonviolence as a tactic: Ella Baker, Stokely Carmichael, Bob Moses; and those like Diane Nash, Bernard Lafayette, John Lewis, and Charles Sherrod, SNCC activists who stayed committed to nonviolence as a way of life for years and sometimes decades after the sit-ins of 1960.[4] One question almost always surfaces: "How did students respond with dignity when they were spat on?" Spitting hardly ever happens in the role play, but "thugs" often pretend, evoking a fierceness of response unlike anything other than bodily violence. "Jim Lawson's response is the most interesting one I know," I say. "When spat on outside a bus in Nashville, he turned immediately to the spitter, saying with great calm and politeness, 'May I please have your handkerchief?' The thug actually had one, pulled it out, and handed it to Lawson." Students also comment positively on the creativity of peers, at the different ways they each responded as nonviolent activists.

Next I ask the thugs how they felt. "Why did it take you so long to escalate? How did it feel to be denied what you wanted? Tell us what you felt like when you were yelling at people and humiliating them." Here, it's the variety of answers that help students understand how nonviolence works or doesn't work. There are always a few who talk about being on top and taking control. "That felt good, even though we were wrong." Others talk about how they had to psych themselves up in order to be cruel, how they only did it because I asked them to and they didn't want to let the others in the group down, and how they felt bad and wrong. "If you were a part of a group of white friends in 1960, and your friends went down to a restaurant and did this, what might make you become 'thuggish' too? What might make you turn away?" In this way, the "White South" becomes less of a monolith, and students begin to see how white youth might have acted not only out of learned habits of hatred, but also out of peer pressure, a desire for power, and insecurity.

Debriefing the restaurant owner's experience allows us to consider the wide variety of responses of businesses to the sit-ins—most were eager to end them. They often had to choose between desegregating their operation and risking ongoing demonstrations. The stark choices the sit-inners forced them into often shocks students. "Students had a lot of power. How could we force unfair businesses to reform today?" they ask. "Could we sit-in at Walmart since it refuses to pay people overtime?" This often leads to questions about the media. "Why did newspapers cover this only when people got hurt?" and "Why don't we hear more about the ways people use nonviolence in the US today?"

They ask about the connections between economic boycotts and non-violent demonstrations, given how much pressure the sit-ins put on businesses. If there is time, I ask students to consider how business owners might respond if they had taken out a small business loan requiring a monthly payment, in addition to paying suppliers, utilities, and workers. "How would you find the money to pay these bills if your restaurant was shut down for a whole month?"

Those in the police role often express incredulity. "Wow, we had no power. Horrible." They report expecting respect and feeling frustrated and flummoxed when both the students and the thugs ignore them. In many cases, the owner ridicules or eggs on police, asking them to "Do their job!" When police cannot, they report how easy it would be for police to "arrest everyone, and not make those arrests gentle, either." The powerlessness bewilders them. "If I got into this job to help people and protect my community, I would not have been able to do that in this situation," a person said once. "Why did people stay police in this time in the South? Why didn't they quit?" This opened up opportunities not only to look at police violence in the South but also to make connections to police violence in uprisings like Watts, Newark, Chicago, and Detroit later in the course and to the current Movement for Black Lives.

I ask the observers to report out: those who watched the sit-inners, then thugs, the owner, and police. Each person needs to put forward some observation, even if class time runs short, and they have to do it "rapid fire." Observers often add highly perceptive comments that deepen the discussion. "I noticed that Jonathan the Thug could only yell at people who refused to look at him. He stopped immediately when Cora looked him in the eye." That allowed us to delve into the idea of putting one's body on the line. "Is it harder to attack someone when they make their humanity visible to you? How does one do that? In what cases might it *not* work? Give me some examples of when this has happened to you." Observers make comments too about how they felt relieved and guilty on the sidelines. "I wanted to jump in," or "I'm glad I wasn't in that scene." We explore that. Why the desire to jump in? What is behind that? Why is it easier to turn away? What might that mean for political engagement on other issues? After the observers share, I ask questions about the role of the media: people had engaged in sit-ins for eighty years prior to 1960. Why did these particular events get picked up by media? Why were they so "photogenic"? How did this media coverage pressure local, state, and national governments? How did the Soviets use these photographs? How do you think this looked to people in Asia, Africa, and Latin America in 1960, as they were trying to establish their own governments free of European and American intervention?

After fifteen to twenty minutes for the first debrief, I ask students to pick anew. First, each observer has to take an active role. I ask if people active in the first round want to try a different role. Often thugs and sit-in people want to switch. Even if it means more actors and fewer observers, I encourage this. It means the second round is rowdier, and the second debrief is often more powerful and insightful than the first.

At the end of the class, I ask people to go back to the orderly classroom. "Pull your seats back into rows. Take a few breaths and clear your mind. I want to ask you to focus on your body for a minute. Is it tense? Where? Relaxed? How's your heartbeat?" They need at least two full minutes here. "Now focus your mind on what just transpired. What's the first feeling or scene that pops into your mind? It doesn't matter what it is, just think about what comes first. On the back of the piece of paper I handed you to record your observations, write it down. Riff on that—what associations can you make to other things we've talked about in class? That you've seen in politics or in your own life?"

Once we share from that reflection, I thank them for taking a time-out from the classroom as usual. "It's brave to take on a role that you don't inhabit, that you would not normally try out. It allows you to experience different approaches and thoughts, and that can be exhilarating, boring, unnerving, scary. All these responses are normal. If other thoughts and feelings occur to you later today or over the course of the week, and you're comfortable sharing, let me know. This is an important and nontraditional kind of learning, and it doesn't always happen in the confines of class. Sometimes you'll be walking to work, or taking a shower, or talking with a friend, and a new insight or image will occur to you. Hold on to those, write them down, bring them back to class. They will help us all get a better understanding of why this tactic works in certain situations, why it fails in others, and, most important, why it is so hard to get people to try it in the context of the United States."

With this encouragement, and the vivid experience of the role play in their minds and bodies, it makes it easy to bring up nonviolence again later in the course. "Would nonviolence work here? If not, why not?" Students easily see, for instance, why nonviolent direct action didn't work to stop business as usual during the 2011 Occupy Wall Street movement, or John Lewis's sit-in on the House floor in 2016, "Duh! No one's money stopped flowing because of those sit-ins!" or "Those sit-ins didn't cause international pressure on the current president!" I often follow up in the next class with photographs from the sit-in training sessions in 1960 to show they were not spontaneous, but took training, dedication, and a process of discerning if one could indeed sit in. If you learned in a test run that you couldn't handle someone spitting on you, you could serve as a support person, making sandwiches, calling the press, or driving people to the site.[5]

Learning this way also allows one to easily contrast this tactic with other movement tools such as boycotts, marches, or self-defense. Nonviolence stops being an "idea" and becomes a vivid reality with definable limits. The role play clarifies one of the most mystifying, often dismissed or ridiculed, and certainly most misunderstood components of the 1960s freedom movement.

RESOURCES

"Ain't Scared of Your Jails (1960–1961)." *Eyes on the Prize*, part 1, episode 3, February 4, 1987. Vimeo, https://vimeo.com/11879868.

Hogan, Wesley. "Freedom Now: Nonviolence in the Southern Movement, 1960–1964." In *Civil Rights History from the Ground Up: Local Struggles, a National Movement*, edited by Emilye Crosby. Athens: University of Georgia Press, 2011.

"Jim Lawson Conducts Nonviolence Workshops in Nashville." SNCC Digital Gateway, https://snccdigital.org/events/jim-lawson-conducts-nonviolent-workshops-in-nashville/.

Lewis, John. *Walking with the Wind: A Memoir of the Movement*. New York: Simon & Schuster, 2015.

Robinson, Phil Alden, dir. *Freedom Song*. TNT Original, 2000. DVD.

Waging Nonviolence: People-Powered News & Analysis (understanding nonviolence in current events), https://wagingnonviolence.org.

Zinn, Howard, ed. *The Power of Nonviolence: Writings by Advocates of Peace*. Boston: Beacon Press, 2002.

NOTES

The passion and creativity of hundreds of people as they respond to this role play has given this essay so much more power. I am grateful to that collective knowledge, as well as to those who have pushed me hard, sometimes because they strongly disagree, to rethink why and how a role play on nonviolence matters, particularly Hasan Jeffries, Emilye Crosby, LaTaSha Levy, Tim Tyson, Courtland Cox, Judy Richardson, Benj Demott, Dirk Philipsen, Nishani Frazier, and the young activists animating so much grassroots work in North Carolina, particularly Tyler Swanson, William Barber III, Ajamu Dillahunt-Holloway, Rebekah Barber, and Kenneth Campbell.

1. For recent work on the prevalence of self-defense in the civil rights movement, see Emilye Crosby, "It Wasn't the Wild West: Keeping Local Studies in Self-Defense Historiography," in *Civil Rights History from the Ground Up: Local Struggles, a National Movement*, ed. Emilye Crosby, 194–256 (Athens: University of Georgia Press, 2011); Akinyele Umoja, *We Will Shoot Back: Armed Resistance in the Mississippi Freedom Struggle* (New York: New York University Press, 2014); Charles Cobb, *This Nonviolent Stuff'll Get You Killed: How Guns Made the Civil Rights Movement Possible* (Durham, NC: Duke University Press, 2015).

2. H. Rap Brown (Jamil Abdullah Al-Amin), press conference at SNCC headquarters, Washington, DC, July 27, 1967, *Evening Star*, Washington, DC, July 27, 1967, p. 1.

3. For more background on role plays in teaching traumatic histories, see Lisa Woolfork, "Ritual Reenactments," in *Embodying American Slavery in Contemporary Culture* (Urbana: University of Illinois Press, 2010). Grant Farred calls the bodily epistemology I'm invoking in the process of participating in role play "vernacular intellectualism" in *What's My Name: Black Vernacular Intellectuals* (Minneapolis: University of Minnesota Press, 2003).

4. John Lewis and Jim Lawson stretched this longest in the public sphere; Lewis continued to participate in nonviolent direct action to support immigrants and the Voting Rights Act, and most recently he sat-in on the floor of Congress to demand gun control legislation in June 2016; Lawson continued to participate in nonviolent direct action into his eighties in support of campaigns for labor justice, immigration rights, and against police brutality. On Lewis, see "A Sit-in on the House Floor over Gun Control," *Atlantic*, June 22, 2016, http://www.theatlantic.com/politics/archive/2016/06/house-democrats-gun-control-sit-in/488264/, accessed August 11, 2016.

5. Other material that is helpful to use after the role play includes the dramatic scene in the 2000 Phil Alden Robinson film *Freedom Song* where the SNCC veterans are training youth in Quinlan to use nonviolence, https://www.youtube.com/watch?v=QqzjKBoVCtc, accessed August 12, 2016; the website Waging Nonviolence for examples from current events, http://wagingnonviolence.org/; and contrasting examples such as Malcolm X's "Ballot or the Bullet" speech, April 3, 1964, American RadioWorks, http://americanradioworks.publicradio.org/features/blackspeech/mx.html, accessed August 12, 2016.

California Democracy Schools

*A Model for Teaching Civil Rights
to Students of All Ages*

MICHELLE M. HERCZOG

There is little doubt that the civil rights movement was a transformative event in the psyche, culture, and polity of American society. It certainly disrupted the status quo and mainstream interpretation of the guiding principle of "we the people" set forth by the founders of our American democracy. And it laid the groundwork for Americans of all underrepresented groups to take bold steps for their voices to be heard and recognized. Movements to secure equal rights for women, immigrants, farm workers, the physically and mentally challenged, and the LGBTQ community *were* and *are* inspired by the brave leadership of the movement to secure equality for African Americans.

But as time moves on, memories fade and the voices of the frontline civil rights leaders, followers, and bystanders begin to fall silent. And sadly, for millions and millions of young people today who were not witness to the events of the civil rights era or do not have living relatives to retell the stories, this pivotal event becomes yet another chapter to read in their history books. The lines of history often become blurred in children's minds. For many, reading about Martin Luther King Jr. is akin to reading about Abraham Lincoln or George Washington—men honored with parades and a day off from school.

Many students today fail to recognize the enormity of the civil rights movement, especially how significant the risks and personal sacrifices for its leaders and the thousands who joined their ranks. You've undoubtedly heard their questions of incredulity. "What do you mean, African American's couldn't go to the same schools, eat at the same restaurants, or use the same swimming pools as white people?" "How could Americans treat people so unfairly?" "Why was it so difficult to create a change?" It is an exceptional teacher who can help young people contextualize the time and place where these conditions existed; help them see, hear, and study the testimonials and video assets that tell the story; help them fully understand the reality of the times and the enormous risk and courage many took and sacrificed in the name of equality and justice for all.

But truly understanding the context and impact of the civil rights movement *then* and what it means in today's world requires more. Much more. It is a skilled teacher who can help students delve into the complexities of the movement, recognize the successes and failures, the setbacks and advancements of the cause—and most importantly, help students understand the enormity of the impact then and the enormity of the impact today. *How far have we come as a nation? How far do we still need to go?* These are the difficult and compelling questions of our time. And if we do not guide students to this level of conversation and do not guide them to a place where they are empowered to address the complex civil rights issues in today's society, we have lost the opportunity to make history meaningful, powerful, and relevant. We will, in essence, offer students a "story well told" rather than a "story that can be learned, acted upon, and realized in today's world."

The future of our democracy depends on a citizenry that is informed, responsible, and actively engaged. As retired Supreme Court justice Sandra Day O'Connor is noted for saying, "Knowledge of our system of government and rights and responsibilities as citizens is not passed down through the gene pool, it must be taught." By teaching social studies—history, geography, economics, civics, and the humanities—in ways that intentionally compel students to apply what they have learned to address the ills and issues of our world today, we will truly learn not to repeat the mistakes of the past and will be able to improve the lives of all people around the globe.

The California Democracy School
Civic Learning Initiative

Was the civil rights movement a success? This is a great way to launch an investigative study of the civil rights movement for students of all ages. Utilizing an inquiry-driven approach engages students in deep analysis of this historic period and allows them to make connections to the world today. It is this approach to teaching and learning that inspired the creation of the California Democracy School Civic Learning Initiative.[1]

The instructional approach of the Initiative, directed by the Los Angeles County Office of Education and funded by the S. D. Bechtel, Jr. Foundation, was informed by the C3 Framework for Social Studies State Standards,[2] the Common Core State Standards,[3] the Guardian of Democracy Report of the Civic Mission of Schools,[4] and the Partnership for 21st Century Learning.[5] This three-year program was designed to institutionalize high-quality civic learning in ten high schools in Los Angeles County and two high schools in Orange County to ensure that *all* students engage in a high-quality civic inquiry and investigation at least once in their high school career.

The schools represented a wide spectrum of geographic, economic, and demographic diversity including a continuation high school in Compton and a school for incarcerated girls at a juvenile hall camp. Teachers from all twelve schools were provided intensive professional development and ongoing coaching and technical assistance to deliver curriculum as described by the Four Dimensions of the C3 Framework but with a civic learning twist.

The Civic Inquiry and Investigation Model

The process begins with a *civic inquiry* that frames a public problem or issue that is relevant to students and can lead to civic action. This leads to *research and investigation* led by students to identify multiple perspectives of the causes and implications of the identified issue. From there, students engage in *civil dialogue* that reveals information, pro and con arguments, and evidence to support a conclusion. The last step is to allow students to strengthen their "civic muscles" by *taking informed civic action* based on their deep analysis of the issue and the various implications of the public policy solution they propose.

This inquiry-based approach to instruction should sound familiar. Like the Common Core State Standards and the Next Generation Science Standards, civic learning described this way focuses on the same pedagogical principles—inquiry-driven instruction that promotes deep learning, critical thinking and analysis of findings, and the development of conclusions based on evidence leading ultimately to the application of acquired knowledge and information in the real world to solve real-world problems.[6]

What Does It Look Like in the Classroom?

Bellflower Middle/High School in the Bellflower Unified School District in Bellflower, California, embraced this approach as one of twelve California Democracy Schools. As a result of their participation, the school has successfully institutionalized the civic inquiry and investigation model in all social studies classes in all grades, seven through twelve.

In all eleventh-grade social studies classes, students begin their study of the civil rights movement with this compelling question: *"How has the United States met the goals set forth by the civil rights movement of the 1960s?"* This opening question begs further inquiry—*What WAS the civil rights movement of the 1960s about? What was happening at that time to propel the movement? What happened in the movement? Was it a success? Was it a failure? What was learned?*

At this point, students are motivated to investigate the history and the complexities of the movement but are still drawn to the opening inquiry—*What were the goals and were they met?* Through deep research and investigation, students begin to come up with conclusions based on the evidence they have found.

An important next step in the civic inquiry and investigation process is to engage students in dialogue that is civil, respectful, and informative. We all know that the political landscape is littered with poor modeling for this important civic attribute. How can we as a nation learn to respect differences of opinions and differences in lifestyles if we cannot learn how to listen, learn, and respond in a respectable manner? It is an important skill that must be learned and mastered in a civil society.

Diana Hess, dean of the School of Education at the University of Wisconsin–Madison is considered a national expert on this subject and has valuable research and tips for the importance of dialogue in the classroom in her books, *Controversy in the Classroom* and *The Political Classroom*, coauthored with Paula McAvoy.[7]

The teachers in our Democracy Schools are trained in the use of Socratic Seminar, Philosophical Chairs, and the Structured Academic Controversy approach highlighted in the Deliberating in a Democracy program.[8] Professional development online modules are now available at no cost for others to learn these techniques.[9] The teachers at Bellflower engage their students in this type of civil dialogue and reach their conclusions about the guiding inquiry question.

Now comes the exciting part. Students have not all reached consensus about whether the goals of the civil rights movement have been fully met for all African Americans. But they begin to think about what can be done now, today, to close the gaps for African Americans. And their thinking goes further as they speculate about the civil rights of other groups. *Have the same goals of equality and justice been achieved for others? For Latinos in America? For Muslims in America? For women? For members of the LGBTQ community?* The list goes on and on, and students are compelled to investigate the civil rights of these different groups and also the civil rights of immigrants, the disabled, and homeless veterans. They go through the same process of investigating the issue, analyzing and discussing different points of view, and coming up with conclusions; finally, and most significantly, they find ways to take informed action to address the problems they uncover.

For some, the action is as simple as raising awareness in the surrounding community of the discrimination faced by different groups. For others it is about forming and facilitating forums and town halls to educate the public. For others still, it is reaching out to local and state policymakers to introduce legislation to combat the problems raised. Some of these efforts are successful. Some are not. That, too, is a lesson in democracy. What can be learned by being an informed, engaged citizen? It is not always easy to achieve your goals, but integrity and persistence are traits that all Americans should embrace as responsible citizens in a democratic society.

The culminating event at Bellflower Middle/High School is the annual Civics Fair. Student projects from across the school are displayed. The various civic inquiries include the following:

- What can residents do to enhance and improve their communities?
- How has local government been responsive to the needs of its citizens?
- How has the United States met the goals set forth in the Preamble of the US Constitution?
- What are the most challenging obstacles facing immigrants to the United States today?
- How has the United States achieved a democratic society for all?
- How should governments respond to epidemics?
- Is the international community doing enough to prevent, suppress, and punish the crime of genocide?

The Civic Learning Arc

Marshall Croddy, president of the Constitutional Rights Foundation, and Peter Levine, director of the Center for Information and Research on Civic Learning and Engagement at Tufts University, brilliantly qualify this approach, modeled after the College, Career, and Civic Life (C3) Framework for Social Studies State Standards as a "civic learning arc" that "anticipates the concepts and tools necessary for informed, skilled, and engagement participation in civic life" in the following ways.[10]

Dimension 1: Developing Questions and Planning Inquiries

On a daily basis American citizens are confronted with a dizzying array of compelling civics-related questions: What is justice? What does equal protection really mean? What are the appropriate limits of government power? What foreign policy should the United States pursue? Dimension 1 helps prepare students identify and construct compelling and supporting questions and make determinations about the kinds of information sources that will be helpful in answering them. These capacities are essential for informed and engaged participation in civic life.

Dimension 2: Applying Disciplinary Concepts and Tools

Dimension 2 provides another set of lenses for a student preparing for civic life to utilize. The C3 Framework emphasizes essential concepts and skills drawn from the disciplines of civics, economics, geography, and history, all of which are critical for an understanding of the problems, issues, and controversies that confront policy makers and citizens alike.

Dimension 3: Evaluating Sources and Using Evidence

In this, the Information Age, with its vast array of print, electronic, and emerging media, the ability of participants in civic life to evaluate a multitude of sources is more important than ever. Moreover, in times of highly charged and partisan political discourse, when one-third fewer people work as professional journalists than in 1989, but billions are spent on campaign advertising, claims often stem from polemics and ideology rather than facts or evidence. Any citizen seeking to be informed on an issue, advocate a position, or decide on candidates for office must be able to develop and evaluate claims by the use of evidence.

Dimension 4: Communicating Conclusions and Taking Informed Action

From the point of view of a civics educator, Dimension 4, Communicating Conclusions and Taking Informed Action, is among the most bold, important, and innovative aspects of the C3 Framework. With this dimension students learn to apply the learnings from the previous dimensions and develop concepts and skills for active engagement in the real world.

The *civic learning arc* makes two especially important interventions. First, it recognizes the importance of, and articulates concepts and skills necessary for, making and critiquing arguments, debate, and discussion in a plural democracy. These concepts and skills are applicable to the courtroom, the political arena, and all manner of civic discourse.

Second, it recognizes that to be engaged citizens, students need to know how to frame and address real problems, deliberate and collaborate with others, and plan and take action to address political, societal, and community issues. It might be said that students learn best by doing. For example, civic education research has found that students best develop civic capacities and competencies through active learning such as with the discussion of real issues in the classroom; simulations, in which they take on roles that model civic processes such as trials, hearings, and the legislative processes; and service-learning, linked to the curriculum.

Conclusion

Guiding students through a deep analysis of the complexities of a historic event driven by a compelling question and resulting in the application of knowledge by taking informed action may begin with the standards but can take students so much further. Even young children understand concepts of fairness, equality, and justice. Introducing them to stories of Rosa Parks, Martin Luther King Jr., Cesar Chavez, Fred T. Korematsu, and other civil rights leaders of the past will inform their ability to grapple with inequities that exist today. Furthermore, it will inspire them to address the myriad issues they confront in their everyday lives.

Students find the approach engaging and inspiring—young people *want* to talk about and study these complex issues that are not just chapters in a history book but issues they confront on a daily basis. *Are there challenges for teachers?* Of course there are. Introducing topics that are controversial or even contentious can raise the hair on the necks of teachers, parents, and administrators alike. But careful facilitation of the instruction with intentionality around analysis of multiple perspectives in a neutral unbiased way is essential. If we want students to be critical thinkers and informed citizens, we need to allow them the time and space in a "safe environment" to grapple with points of view that may be different than their own.

If every teacher can transform the teaching of the civil rights movement into a teachable moment that will empower students with the knowledge and skills they need to be engaged, responsible citizens, the future of democracy will be strengthened and the hopes and dreams of all groups will be realized. That is our hope and our dream for America.

NOTES

1. California Democracy School Civic Learning Initiative, Los Angeles County Office of Education, http://www.lacoe.edu/californiademocracyschool, 2016.

2. *College, Career, and Civic Life (C3) Framework for Social Studies State Standards* (Silver Spring, MD: National Council for the Social Studies, 2013).

3. *Common Core State Standards*, Common Core State Standards Initiative, http://www.corestandards.org.

4. *Guardian of Democracy: The Civic Mission of Schools*, Campaign for the Civic Mission of Schools in partnership with the Leonore Annenberg Institute for Civics of the Annenberg Public Policy Center at the University of Pennsylvania, the National Conference on Citizenship, the Center for Information and Research on Civic Learning and Engagement at Tufts University, and the American Bar Association Division for Public Education, https://www.carnegie.org/publications/guardian-of-democracy-the-civic-mission-of-schools/.

5. Partnership for 21st Century Learning: A Network of Battelle for Kids, http://www.battelleforkids.org/networks/p21.

6. Michelle Herczog, "Next Generation Citizens: Promoting Civic Engagement in Schools," *Leadership* (Association of California School Administrators) 45, no. 5 (May/June 2016): 24–28.

7. Diana E. Hess, *Controversy in the Classroom: The Democratic Power of Discussion* (New York: Routledge, 2009); Diana E. Hess and Paula McAvoy, *The Political Classroom: Evidence and Ethics in Democratic Education* (New York: Routledge, 2015).

8. Deliberating in a Democracy in the Americas, Constitutional Rights Foundation, http://www.deliberating.org.

9. California Democracy School Professional Development Series, Los Angeles County Office of Education, 2016, http://www.lacoe.edu/cds-onlinepd.

10. Marshall Croddy and Peter Levine, "The C3 Framework: A Powerful Tool for Preparing Future Generations for Informed and Engaged Civic Life," *Social Education* (National Council for the Social Studies) 78, no. 6 (2014): 282–85.

Walking in Their Shoes

*Using #BlackLivesMatter to Teach
the Civil Rights Movement*

Shannon King

On August 9, 2014, Darren Wilson, a white police officer, fatally shot Michael Brown, an African Ameri-
can eighteen-year-old, on the streets of Ferguson, Missouri, a suburb
of St. Louis. Brown's death set off a social movement against antiblack
violence during President Barack H. Obama's second term. Since
then, across the nation and across the globe, African American activists
and their allies have participated in a range of political protests—from
candlelight vigils to die-ins—coalescing under the umbrella of the Movement for Black Lives, which has profoundly shaped not only black politics but also American politics, from local elections to the 2016 presidential election. From the very beginning, the Black Lives Matter movement
(BLMM) has been compared to the civil rights struggles of the 1960s.
These comparisons have often been used to denigrate the BLMM as well
as to highlight the uniqueness of this particular phase of the much longer
black movement for "freedom," what both activists and scholars call
the black freedom movement.

Although the Black Lives Matter slogan became popular in the
wake of the Ferguson protest, the phrase was birthed in July 2013 on
Facebook in a post by Alicia Garza, one of the three cofounders of the
Black Lives Matter network, after news of the acquittal of George Zim-
merman, who had killed Trayvon Martin, an African American teenager in Sanford, Florida, the year before. Garza, Patrisse Cullors, and

Opal Tometi, the cofounders of the BLM network, had been involved in different areas of the struggle well before the birth of the BLMM. Like Student Nonviolent Coordinating Committee (SNCC) adviser Ella Baker, who believed that "strong people don't need strong leaders," they embraced a group-centered form of leadership. As Cullors explains, the BLMM "is leader-full," not leaderless. Indeed, these two movements share much in common.[1]

This chapter uses my first-year seminar course, #BlackLivesMatter, which I taught during the fall of 2015 at The College of Wooster, to consider how educators might use the BLMM to teach the civil rights movement. In addition to discussing the conceptual framework and historical thinking behind the syllabus and the course, this chapter foregrounds the ways that the BLMM helped us make comparisons to 1960s activism and, in many cases, think more deeply about the civil rights movement. This chapter builds on and further develops the themes and ideas that came up throughout the semester.

The impetus to teach this course came from one of my students, Chadwick Smith, himself a young activist. During the spring of 2015, I told him that I was teaching a first-year seminar (FYS) and asked if he would be willing to be my teacher's apprentice, as well as asking what he thought I should teach. He quickly said: "Yes! A course on the Black Lives Matter movement!" One of the learning objectives of all FYS courses is to prepare incoming students for undergraduate learning at a liberal arts college. To do this, I tried to create a syllabus and assign readings that enabled them to lead discussions and control the tempo of the classroom. In this course, I lectured infrequently, and the students generally read essays under thirty pages. While there were often moments of silence, we generally had robust conversations. Because students controlled the focus and pace of the discussions, they were able to immerse themselves in the readings, films, social media, and the BLMM itself on their own terms.

Syllabus and Pedagogy

I designed a syllabus that provided a historical background to the BLMM. The syllabus highlighted the ways that the civil rights movement and the post–civil rights era created a context for the BLM era. Our first-year seminars are designed to teach students to think of writing as a process, including notetaking, drafting, and revision.

This course introduced students to the variety of primary sources, including oral histories, memoir, autobiography, and speeches, and secondary sources, such as scholarly articles, magazines, online essays, and films. By providing an array of source materials, we were able to address some of the key learning goals of the course. First, we interrogated the Master Narrative, trying to understand why it centers Martin Luther King Jr.'s leadership and organizational style and lifts up nonviolent resistance as the signature characteristic of the movement. Second, I introduced students to alternative forms of leadership and organization such as Baker's and Cullors's as foundational to the movement. And third, I foregrounded the problem of antiblack violence as an ongoing aspect of the black freedom struggle.[2]

"Did we stop at anytime?"

I began by pointing out to students the glaring gulf between how scholars understand the civil rights movement and the Master Narrative so that they could begin thinking about the civil rights movement, not as a singular national effort led by Dr. King, but rather as a series of concurrent and overlapping local movements, linked by national organizations—the NAACP, Congress of Racial Equality (CORE), Southern Christian Leadership Conference (SCLC), and SNCC—and spearheaded by grassroots leaders who remained active long after the 1960s ended. By centering local movements, students saw how grassroots politics contributed to the struggle at the local level and shaped the larger national struggle. This approach also helped students learn about the various roles that local, state, and federal governments played in the movement, sometimes helping it, other times hindering it.

I scheduled three weeks on civil rights history. During this time, I had the students watch several episodes of *Eyes on the Prize*, examine oral histories from the *Eyes* companion reader, review journalists' accounts, and read essays and speeches.[3] We began this unit with the 1961–1962 Albany Movement in Albany, Georgia, and ended with the voting rights campaign in Selma, Alabama, in 1965. I chose these iconic campaigns involving Dr. King as a way to encourage students to consider him as a part of a cast of leaders from different national, state, and grassroots organizations with their own distinctive political orientations, strategies, tactics, and ideas. By examining these local battles, students became familiar with Ella Baker, SNCC, and the "local people" who often made up grassroots insurgencies. I centered Baker so that students learned not only how she mentored SNCC's young activists, instilling in the organization a commitment to democratic leadership, but also so that they became familiar with her long history of activism before the 1960s. Although we began in the 1960s, I tried, whenever possible, to introduce the students to important civil rights leaders, intellectuals, and activists from previous decades without spending too much time lecturing. Also, by foregrounding the local movements, students learned about grassroots efforts that preceded the 1960s and extended beyond the South.[4]

In Albany, for example, SNCC's Charles Sherrod and Cordell Reagon, working with a network of professional, religious, and secular organizations, formed the Albany Movement. This local movement was led by Dr. William Anderson, a doctor and drugstore owner. Thus SNCC, not Dr. King's SCLC or the NAACP, planted roots first in Albany. I also introduce here the important differences between these groups. Whereas SCLC was led by black ministers and used nonviolent protest to bring about desegregation, mainly in the southern cities, SNCC organized in urban and rural areas, developed local leaders, and stayed in town long after national attention faded away. Although Dr. King eventually came to Albany in December 1961, he left the following year after he and SCLC were unable to desegregate the city. Once they were introduced to grassroots campaigns, my students began to understand the nuances and complexities of local politics and the problems and possibilities they posed for leaders and the movement.[5]

As we interrogated these questions through the course material, similar questions about leadership were being raised about the BLMM. Many of the students, even those following well-known activists such as DeRay Mckesson on different social media platforms, were unclear about its leadership structure and philosophy. We read Oprah Winfrey's interview with *People* magazine about Ava DuVernay's *Selma*, which sparked a particularly passionate discussion of the BLMM's leadership. Although Winfrey thought it was "wonderful to march and to protest and it's wonderful to see all across the country, people doing it," she believed that BLMM lacked leadership. She told *People*, "what I'm looking for is some kind of leadership to come out of this to say, 'This is what we want. This is what has to change, and these are the steps that we need to take to make these changes, and this is what we're willing to do to get it.'"[6]

Winfrey's comments raised questions about the BLMM's prepared-
ness to negotiate with public officials, as well as whether they could
manage tactics, strategies, and political objectives. We also read edito-
rials written by established scholars in the subfields of civil rights and
Black Power studies. By situating the BLMM in the context of the leadership styles of Dr. King and SNCC, historians Barbara Ransby and Peniel
Joseph proffered a corrective to Winfrey's characterization of the BLMM.
In *Colorlines*, Ransby explained that the BLMM was, in fact, "leader-
full," as BLM network cofounder Patrisse Cullors had announced.
Ransby noted that the movement might seem "leaderless" to Winfrey,
since she was "describing the King style of leading, . . . as the strong,
all-knowing, slightly imperfect but still not-like-us type of leader." Joseph, writing in the *Root*, made similar points, explaining that "the call
for vertical or top-down leadership . . . ignores the horizontal, grassroots organizing that transformed American democracy during the
civil rights era." While acknowledging the movement's demands for
broad objectives for racial and economic justice and de-incarceration,
Joseph agreed with Winfrey's concern that now was the time for the
BLMM to propose specific policy initiatives.[7]

As we discussed the significance of public policy and the probable
tepid response of the Obama administration, the discussion returned to
leadership styles, particularly the significance of grassroots leadership
during the early 1960s. We discussed the conflicting portrayals of the
movement in Albany, a local struggle many have judged as a failure.
We revisited Juan Williams's chapter on the Albany Movement in *Eyes
on the Prize* and the oral history in the reader *Voices of Freedom*. It is often
said that Albany taught King and SCLC a lesson in tactical and strategic
planning, and, more importantly, it established the groundwork for the
success of the campaign in Birmingham, Alabama, in 1963. This particular framing of the Albany Movement, however, privileges King and
SCLC as the principal protagonists of the historical narrative and ignores the voices of the local people and grassroots leadership.

As Ransby and Joseph explained, other leadership styles, particularly SNCC's, played a central role in civil rights struggles. Committed
to cultivating indigenous leadership, Sherrod viewed the Albany Movement differently and questioned contemporary portrayals of the movement. He asked, "Where's the failure? Are we not integrated in every
facet? Did we stop at any time?"[8] Sherrod's perspective required a
group-centered or "leaderfull" form of leadership that prioritized the

self-mobilization of local people. As Dr. William G. Anderson, the president of the local movement organization stated, "the Albany Movement was a qualified success." Acknowledging that "none of the facilities had been voluntarily desegregated [after SCLC departed]," Anderson spoke about how the movement, nonetheless, raised the consciousness of the black community. So, although the Albany Movement ended with King and SCLC, the freedom struggle in Albany lived on. As Sherrod rightly queried, "Did we stop at anytime?"[9]

Discussing Winfrey's comments and the popular framing of the Albany Movement as a failure forced us to reconsider the BLM activists' demands on their own terms as well as the pacing of their decisions, particularly since they have chosen a horizontal, decentralized leadership structure that privileges local people. It also forced us to think about the ways in which sit-ins, marches, and other forms of civil disobedience sometimes unintentionally mask the often invisible, slow, and developmental work of the organizing tradition. Our discussion pushed us, as historians and writers, to rethink how to understand and write about historical narratives that require us to center historical actors at the local and national levels of the story.[10]

"When King was alive we had the Watts riots"

As we began to discuss the murder of Michael Brown by officer Darren Wilson in Ferguson, Missouri, the class returned once again to the role of King as a proponent of nonviolence. After Brown was killed and his body was left unceremoniously in the street, half covered, for four hours, with "a stream of blood winding its way across the asphalt," residents from the block led candlelight vigils, but as their anger intensified over not only the loss of one of their own but also over the persistence of police brutality and the militarized response to peaceful protest, young people erupted, setting a couple of buildings on fire and tossing bottles at riot police.[11] The Ferguson Police Department (FPD), whose heavily weaponized presence antagonized protestors from the beginning, responded by firing tear gas and rubber bullets into the crowds, while a SWAT team patrolled the area in armored vehicles. Ferguson residents took to the streets and rebelled again when the St. Louis County grand jury refused to indict Officer Wilson.[12]

On the cable news station CNN, Don Lemon, covering the story of the looting, interviewed veteran civil rights leader Reverend Jesse

Jackson. Lemon described the looting singularly as an expression of criminality. Lemon subtly employed "law and order" rhetoric signaling Barry Goldwater's efforts to criminalize black activism and black uprisings in his run for the presidency in 1964. Jackson knew better. Reminding Lemon that while he was "fundamentally an advocate of nonviolence," he "underst[oo]d how pain play[ed] out when it's compounded, and it is a long train of abuses." Concluding the interview, Lemon compared Ferguson's explosion to the nonviolent protests of the 1960s. "Reverend, part of your legacy is that you marched with Dr. King peacefully, nonviolently. . . . What has changed in our culture and our society that people result—resort to things that played out here last night in Ferguson?" Jackson promptly called Lemon's attention to the fact that there were riots during the civil rights era, asking rhetorically, "You do know that when King was alive we had the Watts riots and the Newark riots and the Detroit riots and Chicago?"[13]

Since we had watched Ava DuVernay's *Selma* and had all been moved by the opening scene of the bombing of the 16th Street Baptist Church and her depiction of Bloody Sunday, the courageous march of Selma demonstrators across the Edmund Pettus Bridge, the students understood that nonviolent resistance lived alongside legal and extra-legal violence. DuVernay's film, as well as the episodes of *Eyes on the Prize*, provided visual evidence of the complicated politics around anti-black violence in the black freedom struggle. In order to place Lemon's comments about peaceful, nonviolent resistance in historical context, we revisited the Birmingham campaign, another well-known struggle associated with King. Although he embodied nonviolence, King persistently challenged the "law and order" rhetoric of white southern segregationists. Reverend Fred Shuttlesworth, the chairperson of the Alabama Christian Movement for Human Rights, invited King and SCLC to Birmingham to help desegregate the city and rehabilitate King's reputation following his inability to change things in Albany. Beginning the demonstrations in early April 1963, SCLC implemented Campaign C (for confrontation), targeting first the city's business district and then marching to city hall and through the streets of downtown. From the start, however, Theophilus Eugene "Bull" Connor, the city's commissioner of public safety, met nonviolence with violence. On April 6, 1963, Reverend A. D. King, Dr. King's younger brother, led a prayer march through the streets of downtown Birmingham, where Connor's police force met them with raised batons and barking dogs.

After Dr. King was arrested for ignoring an injunction by leading a march through the streets, eight white ministers from Birmingham castigated him and denounced the demonstrations, which they described in a letter published in the *Birmingham News* as "unwise and untimely." On April 12, 1963, in a "Letter to Martin Luther King," the clergymen framed the demonstrations as transgressions of law and order. At the same time that they condemned the movement, the ministers applauded "law enforcement officials in particular" and asked them "to remain calm and continue to protect [their] city from violence." They urged Birmingham's black community to withdraw from the demonstrations and to use the courts rather than the streets. Employing language similar to Don Lemon's, the ministers appealed to both blacks and whites to "observe the principle of law and order and common sense."[14]

As a rejoinder to their letter, Dr. King penned his "Letter from Birmingham Jail." Rejecting the notion that the demonstrations were "unwise and untimely," he explained, "Frankly, I have yet to engage in a direct-action campaign that was 'well timed' in the view of those who have not suffered unduly from the disease of segregation." More significantly, he revealed the white ministers' law-and-order rhetoric as a liberal strategy of legitimating segregation and the status quo. Challenging the presumption that laws were intrinsically just, Dr. King wrote that there were "just and unjust" laws and that "any law that degrades human personality is unjust."[15]

Discourses of law and order reinforced rather than eroded segregation. Law-and-order rhetoric, in this sense, as Jesse Jackson expressed to Don Lemon, was a way to erase and ignore the violence that precipitated the protests in the first place—whether it be in Ferguson or Baltimore. Furthermore, Dr. King also questioned the ministers' commitment to civility and "order," stating that he doubted that the ministers "would have so warmly commended the police force if you had seen its dogs sinking their teeth into unarmed, nonviolent Negroes."[16] While Dr. King would not have supported the looting and violence in Ferguson, he, like Jesse Jackson, would have focused on the repressive behavior of the police and would have been more than sympathetic to Ferguson's explosive rejection of St. Louis County's decision not to indict Darren Wilson, which many interpreted as sanctioning the murder of Michael Brown. As King once said, "a riot is the language of the unheard."[17]

In fact, as the movement leveraged greater pressure on the city's law enforcement agencies, Bull Connor expanded the scale of violence he leveled at nonviolent demonstrators. My students made two observations about the Birmingham campaign. First, they saw brief instances of retaliation on the part of black youth watching the repression of nonviolent demonstrators, highlighting how self-defense often coexisted with nonviolence. And second, they commented on how the actions of law enforcement officers in Birmingham and Selma reminded them of what they had seen in Ferguson. As the protesters filled the jails to capacity and SCLC's Rev. James Bevel convinced Birmingham's black youth, ranging in age from six to eighteen, to join the movement, Connor called on the city's firefighters to turn their hoses on the children. Peaceful protest, in other words, was met with powerfully violent streams of water and police violence. These images of brutal police officers, vicious barking dogs, and vulnerable yet valiant black children were broadcast nationally and internationally, spotlighting white supremacy and police lawlessness. Indeed, those images were not too different from what we all watched on our computers, televisions, and cellphones—a police-created war zone in the streets of America.[18]

"Those deaths were forgotten"

After we examined the killing of Michael Brown, we discussed the history of Ferguson's police department in order to locate the death of Brown in the area's social, political, and economic context. Although Officer Wilson was not indicted, the Department of Justice (DOJ) investigation into the Ferguson Police Department found that its practices were "shaped by the city's focus on revenue rather than by public safety needs" and that "African Americans experienced disparate impact in nearly every aspect of Ferguson's law enforcement system." In other words, the city of Ferguson criminalized the black community and used court fees, arrest warrants, and other kinds of fines to fund the city's budget.[19] Similar patterns of police violence appeared in Baltimore too. Before black Baltimore resident Freddie Gray died in police custody, there were multiple cases of police brutality in that city. The *Baltimore Sun* reported that since 2011, the city paid nearly $6 million in court judgments and settlements in 102 lawsuits "alleging police brutality and other misconduct." The findings of the DOJ and *Sun* investigations shocked the students, for, in different ways, the deaths of Brown and Gray revealed the stubborn persistence of police violence in the post–civil rights era.[20]

These narratives of unrelenting antiblack violence and state-sanctioned racism reminded us of the harrowing stories told by CORE's Dave Dennis and SNCC's Kwame Ture (nee Stokely Carmichael) about how the government failed to value black life. In order to bring greater attention to the movement in Mississippi in the summer of 1964, national and local civil rights groups formed the Council of Federated Organizations (COFO) and invited white students from prestigious northern colleges and universities to participate in Freedom Summer, a summer-long campaign to empower black Mississippians through freedom schools and voter registration. At the start of Freedom Summer, three CORE activists, James Chaney, Michael Schwerner, and Andrew Goodman went missing. Using the *Voices of Freedom* oral history reader, we discussed Dennis's description of the FBI's search for the young men. Dennis recalled that "they found torsos in the Mississippi River, they found people who were buried, they even found a few bodies of people on the side of the roads. As soon as it was determined that their bodies were not the three mission workers, or one of the three, those deaths were forgotten." Dennis's recollection of the "forgotten" black bodies led some of us to think about the #SayHerName initiative started by the African American Policy Forum.[21] That the FBI ignored the bodies, we thought, was emblematic of the failure of the federal and state governments to protect black southerners from civilian and police violence in the Jim Crow South. Because white violence against African Americans was generally state sanctioned, no one could know how many black lives had been forgotten about by all except their loved ones.

Dennis's memories of the forgotten speak to how little black life mattered in the Jim Crow South. Ture felt the same way. He remarked:

> We've died out of proportion to numbers, and yet even today when people speak they will tell you once again about Goodman and Schwerner. Everybody forgot about Chaney. The names are recorded—Jimmy Lee Jackson, Herbert Lee—and so many, many, many names are not even known. Even the names of the children blown up in the church in Birmingham, Alabama, are not as well known as the names of Chaney and Goodman and Schwerner. Of course, we're still bitter to this day about it, because it still means that our life is not worth, even in death, the life of anybody else—that their life is still more precious.[22]

Collectively, these stories of antiblack violence, both civilian and state sanctioned, signaled for the students how the American government—at every level and across every region—has failed to protect its black citizens. And reflecting on the BLMM in the classroom setting, especially its leadership structure, strategies, and tactics, helped them make better sense of the civil rights movement. More significantly, the forgetfulness that Dennis spoke of and Ture's notion that "our life is not worth, even in death, the life of anybody else" exemplified, for many students, exactly why the slogan "#BlackLivesMatter" is such a powerful expression not only of this present struggle but the overall history of Africans in America.

NOTES

1. Alicia Garza, "A Herstory of the #BlackLivesMatter Movement," *Feminist Wire*, October 7, 2014, http://www.thefeministwire.com/2014/10/black livesmatter-2/, accessed July 30, 2016; Jelani Cobb, "The Matter of Black Lives," *New Yorker*, March 14, 2016, 35.

2. For variations of the "grand narrative," see Jacquelyn Dowd Hall, "The Long Civil Rights Movement and the Political Uses of the Past," *Journal of American History* 91, no. 4 (March 2005): 1233–63; Renee C. Romano and Leigh Raiford, eds., *The Civil Rights Movement in American Memory* (Athens: University of Georgia Press, 2006); Emilye Crosby, ed., *Civil Rights History from the Ground Up: Local Struggles, a National Movement* (Athens: University of Georgia Press, 2011); Jeanne Theoharis, *A More Beautiful and Terrible History: The Uses and Misuses of Civil Rights History* (Boston: Beacon Press, 2018); Julian Bond's quote found in Wesley C. Hogan, *Many Minds, One Heart: SNCC's Dream for a New America* (Chapel Hill: University of North Carolina Press, 2007), 7.

3. Juan Williams, *Eyes on the Prize: America's Civil Rights Years, 1954–1965* (New York: Penguin Books, 2002); Henry Hampton, Steve Fayer, and Sarah Flynn, *Voices of Freedom: An Oral History of the Civil Rights Movement from the 1950s through the 1980s* (New York: Bantam Books, 1991).

4. Charles Payne, *I've Got the Light of Freedom: The Organizing Tradition and the Mississippi Freedom Struggle* (Berkeley: University of California Press, 2007), 77–102; Barbara Ransby, *Ella Baker and the Black Freedom Movement* (Chapel Hill: University of North Carolina Press, 2003); see first three chapters of Charles E. Cobb Jr., *This Nonviolent Stuff'll Get You Killed: How Guns Made the Civil Rights Movement Possible* (New York: Basic Books, 2014).

5. Williams, *Eyes on the Prize*, 164–165.

6. "Oprah Winfrey's Comments about Recent Protests and Ferguson Spark Controversy," *People*, January 1, 2015, https://people.com/celebrity/oprah-on -recent-protests-and-ferguson/, accessed August 27, 2018.

7. Barbara Ransby, "Ella Taught Me: Shattering the Myth of the Leaderless Movement," *Colorlines*, June 12, 2015, http://www.colorlines.com/articles/ella -taught-me-shattering-myth-leaderless-movement, accessed July 28, 2016; Peniel Joseph, "Time for #BlackLivesMatter to Turn Protest into Policy," *Root*, January 7, 2015, http://www.theroot.com/articles/culture/2015/01/_black livesmatter_turning_protest_into_policy/, accessed July 28, 2016.

8. Hampton, Fayer, and Flynn, *Voices of Freedom*, 114.

9. Hampton, Fayer, and Flynn, *Voices of Freedom*, 114; my thoughts on the Albany Movement were informed by J. Todd Moye, "Focusing Our Eyes on the Prize: How Community Studies Are Reframing and Rewriting the History of the Civil Rights Movement," in Crosby, *Civil Rights History from the Ground Up*, 157–62.

10. See Payne, *I've Got the Light of Freedom*, chapter 3; Crosby, "Introduction: The Politics of Writing and Teaching Movement History" and "That Movement Responsibility: An Interview with Judy Richardson on Movement Values and Movement History," in *Civil Rights History from the Ground Up*; and Cobb, *This Nonviolent Stuff'll Get You Killed*. In August 2016, the BLMM would eventually put forth a platform. See "Platform," The Movement for Black Lives, https:// policy.m4bl.org/platform/, accessed August 27, 2018.

11. Quote from Jelani Cobb, "Anger in Ferguson," *New Yorker*, August 13, 2014, http://www.newyorker.com/news/daily-comment/anger-ferguson, accessed July 29, 2016.

12. Jamelle Boule, "The Militarization of the Police," *Slate*, August 13, 2014, http://www.slate.com/articles/news_and_politics/politics/2014/08/police _in_ferguson_military_weapons_threaten_protesters.html, accessed July 30, 2016; Jelani Cobb, "Chronicle of a Riot Foretold," *New Yorker*, November 25, 2014, http://www.newyorker.com/news/daily-comment/chronicle-ferguson -riot-michael-brown, accessed July 30, 2016.

13. Caitlin Macneal, "Jesse Jackson Explains Civil Rights History to Confused Don Lemon," *Talking Points Memo*, November 25, 2014, http://talking pointsmemo.com/livewire/jesse-jackson-explains-ferguson-don-lemon, accessed July 29, 2016; Michael W. Flamm, *Law and Order: Street Crime, Civil Unrest, and the Crisis of Liberalism in the 1960s* (New York: Columbia University Press, 2005).

14. A Group of Clergymen, "Letter to Martin Luther King," April 12, 1963, *Birmingham News*, http://teachingamericanhistory.org/library/document /letter-to-martin-luther-king/, accessed July 30, 2016; Greg Garrison, "Fifty Years Ago, Eight Clergy Asked the Rev. Martin Luther King, Jr. to Delay Demonstrations," *Alabama Living*, April 12, 2013, http://www.al.com/living/index .ssf/2013/04/post_108.html, accessed July 30, 2016.

15. Martin Luther King Jr. "Letter from Birmingham Jail," *Atlantic*, https:// www.theatlantic.com/magazine/archive/2018/02/letter-from-birmingham -jail/552461/, accessed July 30, 2016.

16. King, "Letter from Birmingham Jail."

17. "MLK: A Riot Is the Language of the Unheard," *60 Minutes: Overtime*, August 25, 2013, http://www.cbsnews.com/news/mlk-a-riot-is-the-language -of-the-unheard/, accessed July 30, 2016.

18. Cobb, *This Nonviolent Stuff'll Get You Killed*.

19. Mark Berman and Wesley Lowery, "The 12 Key Highlights from the DOJ's Scathing Ferguson Report," *Washington Post*, March 4, 2015, https:// www.washingtonpost.com/news/post-nation/wp/2015/03/04/the-12-key -highlights-from-the-dojs-scathing-ferguson-report/?utm_term=.3fcb530fe558, accessed July 30, 2016.

20. Mark Puente, "Justice Officials Outline How They Will Investigate the Baltimore Police Department," *Baltimore Sun*, June 25, 2015.

21. #Sayhername Initiative, African American Policy Forum, http://www .aapf.org/shn-campaign/, accessed July 31, 2016.

22. Kwame Ture quoted in Hampton, Fayer, and Flynn, *Voices of Freedom*, 233–34.

Contributors

SHAWN LEIGH ALEXANDER is the director of the Langston Hughes Center and a professor of African and African American studies at the University of Kansas. He is also the author of a number of books, including *An Army of Lions: The Civil Rights Struggle Before the NAACP* and *W. E. B. Du Bois: An American Intellectual.*

JULIE BUCKNER ARMSTRONG is a professor of literature and cultural studies at the University of South Florida St. Petersburg, where she teaches courses in American, African American, and women's literatures. She has authored and edited multiple publications on the literature of civil rights and racial justice, including the *Cambridge Companion to American Civil Rights Literature* (2015), *Mary Turner and the Memory of Lynching* (2011), *The Civil Rights Reader: American Literature from Jim Crow to Reconciliation* (coedited with Amy Schmidt, 2009), and, with Susan Hult Edwards, Houston Roberson, and Rhonda Williams, *Teaching the American Civil Rights Movement: Freedom's Bittersweet Song* (2002).

STEVE BANDURA is the director of Philadelphia Youth Organization in the Philadelphia (PA) Department of Parks and Recreation. In 1995, after several years of volunteering at the Marian Anderson Recreation Center, he founded the Anderson Monarchs, a sports-based youth development organization based in South Philadelphia that has provided athletic and educational opportunities to thousands of underserved youth in the city. The program has become one of the top youth sports programs in Philadelphia, producing athletes who are as well prepared academically as they are athletically.

STEPHEN A. BERREY is an associate professor of American culture and history at the University of Michigan. His research, writing, and teaching explore the relationship between race and culture in the United States. He is the author of *The Jim Crow Routine: Everyday Performances of Race, Civil Rights, and Segregation in Mississippi.*

NICOLE A. BURROWES is an assistant professor in the African and African Diaspora Studies Department with affiliations in history and Latin American studies at the University of Texas at Austin. Her research and teaching interests include comparative histories of racialization, social justice movements, Black transnationalism, and the politics of solidarity. Nicole served as assistant director for the Schomburg-Mellon Summer Humanities Institute in Harlem mentoring underrepresented students to pursue graduate studies related to Africa and the African diaspora. Beyond academia, she draws on an extensive portfolio of experience in documentary film and community organizing. Nicole served as a site coordinator for the inaugural year of the Harlem Freedom Schools and later cofounded Sista II Sista Freedom School for Young Women of Color in Brooklyn, where she worked in various capacities for ten years.

CHARLES E. COBB JR. is a distinguished journalist, educator, and activist. As a field secretary with the Student Nonviolent Coordinating Committee (SNCC) he originated the idea of freedom schools as a part of the 1964 Mississippi Freedom Summer Project. He began his journalism career in 1974 as a reporter for WHUR Radio in Washington, DC. In 1976 he joined the staff of National Public Radio as a foreign affairs reporter, bringing to that network its first regular coverage of Africa. From 1985 to 1997 Cobb was a National Geographic staff member. He is the coauthor, with civil rights organizer and educator Robert P. Moses, of *Radical Equations: Civil Rights from Mississippi to the Algebra Project* (2001) and the author of *On the Road to Freedom: A Guided Tour of the Civil Rights Trail* (2007) and *This Nonviolent Stuff'll Get You Killed: How Guns Made the Civil Rights Movement Possible* (2014). While a visiting professor of Africana studies at Brown University in the 2000s, he designed and taught a course called "The Organizing Tradition of the Southern Civil Rights Movement."

EMILYE CROSBY is a professor of history at the State University of New York (SUNY), College at Geneseo. She is the author of *A Little Taste of Freedom: The Black Freedom Struggle in Claiborne County, Mississippi* (2005) and editor of *Civil Rights History from the Ground Up* (2011). Her article "White Privilege, Black Burden: Lost Opportunities and Deceptive Narratives in School Desegregation in Claiborne County, Mississippi" was published in the *Oral History Review* and awarded the Oral History Association's 2013 Article Award. She is currently working on a book-length project, "Anything I Was Big Enough to Do: Women and Gender in the Student Nonviolent Coordinating Committee," which has received support from the James Weldon Johnson Institute at Emory University, the National Humanities Center, and the National Endowment for the Humanities. Crosby has been recognized with many awards, including the Chancellor's Award for Teaching, the Chancellor's Award for Service, the Harter Mentoring Award, the Spencer Roemer Supported Professorship, and the President's Award for Scholarship.

KARLYN FORNER is a historian and the author of *Why the Vote Wasn't Enough for Selma* (2017). For five years, she worked as the project manager for the SNCC Digital Gateway: Learning from the Past, Organizing for the Future, Making Democracy Work and is a continuing collaborator in the ongoing partnership between the SNCC Legacy Project and Duke University.

JOHN B. GARTRELL is the director of the John Hope Franklin Research Center for African and African American History and Culture of the David M. Rubenstein Rare Book and Manuscript Library at Duke University. He has held this position since 2012 and has been a professional archivist for more than a decade. His primary responsibilities within the Franklin Research Center include the acquisition of rare book and manuscript collections, the promotion of use of the collections, development of public programing and events, curating exhibitions from collections, and management of research services requests. He also serves on the editorial board of the SNCC Digital Gateway Project and One Person, One Vote: The Legacy of SNCC and the Fight for Voting Rights.

MICHELLE M. HERCZOG is the History-Social Science Coordinator III for the Los Angeles County (CA) Office of Education, responsible for providing professional development, resources, and support for K-12 social studies educators throughout the eighty school districts of Los Angeles County. She is the past president of the National Council for the Social Studies (NCSS), and as a member of the Council of Chief State School Officers she helped develop the College, Career, and Civic Life (C3) Framework for Social Studies State Standards published by NCSS.

WESLEY HOGAN is the director of the Center for Documentary Studies at Duke University and a research professor at the Franklin Humanities Institute and Department of History. Her most recent book, *On the Freedom Side: How Five Decades of Youth Activists Have Remixed American History*, draws a portrait of young people organizing in the spirit of Ella Baker since 1960. She co-facilitates a partnership between the SNCC Legacy Project and Duke—The SNCC Digital Gateway: Learning from the Past, Organizing for the Future, Making Democracy Work—whose purpose is to bring the grassroots stories of the civil rights movement to a much wider public through a web portal, K-12 initiative, and set of critical oral histories.

CHARLES L. HUGHES is the director of the Lynne and Henry Turley Memphis Center at Rhodes College, where he designs courses, programs, and partnerships focused on the human experience of Memphis and the Mid-South region. His first book, *Country Soul: Making Music and Making Race in the American South*, was named one of the Best Music Books of 2015 by *Rolling Stone* magazine. He is a voter for the Rock & Roll Hall of Fame and a participant in *Nashville Scene*'s Year-End Country Music Poll.

HASAN KWAME JEFFRIES is an associate professor of history at The Ohio State University. He is the author of *Bloody Lowndes: Civil Rights and Black Power in Alabama's Black Belt* (2009). He has won several prestigious awards for teaching, including The Ohio State University College of Arts and Sciences Outstanding Teaching Award (2019) and The Ohio State University Alumni Award for Distinguished Teaching (2012), the university's highest award for teaching. He has worked on several public history projects, including the five-year, $27 million renovation of the National Civil Rights Museum at the Lorraine Motel in Memphis, Tennessee. He also hosts the podcast *Teaching Hard History* for Teaching Tolerance, a project of the Southern Poverty Law Center.

PATRICK D. JONES is an associate professor in the Department of History and Institute for Ethnic Studies at University of Nebraska, Lincoln, where he researches, writes, and teaches about the civil rights and Black Power era. He is the author of *The Selma of the North: Civil Rights Insurgency in Milwaukee* (2009). He is currently working on a new monograph that looks at the contested meanings of civil rights and Black Power in Cleveland, Ohio.

SHANNON KING is an associate professor of history at Fairfield University and author of *Whose Harlem Is This, Anyway? Community Politics and Grassroots Activism during the New Negro era* (2017), which won the National Council for Black Studies Anna Julia Cooper/CLR James Award for Outstanding Book in Africana Studies.

CLARENCE LANG is the Susan Welch Dean of the College of the Liberal Arts and a professor of African American studies at the Pennsylvania State University. A former distinguished lecturer of the Organization of American Historians, he is the author of *Grassroots at the Gateway: Class Politics and Black Freedom Struggle in St. Louis, 1936–75* and *Black America in the Shadow of the Sixties: Notes on the Civil Rights Movement, Neoliberalism, and Politics*. He is the coeditor of two books: *Anticommunism and the African American Freedom Movement* and *Reframing Randolph: Labor, Black Freedom, and the Legacies of A. Philip Randolph*. His work also has appeared in such periodicals as *Journal of African American History*, *Journal of Social History*, *Journal of Urban History*, *The Black Scholar*, *Journal of Civil and Human Rights*, and *Critical Sociology*.

LA TASHA B. LEVY is an assistant professor in the Department of American Ethnic Studies at the University of Washington. Her research and teaching interests include post–World War II African American political history, social movements, Black intellectual traditions, and intersectional racial discourse. She is completing a book that explores the dramatic shift in black Republican politics from liberal to conservative during a period of heightened black political consciousness and a burgeoning conservative movement in the United States from the late 1960s through the 1980s.

CHARLES MCKINNEY is the Neville Frierson Bryan Chair of Africana Studies and an associate professor of history at Rhodes College. He is the author of *Greater Freedom: The Evolution of the Civil Rights Struggle in Wilson, North Carolina* (2010) and coeditor, with Aram Goudsouzian, of *An Unseen Light: Black Struggles for Freedom in Memphis, Tennessee* (2018).

LEONARD N. MOORE is the George Littlefield Professor of American History at the University of Texas at Austin, where he regularly teaches a class on the Black Power movement and a signature course titled "Race in the Age of Trump." He has received a number of teaching awards at the University of Texas, including the Jean Holloway Award for Excellence in Teaching and the John Warfield Teaching Award. His most recent book is *The Defeat of Black Power: Civil Rights and the National Black Political Convention of 1972* (2018).

J. TODD MOYE is a professor of history and director of the Oral History Program at the University of North Texas. A past president of the Oral History Association, he has authored several books and articles on the history of the civil rights movement, including *Let the People Decide: Black Freedom and White Resistance Movements in Sunflower County, Mississippi, 1945–1986* (2004), *Freedom Flyers: The Tuskegee Airmen of World War II* (2010), and *Ella Baker: Community Organizer of the Civil Rights Movement* (2013).

JOHN RURY is a professor of education with courtesy appointments in history and African and African American studies at the University of Kansas. His published work has dealt with educational inequality in American history and its consequences, focusing on questions of race, gender, and socioeconomic status.

ADAM SANCHEZ is a social studies teacher at Harvest Collegiate High School in New York City. He is also an editor of *Rethinking Schools* magazine and the author of *Teaching a People's History of Abolition and the Civil War* (2019), a collection of ten classroom-tested lessons on Reconstruction.

CHRISTOPHER B. STRAIN is a professor of history and American studies at the Harriet L. Wilkes Honors College of Florida Atlantic University. He has written four books: *Pure Fire: Self-Defense as Activism in the Civil Rights Era* (2005), *Burning Faith: Church Arson in the American South* (2008), *Reload: Rethinking Violence in American Life* (2010), and *The Long Sixties: America, 1955–1973* (2016).

JAKOBI WILLIAMS is Ruth N. Halls Associate Professor in the Department of African American and African Diaspora Studies and the Department of History at Indiana University–Bloomington. He is the author of *From the Bullet to the Ballot: The Illinois Chapter of the Black Panther Party and Racial Coalition Politics in Chicago* (2013). He has received several notable awards, including a National Endowment for the Humanities grant, a National Humanities Center fellowship, and a Big Ten Academic Alliance-Academic Leadership Program award.

Index

Poor People's Campaign, 109, 190–91
pop, 212–17. *See also* music
Populist Party, 65
Powell, Adam Clayton, Jr., 101, 237
"Power and Racism" (Carmichael), 150
The Power Broker (documentary), 237
Powledge, Fred, 85, 88
presidential election, 2016, xi–xiii. *See also* Trump, Donald
Presley, Elvis, 214
primary sources, 241–46
privilege, 49, 60–62, 88, 192, 226, 268–69, 273–74
The Pruitt-Igoe Myth (documentary), 229
Public Enemy, 161, 217
Pulido, Laura, 191

queer rights, 109, 190, 193–94, 203–4, 291. *See also* class; feminism; sexuality

race. *See* civil rights teaching; Jim Crow; police abuse; white supremacy
Race (documentary), 225
Race (film), 189, 230
Radical Equations (Cobb, Moses), 14–16
Radio Free Dixie (Tyson), 85, 187
Raiders of the Lost Ark (film), 241
Rainbow Coalition, 191
Raines, Annie, 17
Raines, Howell, 123
Raisin in the Sun (Hansberry), 261, 269
Ralph J. Bunche Oral History Collection, 199–200
Randall, Dudley, 273
Randolph, A. Philip, 79, 97, 136, 228
Rankine, Claudia, 262–63
Ransby, Barbara, 147, 304
rap. *See* hip hop
Ready for Revolution (Carmichael), 18
Reagon, Cordell, 303
The Rebellious Life of Rosa Parks (Theoharis), 117, 142n7
Reconstruction, 26, 61, 69
Reddick, Lawrence D., 86
Redding, Otis, 218

redlining, 67, 71, 72nn10–11, 104. *See also* housing discrimination
Redmond, Shana, 222n6
A Red Record (Wells), 186, 267
Red Squads, 106–7, 192
Red Tails (film), 229
Reeves, Martha, 214
Remembering Malcolm (Karim), 165
Remember the Titans (film), 230
"Respect" (song), 209, 218
Rethinking Schools, 41–42
Revolution '67 (documentary), 237
The Revolution Has Come (Spencer), 190–93
Rich, Adrienne, 264
Richardson, Gloria, 85, 88, 122, 170
Richardson, Judy, 43
Richmond, David, 279
Rickford, Russell J., 166
Ricks, Irene, 139–40
Ricks, Willie, 84
"The Riddle of the Zoot" (Kelley), 164
Rioting in America (Gilje), 179
The Rise and Fall of Jim Crow (documentary), 226
Roach, Max, 155, 216
The Road to Brown (documentary), 231–32
Robertson, Carole, 72n14
Robeson, Paul, 212
Robinson, Jackie, 24–25, 79, 87, 213, 230
Robinson, Jo Ann Gibson, 17, 84, 116–18, 133, 138–40
Robinson, Lewis, 104
Robinson, Phil Alden, 290n4
Robinson, Shae Goodman, 14
ROCC, 201
rock 'n' roll, 214–15. *See also* music
Rogers, Lettie Hamlett, 273
role play, 42–45, 276–89
Roof, Dylann, 278
Roosevelt, Franklin D., 79, 164
Root (news site), 304
Roots (television series), 26
Rosa Parks Museum, 32
Rosewood (film), 227
Rothstein, Richard, 163

The Harvey Goldberg Series
for Understanding and Teaching History